KARLA A. ERICKSON

THE HUNGRY COWBOY

SERVICE AND COMMUNITY IN A NEIGHBORHOOD RESTAURANT

UNIVERSITY PRESS OF MISSISSIPPI / JACKSON

www.upress.state.ms.us

Designed by Todd Lape

The University Press of Mississippi is a member
of the Association of American University Presses.

First printing 2009

∞

Library of Congress Cataloging-in-Publication Data

Erickson, Karla A., 1973–
The Hungry Cowboy : service and community
in a neighborhood restaurant / Karla A. Erickson.
p. cm.
Includes bibliographical references and index.
ISBN 978-1-60473-206-1 (cloth : alk. paper)
1. Hungry Cowboy (Restaurant)
2. Restaurants—Social aspects—United States.
I. Title.
TX945.5.H86E75 2009
647.9573—dc22   2008037323

British Library Cataloging-in-Publication Data available

CONTENTS

ACKNOWLEDGMENTS

This work is a coproduction. This study has been supported and made possible by friends, colleagues, and sometimes even by strangers. First, Jennifer Pierce, advisor and friend extraordinaire, convinced me early on to make the Hungry Cowboy the subject of my dissertation research. Jennifer guided me through all the steps of ethnographic research. More than that, she provided a model for how to work in the academy with integrity and how to produce research that honors and respects the lived experience of the people whom one studies. Jennifer's dissertation group provided an incubator for this research. Members of that group—Hokulani Aikau, Felicity Schaffer-Grabiel, Amy Tyson, Peter Hennen, Sara Dorow, Wendy Leo-Moore, Miglena Todorova, Deborah Smith, and Nalo Jackson—helped the work grow through innumerable drafts. Hokulani Aikau's friendship and collaboration has been instrumental to shaping this work. Through our years of collaboration, often with the help of Felicity Schaffer-Grabiel, we have come to know each other's work as well as our own. Such partnerships are rare, and incredibly valuable.

My partner in life, Matthew Karjalahti, escorted the work, and perhaps more important, me, through too many steps and highs and lows to name. He has read and reread every word here, coming to know the Hungry Cowboy first through me and later through this study. Like so much else of our lives, my sister, Kate Erickson, and my best friend, Danielle Sadler, both accompanied me first into the Hungry Cowboy as coworkers and later as editors and welcome critics of this study. Danielle contributed her extraordinary patience and wisdom at several key points, when I was not sure what step to take next. Kate lent her passion and enthusiasm, and memories of working at the Hungry Cowboy when she was just a teenager. My mother, Cathie Corcoran, and my father, Darrell Erickson, raised me with the audacious belief that I could do any number of things. I do not think they envisioned that being a waitress would come to be one of my more important life experiences. Despite that, both my parents visited the Hungry Cowboy innumerable times over the years, read drafts of my work, and my mom even attended conferences where I presented my work. My belief that education is transformative belongs entirely to my parents. And indeed, for me, it has been.

Over the last eight years, I have been supported by social and professional networks made up of outstanding individuals. Specifically, Vicki Smith has offered her generous insights at several critical stages of this work. Vicki's ability to imagine an analytical framework that does justice to the ethnographic details of this study has been invaluable. Early on, Arlene Kaplan Daniels and Eileen Boris provided critical support for this work. Along the way, anonymous reviewers from the University Press of Mississippi, Routledge, and Cornell University Press helped shape the manuscript, as did Frances Benson of Cornell University Press, Rob Shields of *Space and Culture*, and Javier Auyero of *Symbolic Interaction*. Craig Gill of the University Press of Mississippi has been an enthusiastic advocate of this work from the very beginning. Working with Craig and the editorial team at University Press of Mississippi has been enjoyable in ways that I think few first authors get to experience. I am grateful for their frank and honest support and guidance. Thanks specifically to Tammy Oberhausen Rastoder, who skillfully edited the manuscript, improving the clarity of this tale, while Anne Stascavage guided the manuscript through all the necessary stages. David Sutton of Southern Illinois University, Carbondale has been enormously supportive of my work. We share a conviction that food and sociability matter enormously. Sharon Bird has been a great colleague and friend throughout these early stages of my career, and introduced me to a network of feminist scholars at Iowa State University. Marguerite Hernandez, Griff Tester and Ryan Murphy, with whom I share an academic interest in the intersections between sexuality, work, and power, all generously volunteered to review previous drafts.

As a student of feminist epistemology, I believe that what we know is intimately shaped by our teachers, cohorts, and mentors. Early into this work, a dissertation seminar taught by Thomas Augst helped me to launch this project. At that time and throughout my graduate training, my professional development was aided by my cohort of graduate friends: Sharon Leon, Hokulani Aikau, Amy Tyson, Scott Laderman, Felicity Schaffer-Grabiel, Mary Rizzo, Matt Becker, and David Gray. My dissertation work and early training in research methods was guided by Catherine Ceniza Choy. Colleen Hennen, as Associate Administrator of American Studies and as my friend, helped me get through and make sense of the graduate school process. Jeani O'Brien, Lisa Disch, and David Roediger have been important models and touchstones during my training as well. My worldview has been profoundly shaped by the teaching, scholarship, and friendship of David W. Noble. In terms of models within the academy, I have been incredibly blessed, going back not just one but two generations. David Noble, my intellectual grandfather because he trained April Schultz, who trained me, along with Arlie Russell Hochschild and Michael Burawoy, my intellectual grandparents because they trained Jennifer Pierce, who trained me, have profoundly shaped the questions I considered worth asking and the shape my own conclusions have taken in my professional life and work. Serendipitously, I worked with Jim Farrell for one year at St. Olaf College, and he quickly became a friend and mentor. Jim and I share a mix of fascination, apprehension, and admiration for the pleasures to be had through consuming.

My colleagues and friends at Grinnell College have been unfailingly supportive of my work. At Grinnell, Chris Hunter, Kent McClelland, Kesho Scott, Susan Ferguson, Derrick Miller, Laura Sinnett, Joyce Stern, Dan Reynolds, Garrett Roche, Nancy Hayes, George Barlow, David Cook-Martín, Betsy Erbaugh, Jon Chenette, Jim Swartz, Alan Schrift, Vicki Bentley-Conduit, Brad Bateman, Eliza Willis, Johanna Meehan, Henry Rietz, Janet Seiz, and Phil Jones have actively supported the completion of this work, have encouraged me in my next second major project on end of life care, and have helped me find a home here in Grinnell, Iowa. My students at Grinnell are a constant inspiration, and I am honored to teach them, advise them, and share my scholarship with them. In particular, Htike Htike Kyaw

Soe and Brock Webb thoughtfully and methodically improved this text through their attention and insights. Finally, Karla Landers (we call ourselves Karla #1 and #2) generously completed the final round of copyediting during the summer of 2007.

Early versions of this manuscript were written with the support of a Harold Leonard Memorial Film Study Fellowship during the 2002–3 academic year. While that fellowship helped launch this project, Judy Hunter, my friend and extraordinary editor, helped conclude this work. Judy acted like a literary midwife during the summer of 2007, helping me to find the right voice with which to convey my observations and conclusions about the Hungry Cowboy.

Having thanked all the individuals who have supported me while I discovered and refined the means to write about the Hungry Cowboy, the most essential thanks goes to all the participants of the Hungry Cowboy who allowed me to watch and question, who explained to me what their involvement in the community of the Hungry Cowboy meant to them, and who made working there such a rich, challenging, and rewarding experience. Thanks especially to Richard, who encouraged me in all things, even when my plans took me away from him, and to Jessica, who more than any other co-worker, cheered, supported, critiqued, and applauded my efforts to describe what we experienced at the Hungry Cowboy. Thanks to Beth who remarkably administered fifty surveys in one night, and to all my friends and co-workers at the Hungry Cowboy who taught me about the possibilities for building community in the marketplace.

1

SPACES IN THE MARKETPLACE

◆◆◆◆◆◆◆◆◆◆◆◆◆◆◆◆◆◆◆◆◆◆

WORKING, DINING, AND BELONGING AT THE HC

One day in the spring of 2000, I walked in the front door of the Hungry Cowboy, the restaurant where I worked, to pick up my paycheck. I noticed that one of the regular customers had posted a sign in the entryway of the restaurant. I was not surprised to see a sign posted by a customer because the general manager, Richard, a good businessman, knows how to capitalize on existing strengths of his business by building ties with local groups. Richard invests in local charity functions, supports school activities, and allows community groups to use the walls of the restaurant to display their advertisements. Still, this sign was unique. This customer had posted an epitaph to his dog, complete with picture and a story about how his dog had lived, the dog's favorite places and activities, and what he would miss about his dog. I recognized the dog being commemorated. This customer used to bring his beautiful Husky with him to the bar a couple times a week. The dog was popular; staff and guests alike stopped to "chat" with him outside, and servers always provided a bowl of water and some tasty scraps to entertain him while his owner had a beer. When the dog, named Alexander Silverstreak River, was dying, his master placed the pills that eased River into death in a Hungry Cowboy burger. Later, to ease his mourning, he put a picture of the dog with an announcement of its death up in the entryway.

The story of River and his owner highlights the sometimes painful, sometimes beautiful moments that take place within restaurant spaces. Restaurants are consumer spaces carefully constructed to entice and then retain customers' attention and dollars. Restaurants are also social spaces, both carefully orchestrated and unpredictably real.

River's epitaph also raises a series of questions about ambience, community, and making connections in public. As a scholar of social life, I wanted to make sense of this event. What inspired this claiming of a public space for a private memorial? What about the Hungry Cowboy encouraged this customer to post an epitaph to his dog? What did this event, along with the daily exchange of pleasantries and sociability I observed, reveal about how Americans produce and consume familiarity, recognition, and care in commercial spaces? These are the questions that began my ethnographic study of the Hungry Cowboy. First as a worker and later as a researcher at the Hungry Cowboy, I became aware of how restaurants function in our culture, sometimes as homes away from home. While people go out to eat more than ever, they simultaneously cast about for security, stability, and recognition. Some restaurants provide a neighborhood feel by offering an always-open door where people remember your name, a welcoming experience for loyal customers like River and his owner.

As a sociologist and scholar of labor, I am deeply curious about the combination of space, location, staff, management, and clientele that combine to produce ambience. I am also interested in how one environment can foster routine, friendly interactions while another encourages limited, business-like social exchanges. In this study, I explore the components, the "building blocks of sociability," that make up the Hungry Cowboy atmosphere. Sociability describes a place or event that is "marked by or conducive to friendliness or pleasant social relations."[1] The building blocks that create this feeling include everything from the lighting and layout of the restaurant to the smiles and spicy salsa delivered by the servers. Exploring all the factors that shape the ambience of the Hungry Cowboy, this study is as much about emotions and identities as it is about trays and tables.

My analysis is based on two years of participant observation, interviews with servers, managers, and customers, and surveys of customers. Here, I use the ethnographic lens to examine the features that make up the Hungry Cowboy, from the arrangement of space to the use of bodies and feelings within the service exchange. I rely on the interview and survey data I collected to explain how individuals make use of the Hungry Cowboy as a restaurant and as a social world. I combine my observations with the self-reports of servers, customers, and managers to analyze how participants practice public social life. Examining social life at the level of practice requires getting social actors to talk about why they do what they do in routine and daily interactions. What practices support an environment that encourages a customer to commemorate his dog's life in the lobby? What are the limitations of relationships that develop in the marketplace?

The Hungry Cowboy is just one place, a place both like and unlike the restaurants you will enter as producers or consumers, and my conclusions reflect that particularity; however, observations and experiences within this one place shed light on larger questions regarding the production and consumption of smiles, selves, and community within the service economy.

THE HUNGRY COWBOY
Your Neighborhood Restaurant

As customers, when we go to a restaurant for the first time, we have to figure out the rules of the space. Customers' first encounter with a restaurant is like a first kiss: will we stay or will we go? As customers, we respond to the rich array of color, light, smell, sound, order and disorder we encounter as we enter a dining establishment. When the doors of the Hungry Cowboy open and customers step in from the sun or the snow, the staged details confront them simultaneously: carefully placed salt and pepper, forks and spoons, hot sauce and barbeque sauce adorn the tables; candles beckon from booths; lively music plays softly; and enticing smells emanate from the kitchen.

One of the first indicators of a particular ambience is the name of a restaurant. I use the name "Hungry Cowboy" to replace the actual name of the restaurant without losing the cultural resonance of the actual name. "Hungry Cowboy" is a pseudonym for a name that alludes longingly to the South, to spicy foods, and to different times.[2] In keeping with this longing for a time that is past, or a place that is different, the walls of the restaurant are layered with paraphernalia from the southwestern United States and Mexico, from dried chilies, saddles, and horseshoes, to sombreros, stuffed coyotes, and cow skulls. The name manages to refer subtly to a different time, a different place, as well as a particular orientation to that time and place: by becoming a customer, one can become a cowboy. Like the real name, the pseudonym "Hungry Cowboy" is meant to capture the odd nostalgia for a rough and rugged frontier that is long since gone from the northern United States but that many Americans assume is still available down on the border.

Ambience is communicated through the food, not only through what is served but also through how the menu and servers describe the food and how it is presented. Located in a western suburb of Minneapolis, Minnesota, the Hungry Cowboy has been promising "Tex-Mex served up with Southern hospitality" since 1990. The Hungry Cowboy serves up hearty cooking, including tender baby back ribs, thinly sliced smoked brisket, gooey nachos, and sizzling fajitas. The margaritas are delicious, and the tap beers are cheap. The food is consistently tasty and decadently fattening. The servings are huge, and even the salads are loaded with meat and cheese. Health-conscious customers perusing the menu ordinarily succumb to the sight of the cheesy and fried delectables being served at the next table. Everything is handmade: the chips are fried on location, the meats are smoked in an enormous smoker, the salsa is made daily in thirty-gallon containers, and the chimichangas are rolled every morning. This commitment to avoiding flash-frozen, fried foods makes the kitchen labor-intensive. First, the kitchen crew must know how to make each recipe, from the cornbread to the barbeque sauce; plus, customers' knowledge that the food they are ordering is assembled by hand results in a high frequency of "special orders."

The high degree of individualization of the menu is one example of customers' intense involvement in the work process at the Hungry Cowboy. This restaurant has a loyal and demanding clientele. Customers' expectations for personalized service produce fanciful inventiveness among regular clientele. Here, customers often take "having it your way" to an extreme. It is not at all unusual for a customer to come in, not look at the menu (a common practice for regulars who prove their insider knowledge by refusing a menu), but instead say something along the lines of, "You know what I feel like today? A chili burrito with steak, so I want my usual Tex-Mex burrito, no veggies, no rice, but replace with the spicy chili and steak." Customer demands for special orders and special treatment range from one man who gets his chili made extra spicy, to a couple who do not like any of the enchiladas on the menu, so the cooks start from scratch, selecting by hand the vegetables that the customers request. Some customers point with disdain at the multicolor tortilla chips; as a result, their server for the evening must sort through the chips in the chip warmer to pick out and deliver only yellow chips to their table. One family of regulars even has their own private reserve of salad dressing, stocked only for their family. Whether or not regular customers fully exploit the "personalized" potential in their ordering, customers' ability to assert their wishes is clearly part of what they pay for when they come back again and again.

Recognizing regular customers has everything to do with Hungry Cowboy's success. The work of recognition falls squarely on the shoulders of frontline service staff.[3] Being recognized by one's server, manager, and bartender is an expectation and a delight for many regular customers. Richard, the general manager, explicitly trains servers and assistant managers to do the work of recognition. As a result, despite competition, the Hungry Cowboy has built a reputation for top-notch, personalized service in a casual restaurant. Many servers take pride in the history of quality service that has made the restaurant successful. A server named Beth says, "We've always had excellent service here, so they aren't comparing us with somewhere else; they are comparing us with the Hungry Cowboy of the early days." Another server named Julia also explains that "people come back because of the service." And a server named Betsy confirms this perception: "I think there are a lot of great servers here, and that is part of what keeps people coming back. Like in the bar right now, I think it is mostly regulars, and I think it is because we have good food and the service is great." Managers explain the restaurant's success in similar terms. The general manager tutors assistant managers and staff alike how to greet people artfully and acknowledge their repeat business, remember special items they like, present service as personalized, and invite customers to return. Customers report that, while they enjoy the food and the "festive" décor, above all, they are most enthusiastic about the quality of the service.

Customers routinely make themselves "at home" at the Hungry Cowboy by taking off their shoes, kicking up their feet, "visiting" other tables, or introducing family members or friends to the staff. These behaviors transgress easy distinctions that separate home from the marketplace, public life from private life, and work from leisure. Describing the daily interactions of customers, workers, and managers at the Hungry Cowboy requires blending concepts and ideas that are ordinarily kept separate. The physical and conceptual space of restaurants functions as something of a no man's land between the public and the private. When Ray Oldenburg studies the behavior of people in public gathering places, he resolves this problem by referring to businesses such as "coffee shops, beauty parlors, general stores and bars" as "third spaces" after work, and before home. Oldenburg has developed the idea of a third space to fill what he perceives as a gap in the American vocabulary. Oldenburg points to the fact that "the American language reflects the American reality—in vocabulary as in fact—the core settings of an informal public life are underdeveloped."[4] By strict definition, restaurants are of course public, yet both customers and workers often break rules of public behavior, treating the restaurant more like a private space.

As social and economic locations, restaurants blend distinctions between work and leisure, home and work, and even sacred and profane. While restaurants are not home, as consumer spaces they seek to replicate aspects of home. Many restaurants purposely create a space where customers feel at home and train the staff to act as if the customers were family, welcomed guests, and friends. Many restaurants present themselves as hangouts, adventures, or homes away from home; in short, they encourage consumers to feel like family guests, in a strategy that alludes directly to the way that entertaining at a restaurant has replaced entertaining at home.

Another feature of a restaurant that contributes to the production of ambience is the mix between regular and "new" customers. Regular customers have established routines and knowledge of the menu, management, staff and sometimes even each other. On any given night, the Hungry Cowboy is peopled with familiar faces. The clientele is primarily drawn from the relatively affluent community in which the restaurant is located. For the first five years it was open, this was one of the only full-service restaurants in this neighborhood, and, since it is tucked away on a smaller street and located in a residential area in a quiet strip mall, people do not often stumble upon it. In the mid-'90s, the neighborhood started to develop; companies opened up previously undeveloped land, and new restaurants and stores sprang up as well. Throughout the 1990s and even during the economic downturn after the terrorist attacks of September 11, 2001, the Hungry Cowboy has endured the competition, making consistent, modest gains in sales, suggesting that customers have developed an attachment to the restaurant that is not easily displaced by the arrival of new restaurant alternatives. In fact, analysis of customer surveys and comment cards suggest that customers continue to travel as far as ninety miles to eat at this restaurant even after they move away from the neighborhood.[5]

As a casual, full-service bar and restaurant, the Hungry Cowboy represents an understudied type of establishment. Research on dining out has focused on both ends of the spectrum: McDonaldized environments and fast-food work processes on the one hand, and high-end dining and formal service on the other. The Hungry Cowboy represents a different type of dining experience. The food is affordable, which means that regular patronage is possible, and the points of contact between customers and workers are more extensive than one would find in a fast-food environment. The Hungry Cowboy offers a snapshot of a consumer space and work space that involves a high percentage of regular customers, habitual interactions between parties who are familiar to one another, and an opportunity to study a locale in the marketplace that offers a feeling of belonging to not only workers but customers as well.

At this restaurant, customers express a desire to perform sociability rather than to rely on the roles available to them solely as consumers. Performing sociability entails a range of behaviors that extend the service exchange. For example, customers express interest in workers' non-work lives, bring gifts to workers, and even attend holiday staff parties. But, despite customers' expressed claims to membership in the Hungry Cowboy, at key moments, what might be called the façade of sociability drops away. For example, a customer who gets "cut off" for drinking too much may quickly remind the server of their economic relationship, "You are NOT getting a tip tonight!" The regularity of social actors offers a specific venue within which to consider the potential and limitations of performing sociability within the marketplace.

COMMUNITY IN THE MARKETPLACE

In an economy marked by conglomeration, supersizing, corporate chains, and increased uniformity, the Hungry Cowboy remains a messy, personal, and small space in the market economy. It places individualized interactions at the center of practice. Here, workers labor and customers consume within a particular culture that calls itself a community and that also offers its members some benefits associated with traditional communities. I conceptualize places like this that succeed at producing a feeling of home as compensatory economies of pleasure.[6] Such places are effective to the degree that they can compensate for a lack of connection in other aspects of social life by offering opportunities for connection within a paid-for experience. Compensatory economies of pleasure do not replace traditional forms, but simulate, or transform our ideas about how we make connections, and the possibilities of paying for care, community, or at least recognition within the confines of the market economy.

Labeling a series of interactions in the marketplace as "community" brings up intellectual and even political concerns. Scholars of community are wary of locating community in spaces where social actors have to pay to belong. Community has traditionally been understood to be something that arises out of neighborhoods, churches, social movements, clubs, or family connections. Ordinarily, community is understood within a context of free association. "Free" here means not only freely chosen but also free monetarily. Historically, academics have identified community as existing only outside of the marketplace, while they have treated the communion, connection, and relations that develop within the marketplace as different and distinct. Identifying aspects of community within a for-pay social realm extends these ideas, and also risks devaluing other forms of community that might develop through more traditional, and sometimes "free," contexts.

Labeling these sets of interactions as community also threatens to further co-opt the idea of community in ways that many corporations are already well-practiced at doing. Examples of products that offer a sense of belonging through purchase abound. Consumers are routinely encouraged to "be a part of the Pepsi/Coke/Ford/Olive Garden family." The Olive Garden promises, "When you're here, you're family," while State Farm Insurance claims, "Like a good neighbor, State Farm is there." In addition to the strategic use of language that promises a feeling of belonging, the marketplace also increasingly offers to replace services that were once supplied for free by families and sometimes by communities. The service sector increasingly offers to fulfill private needs for both workers and consumers. This process, in which tasks, behaviors, favors, and services that have been provided through familial and community-based networks shift to the marketplace has been called "the commodification of care."[7] In the commodification of care, caring tasks are transformed into services to be purchased. For example, individuals can use a shopping service to purchase gifts for family and friends, a birthday planning company to plan their parties, a play date organization to find friends for their children, a dating service to find a partner or date, even, as Arlie Russell Hochschild points out, a "dial-a-Grandparent" service that connects children with elderly workers who will be available on demand to listen and offer grandparently advice.[8] Against this backdrop of constant allusions to and promises of belonging in public, it is difficult not to become skeptical. Being connected to one another through communities is too important a need to be devalued through overuse, and our culture risks losing sight of real community when ideas like home, network, and family are frequently mobilized to sell a range of products.

Despite these reservations about commodification processes, customers and servers make use of service interactions in culturally interesting and personally meaningful ways that are difficult to ignore or dismiss. While the Hungry Cowboy is the focus of this study, such experiences are not limited to this particular locale. As consumers, many of us locate consumer spaces that do not just look, smell, or sound different but actually *feel* distinct from other spaces and mean something to us. Consumers make use of for-profit spaces for a range of purposes, and sometimes they even find ways to build connections with one another through commerce. As scholars of social life, we need a language to talk about those varied experiences. Specifically, we need ways to describe consumer experiences that have not already been claimed by corporate language, lingos, and advertisements that tell us how we could, should, and do feel.

Despite my general distrust of an increasing reliance on the marketplace, my curiosity has been fed by observing moments at the Hungry Cowboy, like the epitaph to River, that represent a use of the restaurant that expands beyond the profit motive and starts to look more like an actual community. Workers, managers, and consumers describe experiences that cannot be contained in a market-based, instrumental model of relationships. In the late 1800s, German theorist Ferdinand Toennies differentiated between two distinct types of relationships between people: gemeinshaft, which roughly translated means community, and gesellshaft, which means society. Gemeinshaft is characterized by close, intimate, kin or kinlike relations, while gesellshaft is characterized by impersonal and sometimes instrumental relations between people.

Toennies's ideas continue to be relevant today when we, as participants in social life, and as scholars, attempt to differentiate between the mood, tone, or substance of interactions between two or more people. The concepts gemeinshaft and gesellshaft—or community and society—provide us with a vocabulary to distinguish between voluntary connections between similar individuals who support one another, and means-to-an-end connections between heterogeneous social actors who have limited connections with or responsibilities for one another. During his lifetime (1855–1936), Toennies was attempting to make sense of the rapid cultural changes wrought by industrialization. Today, the rapid expansion of the service economy means that more and more of our human interactions take place within the marketplace, while more and more of our needs are fulfilled by services for pay.

The distinction between purely market-driven relations and more kinlike or intimate interactions is useful for examining moments at the Hungry Cowboy when customers and servers alike eclipse the roles of server and served. For instance, customers bring in home-cooked treats to feed employees who have access to free food all day. Customers send Christmas and Hanukah cards to the restaurant as if it is another family on their holiday list. Servers and managers gossip about the private lives of customers, express concern when regular customers fail to show up for a couple weeks at their usual dining times, and share milestones in their customers' lives.

Customers, managers, and servers behave in ways that transcend their categorical or instrumental relationship to one another. Whether they are communal or purely instrumental, these interactions are shaped by the specific sociospatial arrangements of the Hungry Cowboy.

FRONT OF THE HOUSE/BACK OF THE HOUSE

At the Hungry Cowboy, there are several important "lines" in the sociospatial arrangement of the restaurant.[9] The first line divides the "restaurant side" from the "bar side." As customers enter through the lobby, they must decide on which side they want to dine, either the more family-friendly restaurant or the rowdier, smoky bar. The second line is where carpet meets tile, the point past which customers do not cross. This line separates customers from workers. The third line is a fifteen-foot metal assembly table that cooks stand behind to do their work. This line physically separates cooks from servers and managers. Servers are not allowed behind the line, and have to step up to the line to communicate with the cooks. This last is literally called "the line."

Space can "discipline" bodies and shape social interactions.[10] Space can also demarcate according to rank, power, and privilege. Imagine a tour from front to back of the Hungry Cowboy that reveals how these disciplining and demarcating spaces are arranged. We move from the brightly lit dining room toward the back of the building: the lights flicker over the beverage preparation station, then dim over "the line" where the cooks dish out the food, finally, in the back there are almost no lights at all, deep in the bowels of the kitchen where the cow parts are stored in freezers and the pig parts are smoked in a huge iron oven that hisses and spits at its operator. The uneven upkeep and attention to the spaces, from polished to haphazard, from mood-lighting to broken fluorescents, parallels the visibility and status of the workers who labor in each space. The line between back and front not only marks the difference between producers and consumers, who pays and gets paid, who serves and is served; at the Hungry Cowboy that line also marks distinctions of status.

The restaurant is designed to define movement, permitting use of certain pathways and preventing others. For example, the entryway to the kitchen must blend with the frontstage of the dining room, yet must be distinct enough to prevent customers from accidentally accessing the behind-the-scenes space.[11] Such an event would be analogous to a member of the audience sneaking behind the curtain in the middle of a scene change. In fact, customers so disturb workers in the backstage area that when customers do accidentally or intentionally enter the prep area, all motion stops. One by one, as servers recognize the intruder, they stop and turn to look, waiting until the offending trespasser realizes he or she has overstepped his or her allocated space and leaves.

The Hungry Cowboy includes a bar side and a restaurant side.[12] The two distinct but connected spaces "sort" between the clientele. Although the two spaces are connected, the bar is an entirely different space than the restaurant. The bar is always darkened, and loud music plays all day long. The décor mixes televisions displaying sports, beer signs, and neon lights with cactuses, cowboy hats, and chili peppers. Above the bar, a stuffed rattlesnake appears to rear up inside a glass cage, while other taxidermic desert creatures hang from the walls and ceiling. The bar and restaurant clientele have developed differently: the well-lit booths attract families on the restaurant side while the smoky eclecticism of the bar attracts single customers and others looking to drink and socialize.[13] Servers sometimes stand up front and guess from physical appearance which "side" customers will choose, and they are usually right. Customers are quickly disciplined by the unspoken rules of each constructed space. Children tend to head to the restaurant where they are provided with kids' menus that feature Spanish-language crossword puzzles and Texas trivia. Elderly people are the easiest to guess; they instinctively head toward the more cheerful, quieter restaurant side. Codes of conduct also establish the ambience; bar servers might saunter up and ask, "What's going on?" regardless of who you are, while in the restaurant, servers are more likely to use a formal greeting if they don't "know" you: "Good Evening, and welcome to the Hungry Cowboy!" Over the years, these formal greetings have become less and less common, as the percentage of regular customers has grown.

Although the distinction between the bar and restaurant allows for two slightly divergent service experiences, the primary division in the restaurant is the front of the house from the back of the house. Every night begins with the rising heat and energy of bodies arriving: the customers arrive through the front door and the staff through the back. As they arrive, their behavior is guided by the rules of the space. Whether on the bar or restaurant side, the space for the customers, who are the recipients of service, is subtly delineated from workspace, where workers prepare to deliver service. The behaviors permissible or encouraged in each of these spaces are roughly equivalent to the identity managing practices that Erving Goffman defines as frontstage and backstage. For Goffman, everyday life is a performance for an audience of other social actors.[14] Individuals perform a self that they want others to believe of them. Furthermore, for Goffman, selves are performed in relation to others, to place and to time. Goffman identifies frontstage behaviors that are consistent and deliberate and contrasts them with backstage places or times when individual performers can step out of character or drop the act. In daily life, backstages are created when the other social actors who make up our audience are not present. For example, adults alone in cars who pick their noses operate in a backstage: they act in a way they would not if other people could see them.

In service work, the backstage and frontstage are physical spaces with distinct audiences and practices. Hostesses, bussers, servers, and bartenders can and do move from the front to the back of the house hundreds of times each night. In doing so, they subtly and overtly alter their affect, bodily display, physical movement, language, tone, sexual innuendo, and performance; these changes that workers manage across the two spaces contribute to the mood of the restaurant. Servers are not just balancing trays; they are balancing performances: one for frontstage consumption and one for back.

As servers juggle competing demands and situations in the front and the back of the house, their movements and alterations between these two define their work. Servers' partial confinement to the backstage of the restaurant obscures many of the steps that go into producing satisfying service and also marks them as "the staff." Like servants in a home, workers enter and leave out the back door and hide much of their labor from the sight from their customers.[15] Despite the constraining functions of the backstage, servers use the space to assemble food and beverages, and also to drop character, if only for a few seconds. Behind the scenes, servers collide and swear, tell stories and holler.[16] The backstage is where workers do much of the labor of serving food and also where they go to forget they are at work, to hide from customers, and to "have fun," all of which include physical and sometimes sexual maneuvering.

The backstage at the Hungry Cowboy is constructed precisely to hide the evidence of workers' labor.[17] Customers are meant to see as little of the work that goes into their meal as possible, and the division between spaces allows for this. The backstage of the restaurant smells stronger and is often up to 20 degrees hotter than the frontstage. The social rules governing inter-action change as a server or manager crosses the line into the kitchen. The already tight spaces grow even tighter, as up to ten workers try to complete their work in areas so cramped that they crawl over one another, push, and squirm. The language behind the scenes is louder, franker, and fouler. Behind the scenes, leftover food that had been carefully prepared is dumped into an enormous garbage can, and the leftovers are splashed on the walls.

The "line" that separates the cooks and dishwashers from the servers and bartenders is often just as deep a divide as the one that differentiates customers from workers. While the line between the front of the house and the back of the house is identified with carpet and tile, no actual "line" is needed: these are two distinct spaces under the same roof. Cooks work rap-idly "behind the line," which is the fifteen-foot metal table that separates the cooks' workspace from the servers' workspace. When the rush begins, the cooks shout out the orders, break the task down into parts, and through combined effort produce anywhere from twenty to two hundred meals per hour. When the food is ready, it crosses the line from cook to server.

At the Hungry Cowboy, not just the physical "line" divides the front of the house staff from the cooking staff but also status lines between who "should" (and does) do what. Job assignments mirror dominant social rela-tions. For example, in the twelve years I worked there, all the servers and bar-tenders were white. White women predominated as servers and hostesses, while white men were more often bartenders and even bussers. During that same time period, 50 to 90 percent of the kitchen workers, both dishwashers and cooks, were Mexican or Mexican-American men.[18] This arrangement of labor reflects two forms of occupational segregation. First, workers are partially "sorted" by gender, with women predominant in the front of the house, and the back of the house staffed solely by men.[19] Second, even more distinct is the occupational typing that situates white workers in the front of the house, and Mexican and Mexican-American workers in the back of the house.[20] This spatial segregation is even more insidious considering the fact that the restaurant serves food that is desirable in part because it is derived from Mexican recipes.

Space can be used to sort between bodies, and in doing so, space communicates the "value" of groups of actors. The sociospatial dynamics[21] of the restaurant become even more important when we consider how spatial arrangements build on and reinforce social hierarchies of race, class, and gender.[22] While white bodies and brown bodies are segregated spatially within the restaurant, it is the Mexican men's cooking that lends legitimacy to the food that is served by white servers. And yet, the Mexican and Mexican-American men who make the food are largely invisible to the customers. While the cooks' recipes and cooking knowledge provide the "authenticity" that customers say they crave, the predominantly white middle-class customers do not ever come into physical contact with the Mexican men who make their food.

The delivery of this authentic Tex-Mex food by white bodies is a complicated performance infused with connection and exclusion. The performance of service includes bodies that collide and bodies that are carefully kept separate. The spatial divides within the restaurant reinscribe social differences between what feminist scholar Chandra Talpade Mohanty calls the "citizen consumer" and the "producer worker": those who can pay to be served and those who offer their service for pay.[23] In her research on Third World women workers, Mohanty draws attention to the "use of racial and gendered logic to consolidate capitalist accumulation."[24] The racial and gendered logic of the Hungry Cowboy insures that the person delivering the food is most likely going to be a woman and will certainly be white. While Tex-Mex may seem somewhat exotic in Minnesota, the food is delivered by recognizable bodies—white women's bodies. But further back in this space is the hidden labor of men of color, who contribute their knowledge and skill of cooking Mexican dishes invisibly, for the customers to consume. This carefully managed difference is part of the specific ambience of the Hungry Cowboy. Ambience grows out of the smells, sounds, and mood of the people and products available in a particular space. Ambience consequently reflects both who is and who is not present and visible. The divisions in the restaurant provide customers with a "friendly, welcoming" feel by allowing some behaviors and preventing some interactions.

STAGING SERVICE

The spatial arrangement of the Hungry Cowboy operates like a stage on which social relations are acted out. Workers, managers, and customers interact in emotionally complicated and intricate ways that vary between the mundane and the profound. These interactions, sometimes smooth and satisfying, sometimes choppy, are reproduced each night, and yet each night is different. The three groups of actors on the frontstage of the restaurant remain the same, but their relations with one another are anything but static. Taken together, the interactions between these three groups sets the social and emotional tone within the restaurant. These interactions are central to the production of ambience, and direct newcomers to the possibilities and limitations of sociability within the Hungry Cowboy space.

Both on the frontstage and in the back, managers, customers, and servers volley for control and negotiate the terms of their exchange in both momentary and lasting ways. As Tammy explains, "On really weird nights, sometimes it can be the waitresses against the customers. Some nights when the kitchen is slow and they are being jerks, then it's us [servers] against the kitchen and some nights, it's [servers and cooks] against the managers. It just depends. It's not a constant thing. You just walk in and see what happens." Power shifts frequently within the service exchange owing to the structure of the work. Rather than a dyadic arrangement in which workers respond to management and vice versa, front-of-the-house service work is characterized by three primary groups of actors: customers, managers, and servers. In his influential study, *Human Relations in the Restaurant Industry*, William Whyte first described this triadic arrangement of power, explaining that the restaurant worker "has two bosses—his supervisor and the customer."[25] Servers are answerable to customers and managers, managers are responsible to customers and responsible for servers, and customers have the most access to servers and some access to managers.

This triadic arrangement alters how power operates in the restaurant. For example, this arrangement obscures management's power and may lead servers to be more interested in the wishes of their customers than of their bosses because customers pay the tip. Customers might take very seriously their "managerial" role in relation to servers and report to management on servers' performances. Managers might direct their servers to set limits on customers' special requests but generously agree to fulfill any request that a customer makes directly to them. Day-to-day and even minute-to-minute, alliances are formed and broken, and this triadic arrangement of power shifts.

The way that service work blends matters of subjectivity—emotions, authenticity, friendship, recognition, and performance—with labor processes—work roles, job requirements, wages, and tips—challenges how scholars have studied work. Service work requires new frameworks of analysis and raises questions about not only the subjectivity of workers, but also the intersubjective interactions among customers, managers, and workers. For example, in *The Great Good Place*, Ray Oldenburg argues that "what attracts the regular visitor to a third place is supplied not by management but by the fellow customers. The third place is just so much space unless the right people are there to make it come alive, and they are the regulars."[26] I agree that regular customers who are loyal to a business are instrumental in the production of ambience. About regulars, Oldenburg writes, "The single essential element of a third place tavern from which all other characteristics derive is a hard core of regular patrons."[27] In Oldenburg's view, a restaurant continues to succeed because of the routine presence of customers who are "into" what the place delivers, the stable core of familiar faces that make the place friendly. But the way Oldenburg isolates those interactions, as if the space is a flat backdrop against which customers perform sociability, overlooks servers' and managers' contributions to the production of ambience.

Unlike Oldenburg, I view customers as merely one contributing social actor in the space of the restaurant. I argue that customers respond to an ambience made possible by location, decorations, flavors, sounds, and style of service, which all combine to produce the mood of a place. That mood is influenced by management strategies and is provided and sustained by frontline service workers. I extend Oldenburg's study of the community that develops among regulars by shifting the focus from the consumers of sociability in third places to include the producers of service. I consider how servers, managers, and regular customers *cooperate* to create a friendly, cozy ambience. I study service interactions as intersubjective performances among three groups of actors: the customers, managers, and food servers.

In my account, service interactions are intersubjective. Intersubjectivity is an agreed-upon common understanding arrived at by two or more actors.[28] While Gerald Mars and Michael Nicod, in their famous account of waiting tables, ask, "Do servers get the jump on customers or do customers get the jump on servers?"[29] I believe that is precisely the wrong question to ask. Instead, I imagine service work not as one group triumphing over another but as something much more akin to a negotiation. Within service interactions, each social actor tries out a range of approaches and reactions to other social actors. A waitress might approach a table cheerfully and remark, "Well, how are you today?" with a decided lilt to her voice. If the couple at the table continues to look down at the menus and fails to react, she might leave the table entirely. When she returns, her approach will likely be muted compared to that first approach. Alternately, if the couple replies, "We are great! How are you doing tonight?" that response sets in motion an entirely different set of responses from the server. If customers become regular, those interactions become more predictable and entrenched. In both first encounters and much more routine associations, service interactions are intersubjective performances co-produced by customers, workers, and managers.

Relying on intersubjectivity as a framework for understanding service interactions moves away from the false distinction made between the scripted interactions of the marketplace and the spontaneous interactions of social life. Instead, this study takes seriously that service interactions are always both market exchanges and social interactions. The terms of those exchanges are like chess matches: they are intersubjective exchanges of cash, of smiles or frowns, of appreciation or need, and of shared or competing ideas about a particular place. Service work combines prescribed behaviors with improvised steps and gestures. Servers repeat a routine, often prescribed by management, that contains common elements but also adjust it to the particular "audience" of each table. For example, a server named Alex explains how she learned to read her audience at each table and adjust her performance: "Learning how to read people, you come to a table and you're all bouncy and happy and they're like ugh [makes dispassionate face] you know in a second, it's like, OK, I gotta chill with these people more. You definitely have to go with your intuition." In *Fast Food, Fast Talk*, Robin Leidner studied the effectiveness of scripts in directing consumer behavior. She also revealed how workers at McDonald's modify scripts to adapt to customer demands. She was interested in the individual and cultural consequences of moving through a marketplace where more and more human interactions are engineered. "Not only does the routinization of interactive service work complicate the problems of alienation traditionally associated with the elimination of self-direction from work, but it alters cultural understandings of acceptable conduct toward others and manipulation of the self."[30] Leidner was the first to examine directly the consequences of the triadic labor structure on the self of the worker; however, Leidner considered customers indirectly rather than as actors in their own right. My analysis of both the scripted and spontaneous exchange in service encounters begins where Leidner's analysis left off. I extend Leidner's model to include the voices of customers as well. I study the work culture of the restaurant as a coproduction resulting from the conflicting needs and collaborative practices of workers, managers, and customers.

In service work, bodies, emotions, trays, tables, smiles, and tears collide and coordinate in second-to-second interactions. Service interactions are intersubjective processes that make specific use of bodies and space. Bodies are intimately engaged in and necessary to the work of waiting tables. In the restaurant space, bodies are both a resource and a liability. In service work, bodies operate as tools of service delivery, literally transporting the materials that customers need. Servers' bodies carry them in the back door to punch in, and their bodies carry heavy trays. The ambience of the restaurant is displayed on their bodies as uniforms and also seeps into their skin as aroma, cuts, burns, and wanted and unwanted touches. Their skin absorbs the smells, the touch, the approving looks, and the insulting glares of their customers and coworkers. In service work, bodies are both a source of skill and a site of vulnerability. Bodies are also resources mined for strength, for agility, for energy when face and feelings grow tired, and for decoration: servers' bodies are part of the scenery. Finally, satisfying service interactions rely on skillful use of the body: a staff that communicates well will eventually get so accustomed to passing each other, switching places, transferring trays, sharing space, and helping each other that words no longer are necessary during the busiest parts of the evening.

To do their work well, servers must be quick on their feet and able to maneuver the small spaces and crowded passages of the restaurant. Servers constantly use physical language and refer to their own and other people's bodies when they narrate their work. For example, one waitress named Jessica explains the intensity of the workplace by saying, "I think that in the restaurant industry there's probably more people in one spot all the time." Jessica's description points to the congested and complicated space that her work requires her to navigate. On a busy night, not only are the forty-two tables in the bar and restaurant peopled time after time, but all open spaces, every nook and cranny, are packed with people either working, eating, or waiting to be seated. Within the congested social and occupational space of the restaurant every player has both a role and a designated area to inhabit.

MANAGING SERVICE

Managers possess the greatest degree of access to space. There is no location in the restaurant to which they do not have access. Managers move between the front and the back many times each night, often in the role of viewing and supervising, rather than delivering or fighting for supplies. Managers are also generally free to sit down or "hide out" in the back of the house. Despite their expansive access to space, managers are both protected and limited by their less immediate contact with customers.

Just as workers have to juggle the demands of customers with the directives of management, managers are buffeted by demands and requests from both customers and employees. Managers must compromise between the demands of customers and the needs of workers, who are also loyal and opinionated. For example, even if managers secretly do not like regulars, they know they must treat them with respect, appear happy to see them, and take their requests seriously.

While servers are expected to be immediately available to customers and managers alike, managers are more remote and their contact with customers is more selective. For example, part of managers' job involves casual conversation with customers to assess their experience. As a result, managers often chat for extended periods with customers. Managers' presence also communicates different meanings than servers'. Servers are expected to be ever-available, while managers might arrive to flatter, to recognize, or to solve a problem for customers.

CUSTOMERS AND REGULARS AT THE HUNGRY COWBOY

On the stage of the restaurant, every player has both a role and a designated area to inhabit. Customers are the most confined spatially. To illustrate, customers who cannot find a place to stand "out of the action" will get bumped and relocated repeatedly as they wait for their table. Once customers have been assigned a table and guided there by an employee, they settle in by establishing a territory that belongs to them for part of an evening. Servers refer to this temporary ownership when they speak of customers who stay so long that they should be charged "rent" on the table.[31] Customers demarcate their space by stretching out, laying out jackets, papers, or photographs, moving around items on the table, or rearranging chairs.

Like servers, customers' attire, demeanor, and movements affect the service exchange. Adult customers' degree of comfort and sense of ownership of their space varies greatly. Some customers perch in their seats, apologize for getting in the way of workers, and leave quickly once they complete the official business of eating. Other customers take off their shoes, put their legs up, hold hands, kiss or cuddle up with their tablemate. Some shout out to other customers they know, turn to talk to the people in the next table, or motion to the manager to come over for a chat. These more comfortable customers move aggressively through the restaurant when going to the bathroom, and do not hesitate to violate the bounds of their assigned table by gathering supplies for themselves, changing the channel on a TV, or moving tables and rearranging chairs.

Within the restaurant, customers have power owing to their position as consumers, while workers have power owing to their familiarity and access to items and even the attention that customers desire. While servers have greater access to the front- and backstages of the restaurant and must act as the liaison for communicating and retrieving the items that customers desire, customers are encouraged to view the entire restaurant as their own space. Yet workers spend more time in the space, know all the nooks and crannies and the location of items, and have access to places to hide away and escape. Consequently, servers also feel a sense of ownership and view the restaurant as their space.

The volleying for control over space plays out in service exchanges. In response to loud noises from the kitchen, an item they are informed they can't have, or slow service, customers often ask, "What is going on back there?" This question points to the limits of customers' movement and gaze. Regular customers often use their privileged access to information to find out about dating habits of employees, secrets of food production, or other private workplace interactions. In asking such questions, customers acknowledge that they are audience to only a portion of the action in a restaurant and recognize servers as workers for whom the interactions at the table are only part of the larger story of their lives. Questions about workers' lives outside the restaurant break through the staged performance that requires servers only to be servile and friendly, absorbed by the need-fulfillment of their customers.

While many of the faces at the Hungry Cowboy change over time, some performers become "regulars." Regulars are seasoned performers: they know how to follow the protocol of service. Over time, interactions between regular customers and servers increasingly resemble not the scripted and predictable exchanges of role functions but rather friendships or other private relationships. For example, "what can I get you to drink tonight?" is replaced by "how was your weekend?" Despite routine associations, exchanged pleasantries, and even fondness between servers and served, the spatial dynamics of the restaurant reinforce distinct and enduring power relations between the groups of performers within the restaurant.

STORIES FROM THE HUNGRY COWBOY

Every night begins with bodies streaming in both doors; customers in the front, workers in the back. For the space of eight hours, often more, as individuals and as groups, they come together in a shared space, making alliances, constructing selves, and seeking out satisfaction. Some will be more satisfied than others. Some social exchanges will lead to future interactions while others will end with that evening. At the end of the night, the lights go down, the chairs go up, the music is silenced, and each group of social actors depart; customers out the front door, workers out the back. When I was working at the Hungry Cowboy, at the end of the night, the servers and bartenders would kick back, have a beer, count our tips, and, as Julia decribed it, "roll out the mental garbage." During those late-night hours relaxing after a long shift, we frequently concluded that "we should write a book about this place," which is another way of saying that we should find a way to expose and explain the nuances, tall tales, and collective memories of this workplace.[32] *The Hungry Cowboy: Service and Community in a Neighborhood Restaurant* began as my story of one restaurant, the work done there, the ways that workers negotiate the terms of their labor and the social world they create in the process. In the following chapters, I explore the subjective experience of each group of participants in turn. Next, in chapter two, I compare the motivations and rewards for servers who emotionally invest in their work to those who choose to detach emotionally from their service. In chapter three, I detail the benefits of being regular and the rewards for customer loyalty to the Hungry Cowboy. In chapter four, I turn my attention to managers, comparing the training regimes and management techniques of the Hungry Cowboy with a chain restaurant named Rosie's. In chapter five, combining the voices and experiences of servers, managers, and customers, I address what these three groups share: loyalty to the HC and a shared way of describing their experience as "like family." Finally, in the concluding chapter, I connect desires for home and belonging to the maintenance and reproduction of social hierarchies: how do our choices and behaviors as consumers and producers of service challenge or reinforce existing power relationships? What do the pleasures to be had in neighborhood restaurants like the Hungry Cowboy tell us about the culture in which we live?

By becoming a researcher, I learned things about the Hungry Cowboy that I never understood as a participant. Sociologist C. Wright Mills identified this new way of seeing as one of the outcomes of the sociological imagination. The sociological imagination provides us with the tools to situate individual experience within larger structures and to understand how structure develops. Mills described the sociological imagination as the ability to "grasp history and biography and the relations between the two within society." At its best, the sociological imagination equips us to do just that: to take a step back and situate our own experiences within the larger institutional, cultural, and historical context of the time and place. In "The Promise" Mills described the effect of using the sociological imagination as having been "suddenly awakened in a house with which [I] had only supposed [I was] familiar."³³ Sociological practice enables us to make the familiar strange, and doing so reveals new insights.

Sitting down across from a fellow employee and saying, "Tell me about your work," produced work narratives that upended my assumptions. As a researcher, I learned new things about the people I had worked alongside for years. For instance, I came to see my own approach to waiting tables as anomalous and in many ways inferior to the way many of my coworkers conducted their work. When I was a server, I loved the vitality of the restaurant as a place where things *happen* constantly: dishes break, relationships take root, angry words are exchanged, people fall down drunk and even fall in love. I liked being in the heart of a place where so much happens, but for me that tenderness ended where the rug started. The front of the house was a place where I performed the role of a server; I preferred to avoid meaningful contact with the guests. I cared deeply about my coworkers, but I did my best to remain distant from the vast majority of the customers. In contrast, many of my fellow coworkers seemed to care personally about their regular customers, welcoming them like long lost friends, sharing details from their private lives, and even talking about customers' lives and welfare when they were not immediately present. I remember standing in the kitchen listening to servers tell stories about customers and thinking, "How can they care so much?" I just did not feel as if I could afford to care about my customers the way they did. I use "afford" here to refer to emotional, not financial, reserves. I did not want to "spend" more attention, affection, and energy on customers than was necessary. I attempted to distance myself from the emotional demands of the job by spending as little of my self as possible on my customers, while many of my coworkers were more generous with their time, attention, and energy. Becoming a researcher reinforced my respect for workers who throw themselves emotionally into their work; I could then see them as being not dupes but rather deliberate and proud workers.

By carefully listening to stories of consumers and producers in this one small pocket of the marketplace, I want to attest to the contradictions of late capitalism: how humans make creative use of the marketplace not only to serve the needs of capital but also to form connections with one another. This is not a heroic tale; it is an account of one workplace, fraught with all the meanness and goodness of the social world in which it is situated and the faces that people it. In what follows, I hope to lift the curtain of the serving life enough so that readers will no longer approach paying to be served in restaurants as an uncomplicated exchange.

2

PRODUCING FAMILIARITY

◆◆◆◆◆◆◆◆◆◆◆◆◆◆◆◆◆◆◆◆◆◆◆

SERVERS AT THE HUNGRY COWBOY

I worked my first job at a little pizza place, and for some reason I always thought it would be really cool to wait on tables. I always wanted to do that. I always wanted to be a waitress or a bartender. I like working with people. I mean, there's just a certain amount of freedom to this job. You go out there on the floor and you have to be presentable and professional and all that stuff, but then when I go back in the kitchen, I just go crazy, and I pretty much just have fun. The job is fun to work.

I think it's a lot more pleasant to wait on people when they know a little bit about you because they actually talk to you like a person. They can understand if you have a bad day. They know just a little bit of your personality, just a little bit of your background; I think that helps a lot. BUT then there's also these people that pretend to be really nice, like, "Ohh, look at you . . ." and before I was going to school, they'd be like, "Oh, what are you going to school for?" and I'd be like, "I'm not going to school," and they'd say, "You just work here?" or people saying, "So when are you gonna get a real job?" and it's like, "Well, is this an imaginary job? Is this real money I make? This is a real job and I probably make more money than you." But I think sometimes people look at you with this waitressing job and they think—it's almost like financial status I guess—it's like you're below them, because they're eating out and you're waiting on them and sometimes you feel totally demeaned, you know what I mean?

I get a lot, A LOT of pressure from my parents to get a real job. Every day I hear from them, "Do you want to carry those trays on your back for the rest of your life?" I mean my parents talk about it in exactly the same way as those snotty customers do: "Who are you and why don't you do something with your life?" They feel really bad for me, my parents do. They feel like it's shameful and they just feel bad for me physically because I already have varicose veins on my legs at the age of twenty-one and I come home with a sore back and my feet hurt. My parents worry because of the physical strain and because it's so demeaning.

About every three weeks, I go through mood swings. I'm all "I hate this place, I hate this place, I'm gonna quit, oh God, what am I doing here? I can't wait to be done with school," and then I'll be like totally happy and satisfied and "Wahoo! I made a hundred and fifty bucks today!" These mood swings last three weeks. Everybody goes through those.

This job, I want to say that it's like the same everyday, but it's not, it's different. But you don't, you know how in other jobs, you get projects, you move up, but in this job, it's just the same old deal. It's like watching a sitcom on TV, it's like the same thing. It's different 'cause you wait on different people and different things happen to you, but it's the same, and it starts rubbing off on you.

In a few short minutes Julia's narration of her work vibrates between excitement—maybe even titillation—and shame. She describes serving as an adventure she sought out as a young woman, one that continues to challenge her in ways that both reward her and discourage her. She gloats a bit when she recites her (unspoken) conversation with the customers who imagine themselves as superior to her; she reverses the logic by implicitly claiming that this is not only real work but work that also pays better than their jobs. On the other hand, at moments in the interview, Julia's voice softens and she seems to confess rather than simply tell her story. In those moments, Julia leans in and lowers her voice a bit. Her story loses some of its bravado, implying perhaps that her coworkers and customers know only parts of her experience, the parts she proclaims loudly. She becomes quiet when she talks about the varicose veins and her parents' shame at how she "carries those trays on her back," as if her work consisted primarily of being hunched over like a turtle.

One of the reasons Julia's parents are dismissive of her work is that the labor is physical; when waiting tables you get sweaty, you get dirty, and you get tired. The use of the body and the filth that accompanies being around food all day combine to make waiting tables appear low-skilled. For this reason, even servers like Julia who are proud of their work sometimes register shame about how they make use of their bodies. Julia's parents are concerned not only about the physical demands but about the low prestige of waiting tables. Her parents worry less about her varicose veins than the "shame" of being "just a waitress."[1]

Julia's tale of adventure, pleasure, and shame also highlights the emotional intensity as one of the key characteristics of her job. She describes moving back and forth between emotional contexts, reacting to her own "three-week" mood swings, while quietly bickering with the voices in her head that suggest or insist that her work is not meaningful. Despite the physical and emotional challenges of the work, serving work remains appealing to her.

In her narration, Julia does not merely tolerate her work, she also fights to love and defend her work. This finding is surprising. Julia's approach flies in the face of assumptions that serving others, especially in a casual context like the Hungry Cowboy, is degrading and depressing. Much like Julia's parents, who view service work as demeaning, most labor scholars approach service work as unwanted and unrewarding.[2] But Julia and the other servers I interviewed insist that their work has meaning and that they tolerate and manage the costly aspects of their job in part because they love their work.

In this chapter, I use servers' narratives and my own observations of their behavior at work to explore the contradictions, costs, and rewards involved in waiting tables at the Hungry Cowboy. I consider how servers like Julia create and perpetuate belonging, recognition, and community through their approach to their work. My conclusions are based on interviews with fifteen servers—five men and ten women—who have worked at the Hungry Cowboy from one to ten years.[3] The appendix provides interviewees' ages, years of experience, and brief descriptions of their life situations. This group of servers, many of whom have a long history at the restaurant and have come to know their customers well, provide a window into how work cultures develop, are reproduced, and are made available to customers and regulars.

Julia and her coworkers offer up their emotional intensity, physical agility, and personality to their customers, and in the process produce a particular ambience. Thus, their approach to their work not only influences how they feel about their work but also provides a central building block of sociability and community.

STUCK IN SERVING AND THE RHETORIC OF "REAL" JOBS

Servers' stories reflect how much of their selves they invest in a job that, no matter how long they stay, others may not consider to be a real job. The "not-a-real-job" mentality is so prevalent that it even shows up in the glossary of terms listed on a national server website called bitterwaitress. com: "Real Job: that which most people assume we do not have. Certainly long hours of stressful labor isn't real work. Of course the skills of dealing with many people at once is not valuable. Training and education are not part of a real job. No, real jobs entail sitting around, getting shat on by an old boss all day, then in turn being an ass to others, getting frustrated and taking it out on your waitress at dinner that night. If that's a real job, I don't want one." This view that waiting on tables is "not a real job" affects how family members and friends perceive servers' work. Meg explains the tension between what her parents had hoped for her and their disregard for serving work.

> I just think my parents, they don't try to be, but they're just a little pompous. They think that it's not respectable, people who don't have college degrees, people who don't really have any future can do it, but most people who waitress do have college degrees, it's just a way to make cash. They just don't respect it, I don't think they think that this job is worthy of what I should be doing. I'm supposed to be daddy's and mommy's little girl. They want to be proud of me, but they can't as long as I'm just a waitress.

Meg is particularly clear: as long as she works as a waitress, her parents cannot be proud of her. Here, she uses her parents' disregard for her work to explain that others view the work she does as appropriate only for people who do not have a college degree, who are not respectable and who have no future prospects.

Servers struggle to enjoy their work and find meaning in it because their work is stigmatized. In 1963, Erving Goffman defined stigma as "an attribute that is deeply discrediting within a particular social interaction."[4] Goffman identified three types of stigma: overt or visible physical deformities, deviations in personal traits that might include drug addiction or criminality, and finally, tribal stigmas, which include ethnic, racial, religious, or national affiliations. Julia and the other servers encounter a stigma that parallels a tribal stigma. Many view waiting tables, especially in a casual setting, as easy work that lacks meaning and that anyone can do. According to this view, the work is low status and a form of employment one should seek to escape as soon as possible. According to Goffman, individuals who possess a particular stigmatized affiliation are subject to discreditation and suffer the effects of having a "spoiled identity" in the eyes of others. Because this group of service workers knows their labor is discredited, they must struggle to bring meaning to their work or to feel proud of their labor.

Although servers work hard for their money, the stigma of "not a real job" endures in part because the economy structures service work as part-time and temporary. Even the Bureau of Labor describes service work as ordinarily part-time, a good "first" job, and explains that many service workers are "full-time students or homemakers."[5] Indeed, many servers are full-time students or homemakers, but many are not. Because some people assume that waiting tables is legitimate only as a support for other pursuits like raising children or getting an education, full-time food servers have difficulty feeling that waiting tables counts as a career or a source of self-esteem and identity.

Servers not only encounter the attitude that serving is not "real work" from others, they also have to defend against internalizing that belief. For example, workers who have two jobs often define the other job (as long as it's not waiting tables) as their real job. A waitress named Alex argues that service work is important but should be a temporary job. "It should be temporary unless you get the big bucks. I think it should be temporary but it is so invaluable as a young person to learn about life, about reality." Even servers who work full-time hesitate to view serving as their career or a primary source of their identity. For example, Patricia was disturbed when a little girl described waitressing as her career.

> Like one night a couple weeks ago, I had this table and a little girl was looking at her cowpoke menu and you had to translate from Spanish and the little girl was like, "Look it, ma'am, I found your career." And I'm thinking, this isn't my career. Waitress? That's a little scary. This isn't my career. I'm like, I make good money though. I'm not trying to put people down, like being a waitress is something to look down on; I just am at a totally different stage of my life than the majority of the people I work with.

Working hard at a job that does not feel like a "real job" is a significant challenge for servers' sense of self-esteem and identity.

TIPS AND SOCIABILITY
Evaluating Service

The uncomfortable fit between serving and "career" is reinforced because the occupational structure of serving offers little or no advancement, benefits, or rewards for seniority. Trevor explains how the lack of benefits influences who can work in restaurants. He says, "Lots of restaurants don't have benefits; it's not a career-oriented position. It's just not suitable for anybody with a family, or with a future outlook." One server confessed that he had never had a job performance review in five years. In larger occupational structures, key servers who excel can be promoted into management ranks, but in smaller restaurants like the Hungry Cowboy, the only structural reward for excellence is access to lucrative shifts that might result in more tips. Jessica explains the stigma that attaches to her for working a job that does not offer insurance to its employees.

> Sometimes I think, I've worked here for seven years and I've never had one day of vacation pay. I think one of the benefits of having a real job that I miss, and that right now is really important to me, is insurance, because I'm paying too much for [private insurance]. You know I pay

two hundred dollars a month in insurance just to have people look
down their noses at me! Like I'm some sort of welfare victim. It pisses
me off, and I get that all the time. I pay all that money for insurance,
and it's like "get a job!"

During my research, I conducted interviews at eight competing restaurants.
Out of the nine restaurants I studied, only one offered insurance, and none
of the restaurants offered vacation pay to tipped employees. The quick cash
that gets many servers into the business of waiting tables in the first place is
the sole reward for the majority of servers in the United States.

Tips are the monthly review, promotion, profit sharing, evaluation, and
academy awards of serving. To serve is to enter the lottery again and again,
betting on the reception of one's skills: the ability to relate to people across
the spectrums of age and mood, to entertain without becoming overbear-
ing, to serve without becoming servile, and to convey a sense of personal
worth to the customers that will convince them to leave a good tip. Author
Bruce Griffin Henderson, a waiter by trade, explains how the power of tip is
always present, sometimes overtly, sometimes as subtext:

> I think the most significant effects of the tipping system are the psy-
> chological ones. As a waiter working for tips, on a certain level you feel
> like a beggar or a servant; scrounging for whatever your benefactors
> see fit to give you. This is not a good feeling. And your customers do
> little to dispel this notion, saying clever things like, "Your tip depends
> on it!" or the ever-popular, "There goes your tip!" In the end, the tip-
> ping system is as psychologically empowering to customers as it is
> debilitating to the waiters. But we all know the score when we tie on
> an apron.[6]

Tipping is the primary source of food servers' income. Servers' wages
are not supplemented but basically provided by their customers. In Minnesota, restaurants have to pay minimum wage; however, some servers work in
states where the law allows tipped employees to be paid as little as $2.13 an
hour.[7] As a pay structure, tipping provides customers with significant power
over servers.[8]

While tips are central to servers' ability to make a living, servers at the Hungry Cowboy rarely mentioned tips in interviews. From their perspective, the currency of tips gets mixed in with customers' qualitative evaluation of their work. Anthropologist David Sutton explains what he calls the "communicative function" of tips: "tipping is an interesting mode of communication between workers and customers, partaking simultaneously of the symbolic and utilitarian, the meaningful and the functional."[9] At the Hungry Cowboy, the majority of servers focus on the symbolic and social aspects of serving rather than the economic and utilitarian. Some servers report that they are more likely to take offense at customers' facial expressions and verbal remarks than at the tip itself. Most of the servers I interviewed attempt to separate pay from performance by ignoring how individual customers "value" their work through tips. In interviews, servers talked about bad tips not as a primary source of abuse but merely as additional insults in customers' treatment of them. During a shift or at the end of the night, servers occasionally acknowledge a particularly good or bad tip, yet when questioned directly about tips they proclaim that tips "do not matter." Instead, servers attempt to obscure the power relations operating within the service exchange by focusing on giving a sincere performance or providing "a good evening" for a guest.[10]

Although many people enjoy being served and look forward to going out, the popular imagination does not view the job of serving and helping people enjoy their experience as one that "matters" or counts as real work. As a result, servers find it challenging to feel proud of their labor, build a positive work identity, and have their labor recognized as having social value.

SERVING UP SMILES

Perhaps the greatest difficulty servers encounter is in learning how to put on multiple emotional performances simultaneously. As servers' bodies move between locations and slip between tables, they adjust their faces and affect to react to irate customers in one booth, a favorite regular celebrating a birthday in the next, and a family in the adjacent table who have come from a funeral. Hochschild defines these adjustments of feeling as "emotional labor."[11] Hochschild uses this term to describe work that "requires one to induce or suppress feeling in order to sustain the outward countenance that produces the proper state of mind in others."[12] Hochschild differentiated the emotion work that all people do privately from the manipulation of feelings in public and for a wage. Individuals often alter their emotions in private. For example, a teenage girl might pretend to be delighted by the sweater that her grandmother buys her as a birthday present, even if she will never wear it. When people do emotion work not to smooth private relationships but rather to mask the work of serving others, Hochschild defines that work as emotional labor.

Sociologists ordinarily use the term "emotional labor" to describe a required aspect of work that is costly to workers. Just as physical labor can tire and wear out the body, emotional labor can estrange workers from the part of themselves they use at work—their emotions. Hochschild worries that manipulating one's emotions at work will essentially wear out a worker's face and feelings. Servers illustrate Hochschild's claim when they describe instances of emotional fatigue. For example, when I ask Betsy what the hardest part of her job is, she describes emotional exhaustion. "Sometimes when you're not in the mood, when you're not feeling good, it's not a phone job where people can't see you and there are times when you just go [sighs deeply], 'I'm tired.' You get burned out." Routine use of one's face and expression to disguise hurt, exhaustion, or lack of concern can take a toll on workers over time.

Learning how to manage one's emotions and perpetually display what one server calls a "perma-grin" is part of the training. Servers are trained with an official document called "the twenty-one points of service." Explicit in this document is the requirement to do what Erving Goffman calls "face work."[13] Goffman uses this term to describe the work that individuals do through interactions to present a desirable image of themselves or one appropriate to the situation at hand. Descriptions like "save face" or "maintain face" derive their meaning from this idea of intentional performances of the self. In the Hungry Cowboy's twenty-one points of service, servers are reminded routinely to present a smile. Three of the twenty-one points are "1. Smile . . . 7. Smile . . . [and] 19. Smile." The requirement to "wear that smile" parallels Hochshild's claim that the workers she interviewed described their smiles as "on them, but not of them."[14] When I asked Betsy what qualities were necessary to be a good server, she replied, "When you walk the floor, you just have to, um, you have to be happy, not really happy, but you have to satisfy the criteria of waiting." Betsy's description reveals that performing pleasant emotions is a job requirement. Her happiness does not have to be deeply felt, but it does have to be visible when she is on the front stage of the restaurant.

Servers refer to this emotion work as a key to the service contract. Servers not only described their own approach to waiting on tables but also explained that they had learned from their coworkers techniques for managing uncooperative customers and demands for deference. Specifically, waiting tables requires servers to perform, or "do deference."[15] "Deference" is another important term derived from Goffman's theories of social inter-action that describes the power dynamics of relationships. To defer is to show regard or respect to another through symbolic gestures. Hochshild refers to it as a symbolic bowing to another.[16] In the service exchange, servers must defer to customers, not vice versa. For instance, Meg explained that she learned how to manage her emotions from Sarah. "Dealing with crabby people because before I would just be kind of a bitch, but now I just kind of say yes, and I have a big smile on my face. In my own way, I can make myself feel OK because I'm not being nice to them; they just think I am. Sarah taught me that. I just watched her. I trained with her and I just watched her, she was the queen of that, of just totally being mean to them, but they think she's nice. She was so funny to watch." Meg's explanation of learning to insincerely perform "caring" also demonstrates the degree to which serv-ers teach each other how to manage emotions. From the moment a server announces, "Hi my name is Meg, I'll be your server today," her emotions become constrained by the requirements of her job. As Meg's story demon-strates, one of the emotional requirements of service work is that servers act as if they are happy to wait on people, even when they are not. To produce excitement, pleasure and interest in one's customers for hours on end is to perform emotional deference.

Labor scholars have used the powerful framework of emotional labor to examine labor relations and work experience, particularly in service work; however, the scholarship on emotional labor tends to examine the costs to individuals of performing caring while ignoring the potential rewards of emotional labor. That is, scholars see this labor not as benefiting workers but as costing them. By contrast, studying service interactions at the Hungry Cowboy reveals how service workers emotionally invest in and potentially take pleasure in the emotional aspects of service interactions. While previous studies of emotional labor have focused on worker strategies for protecting themselves from emotional demands, this study highlights the pleasure to be had in both the social and physical interactions that take place in restaurants.

Servers' accounts challenged me to consider how emotional labor might operate as a "hook," as a positive inducement for workers. What if emotion work were both a cost and an incentive of serving others? At least for some of the workers here, emotional labor operates as an incentive in a job that offers few structural rewards for working hard. For example, Julia's narrative is rife with emotional highs and lows. What she does not say in the interview is just how remarkably good she is at waiting on tables, pouring a drink while she tells a story, getting a customer who is down on his luck to utter a laugh. More than that, Julia's fierce emotionality often buoys up, or drives down, the mood of the entire staff. She is fiery and brilliant, hilarious and sometimes very angry. She brings all of those moods, performances, and passions to work with her. Julia offers up her substantial emotional resources repeatedly even though the pay structure does not reward her for her effort. The work offers Julia no guarantee that she will make more money than workers who are lazy or dispassionate. In fact, her tips might not even reflect her effort. She offers up her emotional resources also knowing that she cannot count on having her tips reflect her efforts: sometimes regular customers tip worse than new customers; sometimes a table she makes mistakes with might tip her more than the one for which she is the most charming.

Despite the unpredictability of working for tips, Julia and many other servers emotionally "show up" night after night, recognizing their customers' needs, remembering their favorites, livening up their evening, or listening to a story or memory. Servers describe the emotional labor they perform as both exhausting and rewarding. In fact, servers seek out emotional high points, from going "crazy" behind the scenes to moments when they feel they have "made someone's night." Servers report that the emotional high points of the job motivate them and inspire their commitment to the work. Servers' choice to perform enthusiastic emotional labor for their customers

contributes to the restaurant's warm atmosphere and fosters emotional connections among staff and with customers.

LOVING WORK DESPITE THE JOB DESCRIPTION

When scholars study work, they often carry with them a set of ideas about
the experience of work that are derived originally from Marxist teachings.
Marx sees the structure of work as alienating: some (the capitalists) own
the means of production, while the workers (the proletariat) work for sub-
sistence. For Marx, this alienation is a multifaceted experience in which
the worker becomes alienated from the product of his labor, from his fellow workers, from nature, and, finally, from himself.[17] Perhaps the simplest
example of Marx's predictions in the contemporary era is a factory worker
who labors to produce one panel of a pickup truck all day long. At the end
of the day, the capitalist owns all the trucks the worker has helped assemble,
and the worker cannot afford to buy even one of the trucks from the capitalist. In this scenario, the worker has lost control not only of the products of
his own efforts but also of his connection to the earth and its products. He
is divided against his fellow man, who profits from his labor, and he eventually (Marx predicts) will become alienated from his body as it increasingly
appears as an object to him. His arm that shapes the truck panel is no longer
his own, and so he is alienated from himself.

Whether scholars work within or against a Marxist tradition, many
carry with them ideas about exploitation, alienation, and revolution that
begin with Marx. While contemporary labor studies need not deal with
Marx in the purest form, studies of work often seek to identify degrees of
exploitation of workers: they contrast exploitation with autonomy, seeing
workers who have less autonomy as more exploited., What I discover at the
Hungry Cowboy, however, is difficult to fit into these categories. Here I find
workers who are structurally exploited explaining that they love their job
because it gives them "pleasure." This work makes hard use of faces, bodies,
and selves; at the same time, workers claim that using their bodies and feelings as resources is part of what makes the job rewarding and even meaningful. In these findings, autonomy and exploitation are not opposites; rather,
autonomy blends with structural disadvantage and even exploitation.

Servers' stories and answers to my questions revealed two distinct strategies for protecting their self-image from the potentially degrading work of serving others: "detachment" and "investment." I identify detachment and investment as distinct approaches servers use to cope with emotional labor and to protect their emotions and sense of dignity while at work. The detached worker views emotions while on the clock as necessary labor but not as a vehicle for producing ongoing connections with customers. The invested worker seeks to throw him- or herself into his or her work and invites ongoing connections with customers.

Workers who invest use emotional labor as a way to give meaning to their labor, seizing on their role in the restaurant as an opportunity to give and receive recognition, care, and concern in the public space of the restaurant. This caring emerges despite rather than because of the official job description.[18]

SWAPPING SMILES FOR FAST CASH
Detaching

Detachment involves setting aside one's own identity while "on the clock." Servers who use this approach exaggerate the difference between the kinds of behavior, practice, and deferential attitude necessitated by the job and those voluntarily produced by the "real" self. Servers who detach seek to maintain a divide between being in role at the table and breaking role "off-stage," beyond the purview of customers. Calling this approach "role distance," Erving Goffman explains that an individual will stay in role in the staging area of his or her performance when he or she is being observed but will "break role or go out of role when he [or she] thinks that no one or no one important can see him [or her]."[19] Servers who detach insist that they prevent customers from "getting to them" by remaining emotionally distant from the service exchange. Joey's story provides one example of what a detachment approach entails:

> I used to feel like [customers were] in control, but now I'm kind of bitter, so now I'm in control. I don't think I'm happy in general right now, so it sort of comes out in my personality. I'm sort of short with people. They know that. I think they have to make up their mind quicker.

People that, you know, they've been waving me down and I go over there and say "Are you ready?" and they go, "Ummm," and I say, "Well, you know, why don't I come back when you're ready." Stuff like that.

I'm getting really sick of regulars. [Laughs] I just want one day with not the same people walking in the place. I'm tired of seeing them. You need something different. You're at the same place everyday, you need something different. You know who takes care of you, so that's who you take care of. I remember people who don't tip me anything, I remember people who tip me huge. The people who don't tip right, they just don't get the service. It's not that we don't serve them, but we know. I don't work for free. I mean I'm not there to have fun, I'm there to make money. It's the money that keeps me there.

Joey reveals an instrumental orientation toward his labor, seeking to remain distant and detached from the requirements of his work role. Goffman predicts that an individual will pretend to embrace a role to protect him- or herself from the "psychological dangers of his [or her] actual attachment to it."[20] Similarly, Joey expresses confidence that his approach protects him. He offers up energy and attention only when he knows there will be a direct reward—in this case, a tip—for his effort.

In keeping with Goffman's description of role distance, Joey is able to continue to play the role required by his job, while simultaneously resisting what a server who invests might describe as "opportunities" to offer more than is required:

I get so sick of it. But I make a lot more money than people I know, who have supposedly respectable jobs. We make too much money for what we do. It's crazy. I can pay for my rent in one night. I'm never going to go to another restaurant and start over. When I'm done with the Hungry Cowboy, I'm done. I have to be. I mean, what kind of goals can you have, doing that night after night? You can't reach goals because there's [sic] no goals to set. You can't set any goals. You can set short-term goals like I'm going to have a good night tonight, I'm going to be in a good mood.

I don't have job security here; nobody does. If you give a drink to the wrong person, you're fired.[21] If somebody brings in a minor and

you serve them, you're going to get fired, I don't care how long you've
been here. It makes you not have commitment. I don't feel really committed to this job. I do when I'm here, because it's my job, but when
it comes right down to it, I'd walk out, because I know they'd do the
same to me.

Joey's rationale for his approach mixes a structural critique of the limitations of the job with his own displeasure at having to cater to the needs
of others. Joey offers several explanations for his approach to his work:
the irritations of serving others, the dull routine and repetition of the
work, the inconsistency of tips, the inability to set long-term goals, and
the instability of employment. In response to these limitations, he has
decided to limit what he will give to his work in terms of energy, enthusiasm, and even attention. He has assessed what he can "get away with"
in terms of what he offers to customers, what will keep him sufficiently
out of trouble with the management, and even what his coworkers will
tolerate. For example, he remembers how his customers tip because, after
all, he doesn't "work for free." Joey's strategy is a rationalized approach to
waiting tables in two ways. First, he rationalizes his work, meaning that
he "attributes to [his actions] rational and credible motives,"[22] by explaining that his work is not his life so it makes sense to do the least amount
of work for the most amount of money. He also rationalizes his work in
the sense of applying "principles of scientific management to [a process]
for a desired result (as increased efficiency)."[23] For example, he streamlines
his efforts and attempts to get his customers to do the same, by saying,
"Why don't I come back when you're ready." Joey's goal is to minimize the
interactions required to complete his work.

    Joey professes to be unaffected by customer insults and mistreatment
because he perceives customers solely in terms of the dollars they will leave
on the table. Joey's detached outlook seems successfully to transport him
away from customers' verbal abuse, because he refuses to acknowledge his
job as part of who he is.[24] When he is attacked or maligned, he emotionally
removes himself as if his "real self" is not even present. Joey disengages from
difficult and demeaning moments by maintaining an attitude that work is,
by nature, a task to be endured.

In the spectrum of detachment and investment at the Hungry Cowboy, Joey is on the extreme end of detaching. Joey talks about his work with a mix of defensiveness, anger, and resignation. The only source of satisfaction that he names is the money he receives and his friendships with co-workers. When it comes to customers, the more distant he is, the better off he is. Of the five workers who detached, Meg is the only other server who shares Joey's deeply held disdain for this particular form of work. Meg said she "used to be a bitch" until she learned from a coworker, Sarah, how to fake being pleasant to customers. Learning how to "fake it" is certainly far from really caring about one's customers, yet Meg's desire to know how to appear concerned about her customer's needs clearly surpasses Joey's interest in strictly rationalized interactions with customers. While Meg and Joey clearly share disdain for their work, Joey remains the extreme example of detaching. In fact, his fellow coworkers routinely complain about how detached he is. Joey is frequently used as a negative example of how not to do their work. Beth says, "Like Joey, you know, he does pretty good for somebody who looks bad. I'll be like, 'Joey, you gotta clean yourself up! You're hung over, you look like shit, you smell like shit, you're bumping around, you always look tired, you never smile.' I've never seen him in a fast pace. Even when we're really busy in the bar." For some of his coworkers, Joey operates as an example of doing the job poorly.

While Joey emphasizes that work is simply a means to an end, other workers who detach focus on the fact that jobs, in general, tend to require alienating conditions. For Billy, Trevor, and Ralph, it is not that this job "sucks" but rather that most jobs are alienating and disappointing. To rationalize their work, these workers point to other types of work that are equally unrewarding and yet do not pay any better. For example, Billy explains that he trained to work in the music industry but soon realized that his music industry job was "just the same as everything else—lots of politics, you need to know somebody to get in, and there's no guarantees." Later he left serving for a while to work at "a desk job," which pained him not only because of "the clothes, the schedule, and the competition" but also because he did not maintain the same income as he had received at the Hungry Cowboy. These two excursions into different work settings have solidified Billy's conviction that service work fits with who he is and the life he wants to lead, while also reinforcing his worldview that work is a necessary evil.

Despite some variation in the logic that drives their detachment narratives, workers who detach have a great deal in common. One striking similarity is that the four men who detach—Billy, Joey, Trevor, and Ralph—rationalize their work through comparison. Note how each of them compares his work favorably to alternatives for employment.

Billy explains that while he does not like his job, he is not eager to join what he refers to as the "cubicle culture" of the 9-to-5 world. He states: "It's kind of a funny, ironic thing, that you can be waiting on someone that's in for lunch in a suit and tie and they're making less a year than you are and they're working thirty more hours a week than you are and giving you attitude like you're some peon, and you go back and laugh at those people; they have no clue."

Trevor also compares himself to the man in the suit to justify his work: "What society deems as normal doesn't do what we do because the hours suck and that section of society that doesn't do this perceives us as being a lower class in a way and you get looked down upon. Normal people just don't do what we do, they just don't, and it's not something for everybody. But a lot of times I'm waiting on a guy in a suit and I make more than him, but he's got no idea!"

Billy describes his disappointment when he interned at a music company: "I felt used. That's sort of what it comes down to. I did, I felt used, big-time. Interning for four months, they had me doing everything from cleaning the bathrooms, and I thought at the end something really good was going to come out of it, but then the next intern just came in and started cleaning the bathrooms. That was it."

Trevor describes feeling out of place at a factory job: "I have worked a lot of jobs, worked in a factory for a while, so the horn sounds, we go to lunch, the horn sounds again and we go home. I'm working like a little ant in a little colony. I got reprimanded for being too social there. Too social! It's like—Jesus, please—so obviously, there, that was a big red flag, that that wasn't my place."

Joey sets up a contrast between "hell" and "freedom" to compare serving work to office work. "It sucked. It really sucked. It was at a wireless company. Oh my god, it was hell. Training that should have lasted four days lasted four weeks. And I'm like, are you kidding me, I'm making $8.50 an hour and I'm ready to kill myself. I have a lot of freedom where I work right now."

What emerges from these comparisons is a shared belief that they have "figured it out" and somehow beat the system by making do with work that allows them specific freedoms not available in the 9-to-5 cubicle culture or to the "man in the suit."[25] These workers believe that they have what Joey describes as the "freedom" to socialize with friends (which often means each other), drink at a reduced price after work, and offer very little of themselves in exchange for cash. The fact that their current job requires as little of their energy as possible has become a benchmark of not only individual identities but also a group mentality among the four men who detach.

These four workers not only share a detached approach to the emotional demands of serving, they also rely on a common language to set up these comparisons. The similarity of linguistic conventions[26] in servers' detachment narratives is remarkable. Greta Foff Paules uses "linguistic conventions" to describe the symbolism of service that surrounds waiting tables.[27] One of the linguistic conventions that emerges from these interviews is the repetition of central ideas and symbols used to narrate this work. For example, servers who detach explicitly compare their "freedom" at work to the "guy in the suit." For instance, Trevor's explanation refers to his work as not "what society deems as normal," just before he uses the "guy in a suit" as a foil against which to compare himself. He argues that even if this work is not for the normal, or the average, at least he does not have it as bad as the guy in the suit.

At first glance, the repeated use of "the guy in the suit" as a measure of another kind of worker who has been duped seems to reflect an air of superiority, like craft pride. Craft pride refers to a worker's sense of his or her own skill and competence, pride in one's craft. In his study of "the blue-collar aristocrats," E. E. LeMasters explains that working-class men often compare themselves favorably to white-collar workers of a certain type: "These blue-collar aristocrats actually feel that they are earning an 'honest living,' that working with your hands is more honorable than 'shuffling papers' or earning a living 'with your mouth.' They recognize the integrity of a good architect or that of a construction engineer, but they still feel that a great many white-collar workers make no substantial contribution to the welfare of our society."[28] While the four men who detach certainly use comparisons with other workers to explain how their work "rates" out of the available options, they do not seem to achieve the sense of superiority that LeMasters identified in his study. Billy, Ralph, Trevor, and Joey do not lay claim to making an "honest living." If anything, their narratives suggest that their triumph is in making an easy living compared to what other dupes, like the guy in the suit, give away to their work. They have a leg up on that imagined adversary because compared to cubicle culture, their work gives them equal or greater rewards while requiring less.

The fact that these workers' narratives share linguistic conventions is significant because, as Richard Sennett explains, "Narratives are more than simple chronicles of events; they give shape to the forward movement of time, suggesting reasons why things happen, showing their consequences."[29] The linguistic conventions these four men rely on reveal a more instrumental approach to work and a cynical attitude toward the potential for any work (or at least work they can imagine being available to them) to allow them to feel proud. Compare their narratives, for example, with John Simmons, a waiter at a different restaurant, who won first prize in an essay contest entitled "Why do you wait?"

> I could get a job that pays more, but would I get this feeling of accomplishment in sitting behind a desk being just another executroid? I don't think so. I am better at this than 99% of all the people I know will ever be at anything. Do you have any idea how it feels to do something so well that you feel invincible? It's amazing. I have days that I'm on such a roll I feel like I couldn't screw up if I tried. That's an awesome feeling of accomplishment that most people can't even begin to imagine.[30]

John Simmons is proud, even arrogant, about his skill and his sense of craft. He seems unafraid to say that he is good at what he does, really good. While Simmons also compares himself with the "exectroid," his evaluation of himself is much less cynical than the four men who detach at the Hungry Cowboy. In their narratives, each of these men downplay the importance of work in general to identity and favorably compare their work to jobs that require more of their selves but turn out to be less rewarding.

REFUSING TO CARE
Limits to Detachment

These servers recast the potential for abuse, lack of benefits and low status of service work as advantageous because it enables them to invest as little energy and attention in work as possible. On the surface, detaching seems like it might shield workers, yet several questions arise about the limitations of such a strategy. First, what does it cost them to abandon work as a source of meaning? Casting the idea of meaningful work as a farce robs them of the opportunity to care about their present job, while simultaneously narrowing their hopes for the future. Second, detachment makes it difficult to register instances of caring, in terms of either feeling wounded on the job or enjoying the emotional demands of the job. Finally, having professed that they do not care about their work, a detached approach might also make it more difficult to express the costs of emotional labor.

Despite these workers' detachment strategies, examples of how they do care occasionally slip out during the interviews. This tension is clear in Joey's description when he complains about customers who signal him rather than speaking to him, and then threatens to react violently, "If one more person whistles at me, I swear I'm going to jump across the table and knock them out." At one point, Trevor admits to resigning himself to drinking just to get through his work at a downtown bar where the "obnoxious" customers were so drunk that he could not hide his disdain for them unless he was also intoxicated. When I ask follow-up questions about these instances of emotional exhaustion or outrage, Trevor and Joey are quick to return to their prevailing sentiment that work does not matter. Goffman describes discrepant reports like Trevor and Joey's as "destructive information": "Given the fragility and the required expressive coherence of the reality that is dramatized by a performance, there are usually facts which, if attention is drawn to them during the performance, would discredit, disrupt or make useless the impression that the performance fosters."[31] Workers who detach must insist that they remain unaffected by the emotional demands of waiting tables because information to the contrary undermines their approach; however, professing not to care constrains their ability to acknowledge or even experience the highs and lows that accompany emotional labor.

USING SERVICE TO MAKE CONNECTIONS
Investing

Servers who rely on an investment strategy tend to be more passionate about their work, insisting on the significance of the social interactions that take place within service transactions. These servers insist that the way they perform service and the relationships that develop as a result are important and give their work meaning. Servers who invest view enjoying their work as part of who they are, not a role that they take on and off. These servers seek to know and remember customers' names, encourage them to "chitchat," and also approach their relations with coworkers as opportunities for meaningful social interaction beyond simply procuring supplies and delivering food and beverages.

For instance, Jessica's work narrative exemplifies how the majority of servers at the Hungry Cowboy invest in the emotional demands of their work:

> I like interacting with the people. I've known so many people for so long, it's not really like a job. I call it my little social life. Half the servers that I work with have been there as long as I have, or close to it. But families, families of children [of regular customers] that were in elementary school when I started are in college now. Just keeping up with what's going on with my customers, yeah, I like it.
>
> If a customer is irritating me, which shows that I'm not at my top par, because I'm letting them irritate me, and they're being dorks, which means they're either being rude, or they're having a bad day too. Basically, looking at it as it's not what they do to me, it's my reaction to it. Trying to keep that in focus. . . . If a customer pisses me off, I smile sweetly at them, and then go back into the kitchen and go, "They're driving me nuts!"

For being a good server, just being aware what's going on with your table, looking around, recognizing what they need, timely, remembering things too. Being a bad server means not knowing what their customer needs or not caring. You definitely have to care about your job in order to do your job well.

Jessica talks with pride about her history at the Hungry Cowboy and her ongoing relationships with customers. For Jessica, good service depends on the skill and level of "caring" of the server. Like Joey, she talks about needing to remember customers, but instead of remembering how much each table is "worth" based on previous tips, she refers to recognizing and remembering what customers need and like.

Jessica's investment strategy also affects her attitude toward the time she dedicates to her job. For Joey, work competes with his "real life," while for Jessica, work is her "social time," a time she looks forward to as a means of interacting with other people, some of whom she knows well.

A lot of regulars come in on Friday nights, so it's my night that I go around and chat with everybody. It's my PR [public relations] night. I enjoy chatting with them, there's always some funny story, some great joke, what's going on with them and vice versa. Yes, [customers] treat me like an acquaintance, like somebody that they've known for a long time, which they have.

Of course, I always like my tip, I can't say I don't like my tip, but I don't expect more from a regular customer because I've known them forever and I like chatting with them. I'm doing the chatting because that's why I like my job. We talk with our customers and we show them our kids and the latest things going on and, you know, they ask about it: "How are your kids? Do you have any pictures?" I just like to show off my kids' pictures.

I also like the challenge of a new table. When there's somebody who hasn't been there before, you can recommend things to them, and tell them what's great and all of that. In fact I have these regular customers, they came in five years ago or so, I think. They were moving

here, from [another country] for a job transfer for her husband and
they wanted to know about schools. So I told them what I thought . . .
and they still come in, they live in the neighborhood, and I email them
and they're cool.

Jessica describes service work as a careful mix of awareness and sociability
that is challenging and rewarding, making use of her wit and conversational
skills. In contrast to Joey's reluctance to commit his emotional energy to the
service exchange, Jessica welcomes opportunities to engage emotionally with
her customers and to get to know them as people, above and beyond the
demands of the service exchange.

    Like Jessica, the majority of the servers report that they have personal-
ized their relationship with both their customers and coworkers. Workers
who invest survive their jobs by believing that the care they offer as part of
the service encounter improved the experiences of customers. For instance,
when I asked Alex if there was anything she did not like about serving, she
said, "No, right now I'm not doing it because I have to, I'm doing it for complete pleasure." Regarding why she does this work, Lisa replied, "The people.
Meeting the people. I love meeting people." They take pleasure in the nature
of their work and their ability to do it well. Charles explains that he feels
satisfied when he can bring happiness to his customers: "There's a warm
quality, the smell of the food, the coffee. It's a pleasure for myself. How I
feel about going to work is that you feel good trying to bring pleasure to
people, too. I kind of empathetically get off on people too—if they're happy."
Like Charles, many servers indicate that their work gives them pleasure.
Similarly, in her study of emotional management in the workplace, Sharon
Bolton discovers that "many front-line workers actually view the provision
of customer service as 'working with people' or 'helping people' and frame it
as a socially relevant activity with all the multiple interpretations and contradictions this brings."[32] Rather than imagining customers as adversaries in
the service encounter, servers who invest describe interactions with customers as primarily enjoyable and a rewarding aspect of their jobs.

    Investment narratives also include reoccurring linguistic conventions,
borrowed, in this case, from the private world of social interactions. Servers who invest recast occupational interactions as personal ones, imagining

customers as friends, and infusing coworker relationships with familial qualities and loyalties. Jessica refers to Friday as her "public relations" night, describing herself much like a hostess at a party who mingles with the guests, catching up on news of friends and acquaintances. Similarly, Alex compares Friday nights to a reunion: "I look forward to working on Friday nights, I like to come in on Friday nights because it's like family reunion time. All of these customers that I haven't seen for a while, I can give them a hug, I can say it's good to see you, oh my god, you're getting so grown up. I have always looked forward to Friday nights. A good night is lots of familiar faces, not a lot of money. Just to have fun and enjoy the people I'm waiting on." Comparing her work to a family reunion, Alex redirects attention from the dirty, physical, and potentially demeaning aspects of waiting tables, focusing instead on the social rewards of service work.

Servers who emotionally invest in their work seek to reimagine service interactions as more than simply an exchange of cash for service. Rather, they describe their work using various metaphors that connote connection and relationships that are not exclusively market-driven. Servers begin with simple rituals, like committing regular customers' preferences to memory, and over time, some servers develop affection for their customers. Servers who invest encourage customers to engage in forms of conversations that transform a market-driven service interaction into an exchange of pleasantries, or friendly "chitchat." These servers attempt to engage customers in behaviors that break the role functions of "server" and "customer," producing a more equal, less market-oriented exchange. Instead, a server who uses successful investment strategies can produce conversations between workers and customers that address areas unconnected to the restaurant, to ordering food or drinks, or even to their roles as customer and worker. Despite unequal occupational power where the worker stands and the customer sits and the worker must attend to work responsibilities while the customer stays still, these conversations sound more like mingling at a cocktail party than the superficial pleasantries associated with many service interactions.

For some customers, then, going out to eat becomes a way to "visit" with people who are familiar, perhaps even interesting, not only a way to avoid cooking at home. This mutual investment is best demonstrated by Jessica's explanation of why she keeps pictures of her kids in her apron. "We talk with our customers, and we show them our kids and the latest things going on and you know; they ask about it: 'How are your kids? Do you have any pictures?' I just like to show off my kids' pictures." Like Jessica, Patricia also carries pictures of her family in her apron. She explains why: "Everybody there—guests that come in there have all seen me pregnant—they know me and they know the kids. When I talk to my customers that I know well, I just say my kids' names. I don't have to say 'my husband' or 'my kids,' they just know." During the years that I worked alongside these two women, I assumed that they carried pictures of their children to remind themselves why they endure this work. But their responses could not be more to the contrary. Because these two women choose the investment strategy, they share pictures to further their connections with customers.

Some servers' enthusiasm for their work proves contagious, and over time they build a loyal "following" of customers. On any given night, a dozen customers request Jessica's section. In surveys, when customers were asked what they like best about eating at the Hungry Cowboy, over a third named Jessica as part of what makes the restaurant a special favorite of their families. Obviously an investment approach appeals to many customers, and encourages them to also view the exchange of cash for food as an opportunity to exchange pleasantries and perhaps even form relationships. These workers' stories suggest that servers who choose to detach may miss out on one of the potential benefits of service work: the two-way exchange of concern made possible by investing in rather than pulling back from their work and the people with whom it brings them into contact.

Along with the social rewards of investing, servers who invest may benefit financially. Jessica emphasizes getting to know customers, helping them and developing long-term connections over and above the money she receives. Yet some of the customers who have "known" her for many years tip her very well, sometimes as much as 40 percent of the bill. At least for Jessica, financial and emotional rewards seem to coexist. Unlike Joey, who frequently refers directly to tips, Jessica prefers to focus on the pleasure of knowing her customers and socializing at work. This focus is reinforced by her behavior on the job. While Joey spends a fair amount of time in the back of the house complaining or bragging about his tips, Jessica does not count any of her money until the end of the night. She trains new servers to do the same because she says it helps to maintain a good mood if you are not too "focused on the money." Clearly, the fact that customers pay for her service is never entirely obscured by her emotional investment. What is striking, however, is the desire of some servers to downplay the dynamics of tipping and instead focus on the social world of the restaurant. Given what invested personal interactions servers like Jessica are attempting to create through their work, it makes sense that they would try to mask the power of the tip.

CARING, CRYING, AND NIGHTMARES
The Downside of Investment

Investing in the emotional demands of service interactions allows servers to feel proud of the work they do. Despite their pride, the narrations of servers who invest reveal several contradictions between the pride they claim and the sadness and sometimes shame that they feel. These dissonant feelings come across when they talk about crying, nightmares, and whether or not they would allow their children to wait on tables. This dissonance between pleasure and pain at work suggests that investment offers only incomplete protection against experiencing emotional costs at work. Servers' investment strategies enable them to feel better about their jobs, but when those costs do leak out, despite their best efforts to contain them, the consequences to workers who invest may be more severe.

Servers who invest present a brave and even cheery view of their work. Each of the ten workers who invest can share touching stories of when they have meaningfully connected with one of their customers over the years; however, servers' investment in their jobs also encourages them to "speed up" their emotional labor.[33] They voluntarily increase the energy and attention they pour into their work with no direct incentive or reward for their voluntary speed-up. Servers who attempt to build a "home away from home" for their customers and themselves often succeed at producing service encounters that are less alienating and impersonal for both consumers and producers in the service economy.[34] Their work intensifies the labor process, simultaneously increasing the company's profits and, therefore, serving the needs of capitalism. To begin to enjoy what one does, to offer more of one's self than is required, is to submit voluntarily to the demands of capitalism. The servers who choose the investment strategy may be doing extra emotional labor with no external benefits such as an increase in wages. One of the dangers, then, of investment is that it makes the work seem easier to both the servers and customers than it actually is.

Servers who invest may also be reluctant to identify or address problems at work. The servers who say they come to work to socialize also use the sociality of their job to overshadow the less appealing aspects of their work. For example, when I asked Patricia, "What's the hardest thing about your job?" she replied, "There's nothing hard about that job." What is interesting about her reply is that the social aspects of her work become not only a source of enjoyment but also the only acknowledged aspect of the work itself. For certain servers, even the physical labor of serving disappears. Alex says, "So I get excited really, just to hang out. I'm more excited really about who's going to be in or what customers come in on a specific night." Servers who invest are less likely to acknowledge aspects of the workplace that are exploitative: the lack of benefits, irregular working hours, and lack of stability or promotion. Lisa says, "It can be hard. It can be hard, but it's only going to be as hard as you make it. I guess my deal is I don't really look at it like a job." If servers come into work to "get the dirt," to "see what is going on," or to "see who is there that night," then they don't have to peer too closely at the requirements of the job or the impossibility of promotion, advancement, or a future that looks any different than the night before.

Servers who invest might also be more vulnerable to customers who are rude or abusive. This limitation to investing matters because, despite the rosy view of servers who invest, sometimes waiting tables can be emotionally exhausting, and sometimes customers can be foul. Regardless of servers' approach to their work, customers retain greater rights to behave in accordance with their own feelings, whether that means yelling at a server for no reason or participating in a pleasant exchange of "chitchat." As Sharon Bolton observes, in service encounters, customers assume greater rights to feeling and display than workers, whose feelings are constrained, "The 'culture of the customer' bestows a superior status to the consumer and the interaction between service provider and customer is an unequal exchange."[35] Servers are expected to smile at customers, appear happy, and respond pleasantly to customers even if customers do not return the favor. In *The Pursuit of Attention: Power and Individualism in Everyday Life*, Charles Derber observed that individuals with lower occupational status talk more frequently in order to get attention from individuals higher up the occupational ladder. Derber's observations can be applied to the status differential between workers and customers at the Hungry Cowboy. While customers can choose a wide range of responses to workers' attempts to get their attention, customers are guaranteed at least some attention by virtue of their role.

Additionally, it is important to recall that the customers whom the servers invite into the restaurant "community" are the same individuals who can exhaust servers' emotional reserves and occasionally make them cry. A remarkable eight out of the ten servers who invest shared stories of crying, while none of the workers who detach did. Tammy refers to crying as a frequent occurrence: "Oh yeah! Lots at the beginning. I'd run in back and cry. One lady made me cry like a year and a half ago, and I'm still so bitter towards her. I wait on her now, and I just feel angry at her. I've cried a lot."

Unlike other emotions that play out on the stage of the restaurant or between workers in the kitchen, crying is something that servers do alone, out back. Crying is something that is done beyond the backstage of the restaurant, which at the Hungry Cowboy means all the way out the back door next to the shed where the supplies are kept. Julia acknowledges the beyond-the-backstage shed area as a private space, "Yeah. You know my little place to go is out back behind the shed on the other side. That's where I go, 'cause I hate crying."

Crying is hidden spatially because it is perceived as a failure and as a loss of control over the situation. For example, after one demanding and drunken customer insulted Julia in front of the whole dining room, she sought refuge out the back door, seeking a place to cry alone before returning to deal with the belligerent man. I asked Julia if crying made her feel like the customer had won, she replied, "Yeah, there's no way. I'll stand out back for a half hour and let all my tables go to hell before I'll go out there with red eyes and let my customers see that I was upset." Crying is clearly marked as a form of defeat for servers who invest, a part of the performance that servers will not allow their customers to see. Crying suggests that they have not transformed but internalized the conflicts that arise through their work. For servers who invest, crying can also be an unwelcome reminder that sometimes customers refuse to participate in positive social interactions. Their refusal to cry in front of either coworkers or customers reflects a desire to hide the evidence of their pain and frustration when things do not go right.

Another way that the costs of caring—both real and imagined—can be measured is by the incidence of server nightmares among all interviewees. Servers uniformly report experiencing anxiety dreams about serving. Describing and comparing nightmares is a routine practice among servers at the Hungry Cowboy. The basic format for a nightmare involves a server working either alone or understaffed, in a space too large for one person to service. The area he or she is responsible for serving is unmanageably large, sometimes as big as a football stadium, and keeps filling against his or her will, making it impossible to "get to" all the customers who are waiting, yelling, or verbally abusing him or her.

The prevalence of these nightmares points to one cost of emotion management that Hochschild did not address, betraying another harmful consequence of servers' emotional labor. Just as Trevor's and Billy's stories include discrepant information, these anxiety dreams suggest that, whether or not they are conscious of it, servers who invest sometimes internalize the degradation of service work. Does their emotional engagement include costs that get quieted and internalized, only to show up at night, when they dream? Servers who invest need to love their jobs and be convinced that investing is a rewarding approach to their work. In order to maintain their investment, they may need to mask the additional costs of their approach not only to others but also to themselves. In order to sustain their commitment to their work, they may suppress evidence of anger or hurt experienced as a result of their work.

Perhaps the most telling measure of the cost of caring is that servers who invest would not wish their work on their children. Even though Jessica professes to enjoy her work, she says she would never let her daughters wait tables. At the end of Jessica's interview, after she had described all the benefits of waiting tables and her attachment to people whom she had served over the years, I asked her if she would let her children work as waitresses when they grew up. Her answer was definitive.

KE: Would you let your girls serve?

JESSICA: Never! Never! My girls have already said they want to grow up and work at the Hungry Cowboy.

KE: And what do you tell them?

JESSICA: Oh honey, just try lots of things in life.

KE: But you would never want your girls to serve?

JESSICA: Never! No way! Not even to go to college. I will bust my ass to pay for them to go to college before I will let them serve.

Patricia, who had said that she looked forward to coming into work, also said that she would never allow her children to wait tables. Patricia and Jessica both narrate their work as being enjoyable, easy, and even pleasurable, and yet they react strongly to the mere suggestion that their children could someday do the same work. Their strong refusal is another form of dissonant information that challenges the integrity of their stories and raises suspicion that perhaps their work is costly in ways they would not want their children to discover.

While servers who invest focus their narratives on the rewarding aspects of their jobs, these same servers also have nightmares, cry when customers are mean to them, and would not wish their work on their children. Thus, while their choice to maintain a positive attitude and to value the emotional demands of their work does seem to improve their work experience, it does not protect them entirely from some of the attendant costs of performing care.

TO INVEST OR DETACH?

Despite the costs of caring that leak through in the shape of crying, nightmares, and even a refusal to allow loved ones to do this work, the majority of servers, ten out of fifteen, chose to invest. What factors contribute to the prevalence of investment at the Hungry Cowboy?

First, peer training perpetuates the propensity to invest. Because many of the servers who invest have worked there for many years, their approach has a profound influence on the work culture as a whole.[36] Servers with long histories are in a position to influence what Susan Porter Benson calls the "realm of informal, customary values and rules," which are "created as workers confront the limitations and exploit the possibilities of their jobs."[37] In addition, workers who invest bond with one another through their shared approach to the work. In short, investment not only improves relations with customers but also helps to form important relationships between the staff members who share the attitude that service work can be pleasurable.[38]

Next, the prevalence of servers who invest creates customer expectations that service at the Hungry Cowboy will be personalized and caring. New workers learn this approach by observing coworkers who find creative ways to anticipate and fulfill customers' wishes and by attending to customers who have come to expect the "cozy, welcoming" ambience daily produced by a culture of investment. When servers pass on the investment approach to newcomers, they reproduce this approach to service and establish investment as the standard for quality service in the work culture.

Finally, management also supports the investment strategy because it advances business goals. Servers who invest in the emotional labor required as part of their jobs assist the larger goals of the restaurant and, in effect, help the bottom line. Managers recognize customer satisfaction as a source of profit. For example, even though "upselling"—the process of pressuring customers to upgrade their food and beverage selections to increase profits—is an industry standard, managers at the Hungry Cowboy do not push this practice because they recognize that customers resent it. They would rather build customer comfort and loyalty than raise a customer's tab by two or three dollars. Rookie servers are initiated into the investment approach through participation in a work culture where managers direct them not to upsell but rather to learn customers' names and preferences.

A strong preference for investing is clearly articulated when managers reprimand servers who attempt to detach. While the general manager, Richard, prefers to leave training up to the servers, one of his pet peeves is an overly casual approach to greeting, welcoming or recognizing customers. For example, if Richard saw Joey shuffling over to a table frowning, Joey would be subject to a "talking to" from Richard. If Richard observes servers noticeably detaching from the demand to act as if the customer who just walked through the door is who they wanted to see and serve, he will reprimand those servers.

In a context like the Hungry Cowboy where the majority of workers invest, detaching may be a difficult stance to maintain or defend. Workers who detach from their work are the minority. For example, Joey's approach often permits him to build a wall of indifference between himself and the people he waits on; however, if many servers took on this instrumental attitude toward service work, the workplace culture might become one where sociability is forced and feels insincere.

The workplace culture at the Hungry Cowboy is a collaborative production: servers are willing to invest; managers allow servers the freedom to determine their work performance; customers enthusiastically support, if not insist, that servers go beyond the basics of the service exchange. When customers remark that they frequent the restaurant because they "like the feel of the place," they are consuming not only food but also a certain emotional experience. The prevalence of servers who invest is a key building block of sociability. Customers seek out the experience of being waited on by servers who make them feel welcome, who acknowledge, recognize, and engage them as familiar people rather than anonymous consumers. Even the servers who detach, while they do not choose to put their own emotional wares as close to the surface, still benefit from this culture of investment.[39]

The pressure to invest thus originates from three sources: coworkers (specifically long-term servers who have quite a bit of occupational power), customers, and managers. Given the institutional pressure to invest, why do a fraction of workers detach? Considering the pressure to invest, the ability of some servers to maintain an alternative approach is notable. In fact, some servers who initially detached eventually found it too difficult to sustain this distance in service interactions and increasingly started to invest. These changes suggest that investment and detachment are not permanently determined approaches to work; rather, they can change over time.

Of the fifteen servers I interviewed, two reported that they had increasingly invested over time. Billy, who has worked at the Hungry Cowboy on and off for eight years, describes his work as "just another dead-end job." Yet he also admits that he has come to accept that the restaurant makes good use of his skills. Billy says, "I like to pour it on and get the customer to come back because they had a great experience. You take pride in people liking you, or at least I do. I take pride in people liking me, and if I can do that, by making them smile, making them see that I'm happy, whatever it might be . . . I will do it." He explains that over the years he has increasingly made sense of his work by thinking of the restaurant as a stage where he can perform a fun-loving self and that he values the ability to make people smile at work.

Meg narrated a shift in her work from a purely instrumental approach to customers to an increasing ability to act as if she cared. At the time of her interview, she clearly detached from her work. At one point she said, "I don't, basically, I don't like serving other people." At that point in time, all she could fantasize about was quitting restaurant work as soon as possible. When I asked her what her plans for the future entailed, she replied, "I look forward to leaving this place with great anticipation. I'm going to burn my apron, like a flag." Interestingly, by the time she did quit the Hungry Cow-boy, three years after I interviewed her, she had become close enough to her customers that she hugged several of them, invited them to her going-away party, and cried when she said good-bye to them. Her behavior at the end of her time at the restaurant suggests that perhaps she invested more the longer she worked there. Meg and Billy's stories indicate that duration of employment may influence servers' propensity to invest. As a result of the implicit pressure from coworkers to invest and of customers' expectations to be recognized and to engage in familiar, friendly exchanges, the prevailing investment strategy seems to be easier to embrace than to resist.

SERVING UP SOCIABILITY

Having observed these two approaches in action, I argue that workers who choose to detach miss out on some of the potential benefits of being paid to interact with other people. The stories that servers tell articulate the need for human attachments at work, attachments for which we do not always have a language but which affect us personally and emotionally. Servers are drawn into emotional performances through multiple routes—not only managerial strategies but also their own sense of craft and the collaborative construction of a sense of community.[40] What these servers and customers coproduce is a workplace culture that feels more like a home away from home than simply a successful business, a place where customers and work-ers initially meet in a market exchange but often end up interacting like friends, neighbors, and even family.

3

CONSUMING BELONGING

◆◆◆◆◆◆◆◆◆◆◆◆◆◆◆◆◆◆◆◆◆◆◆◆◆◆◆◆

FEELING "AT HOME" AT THE HUNGRY COWBOY

"This is my place, my home away from home."
—Man at the next booth, Perkins Restaurant and Bakery, New Brighton, Minnesota

At more casual restaurants, such as the Original Pancake House in Edina, Minnesota, the expectations are different. Regular customers expect to be treated like family.
—Jeremy Iggers, "At Your Service"

During the summer of 2003, Mr. and Mrs. Noble, who usually come in every Friday, had been missing their usual dining time for several weeks. The Nobles were ordinarily so reliably present on Fridays that when they did not come in several weeks in a row, servers and managers at the Hungry Cowboy noted their absence. Mrs. Noble had cancer a couple of years before, and their Friday night attendance was spotty during that time. Now she was in remission. Richard and the servers wondered amongst themselves if her cancer had returned. After several weeks of absence, the Nobles returned on a Friday at their regular time.

Although she was not waiting on them, Jessica was quick to ask the Nobles where they had been, "We missed you!" They reluctantly admitted that they had been having some financial difficulty due to the downturn in the economy, and could not afford to come in every week. That night, Jessica bought their dinner with her own money. I said, "That was awfully nice of you." Jessica replied, "All the money they've given me over the years, I owe them. Plus, I want them to be able to come."

When the general manager, Richard, found out the reason the Nobles were not coming in as often, he said next time he would buy their dinner. This is not how all businesses behave, perhaps because they do not recognize their customers, do not know what is happening in their lives, and perhaps do not care. While many restaurants will refund the cost of a meal if something goes wrong during a customer's visit, it is much less common for workers or managers to pay for a customer's bill as a gift.

Regular customers enjoy being recognized and feeling that they belong to the Hungry Cowboy. Servers and managers both work to facilitate a feeling of familiarity and belonging, what I call "the work of recognition." In return for feeling as if they belong, customers exhibit strong loyalty to the restaurant. Customers say they come into the restaurant to see people, to visit friends, and to entertain family. Regular customers proudly claim the Hungry Cowboy as their "favorite place" and their enthusiasm and patronage clearly contributes to the ambience available to workers and to other customers who enter the restaurant. Drawing from analysis of one hundred customer surveys and over five hundred customer comment cards, in this chapter I examine what customers want and what they get by becoming "regulars." I contrast regular customers' loyalty to the Hungry Cowboy with what George Ritzer calls the McDonaldization of everything.[1]

"McDonaldization," the term coined by George Ritzer, describes an increasingly prevalent business approach modeled on the success of the McDonald's franchise. McDonaldization reorganizes processes to emphasize efficiency, calculability, and predictability; it exerts control through nonhuman technologies. Service regimes are made more efficient by putting the customer to work, imploding space, and commodifying time. Customers have become accustomed to making themselves more efficient by ordering quickly at a drive-up window, dumping their trays at fast-food restaurants, and acquiring and eating a meal in less than ten minutes. Customers have come to expect that consumer venues have imploded, so much so that finding a coffee shop, dry cleaners, photo processing service, and grocery store all under the same roof no longer warrants surprise. Increased efficiency allows customers not only to move more quickly through their errands but to internalize the rapid pace of consumer spaces.

Calculability is Ritzer's term for the focus on quantity over and above quality. Wal-Mart and similar superstores emphasize size, variety, and low prices. Within these contexts, value is measured by how *much* one can get for a dollar. Value is about size and quantity, not about originality or quality.

Predictability describes the increasing homogeneity of consumer experiences. Predictability ensures that consumers will know what to expect in all places and times with few surprises. In fact, the spread of corporate chains—from Jiffy Lube to Olive Garden—results in an economy that offers a range of similar "options." The Big Mac you ate in Chicago today will be practically identical to the one you can order in London tomorrow. Predictability can be comforting, but it can also be boring. Perhaps more alarming is that the predictability achieved by corporate spaces risks flattening out cultural differences altogether. Imagine getting off a train in a different country only to find the same stores, businesses, and restaurants you left back at home.

McDonaldization exerts control through the substitution of nonhuman for human technologies. From ATMs to computerized telemarketing, many of the spaces we move through are controlled through nonhuman means. Humans are far less predictable than machines, so McDonaldized locales seek to eliminate as much human control as possible. To illustrate, all of Wal-Mart's distribution centers are automated. Computers that track merchandise at the Wal-Mart down the block "tell" the distribution center to send more of a certain product.[2] Consumers in shopping malls are carefully controlled through temperature, sound, placement of products, lack of clocks, and surveillance cameras and scanners that record what customers do so that the company can learn how to improve sales. One of the most noticeable effects of these changes is that consumers are increasingly comfortable with consuming in the absence of interaction with other humans. Online shopping makes consuming even more isolated and impersonal.

According to Ritzer, the process of rationalizing business practices and interactions also produces irrationalities. McDonaldization speeds up interactions, emphasizes quantity over quality, homogenizes customer experience, and deskills workers. "Most notably, McDonaldized systems tend to have a negative effect on the environment and to dehumanize the world, leading to a series of nonhuman or even anti-human activities and behaviors."[3] Two of the most apparent effects of McDonaldization are the huge quantity of garbage produced by fast food and the disastrous impact of eating fast food on human bodies.[4] But McDonaldization also produces less apparent cultural changes. Streamlined processes often exclude human reason and creativity, destroy workers' sense of craft and ownership, and produce dissatisfaction and boredom alongside satiation for consumers. As Paul Goldberger explains, "A kind of high level blandness begins to take over . . . you begin to yearn for some off-note, something wrong, something even a bit vulgar, just to show individual sensibility."[5] Along with many scholars who study civic life, Ritzer is also concerned that the spread of McDonaldization produces customers who are accustomed to interacting both with machines and with people distant to them in time and in space; such customers may be increasingly uncomfortable with face-to-face interactions.

Within the social landscape of McDonaldized consumer spaces, some businesses resist these trends. Debra Ginsberg reflects on how full-service restaurants reverse the efficient routinization to which so many other services have been subjected.

> Restaurants provide one of the last customer service industries to flourish. These days everything can be done via fax, modem, or phone. I can order my clothes from a catalog, furnish my house through home shopping channels, listen to music samples on my computer, and submit my written work via e-mail. The only thing I really can't do without a human being present is be served dinner in a restaurant. Somehow, there really is no substitute for the person-to-person contact involved in the simple act of sitting down in a restaurant and being waited on. Perhaps this is part of the reason that the interchanges between customer and server are often so highly charged and have emotional content far beyond what seems reasonable given the situation. The expectations for an "experience," be it pleasant or not, are great. On both sides of the table.[6]

The charged atmosphere in restaurants produced by the mix of food, drink, voices, and music, can, when produced successfully, "warm up" the more sterile, predictable, efficient exchanges many contemporary consumers encounter everyday.

While many scholars have studied changes in labor practices, few scholars have considered the power of alternatives to "McDonaldized" service venues. Sharon Bolton argues that consumers are disquieted by the artificiality of some service interactions and can feel "discomfited and alienated from the interaction" if "any leakage intimates that they are not receiving personalized service."[7] My study of the Hungry Cowboy allows me to consider a consumer space that exists alongside those that Ritzer describes. While Ritzer is largely correct in his conclusions about the effects of corporatization, the effects of McDonaldization are in no way absolute. In fact, little "hole-in-the-wall" places—as one customer called them—like the Hungry Cowboy speak to another set of consumer experiences that participants value particularly because they experience them as humanizing. As consumers pick their way through a marketplace that offers an ever-increasing number of similar dehumanized options, they also locate these pockets of humanization, personalization, and sociability in the marketplace. These spaces not only differ from the patterns Ritzer identifies, they are perhaps more valuable to participants because McDonaldization and its attendant effects are so pervasive elsewhere.

The Hungry Cowboy is popular in part because it allows customers to count on being recognized and to have a predictable experience without feeling like one of the thousands of customers being fed and processed by hundreds of workers in chain locations across the country. The work culture is flexible enough to respond to individual customer's needs. As a result, customers can experience a sense of belonging and a sense of ownership.

THE PLEASURE OF BEING REGULAR

The Nobles still come in to eat once a week, and they are quick to tell new servers or other customers about what Jessica and Richard did for them during a hard time. These small tokens of connection, what I call the extras of service work, can deepen the relationship among customers, workers, and managers.[8] Over time, long-term staff and regular customers develop a shared sense of what to expect of each other. They develop routines with one another that, despite the occasional annoyance or misstep, deliver a range of benefits: laughter, a paycheck, a sense of belonging, good food, and a feeling of being known. Some customers are reliably ornery while others are predictably funny; some servers are regularly "bubbly" while others are efficient but dull. Whatever the particular mix, the regulars who return to the restaurant over time tend to be pretty satisfied with what they find there. Their satisfaction and desire to return is one of the building blocks of sociability at the Hungry Cowboy.

Becoming regular requires consistent visits over a period of time, usually several years. In the same way that servers are proud of their own "following" of regular customers, many customers are quick to stake a claim to their own history at the Hungry Cowboy. In surveys, customers report a lengthy history of patronage.[9] Out of the one hundred customers I surveyed, the average number of years of eating at the Hungry Cowboy was 5.9, a remarkable average considering that at the time of the survey it had been open for only twelve years.[10] Like the workers, customers have a low turnover; seventy of the customers surveyed had been dining regularly at the Hungry Cowboy for over four years.

Being a "regular" is achieved by the duration of patronage but is also affected by frequency. Over 50 percent of the customers surveyed come in once a week, many even naming which day of the week that they ordinarily come in, if it is a weekly occurrence. Another 28 percent come in more than once a week, and in the case of three customers, more than once a day. Such routine, habitual, and reliable attendance has been the key to the restaurant's success, as well as the most determinative factor for maintaining and building the business.[11]

The presence of a core group of customers who are happy to return to the Hungry Cowboy warms up the atmosphere in the restaurant. Customers, especially regular customers, contribute to the production of mood, affect and the "feel" of the place.[12] The mood of the place can be thrown off by the absence of key people on either side of the tray. For example, in the back of the house, servers often discuss which regular customers are present or absent on a given evening. A night without a majority of regular customers can feel odd ("Where are all the regulars tonight? I feel like I don't know anybody!"). At a given time, the restaurant and bar will hold up to 70 percent regular customers who are frequent diners. Through the frequency and reliability of their patronage, and through their behavior within the restaurant, customers contribute to the production of a homelike ambience.

Regular customers develop an affinity for the Hungry Cowboy, and over time become attached to spending time there. As such, they are invested in presenting it as an important and successful place and contributing to the ongoing success of the business. There are no fancy slogans or marketing campaigns. Richard made a commercial for local cable television once, but most new customers find the place by word of mouth.[13] Without the prompting of loyal insiders, most would-be customers could easily drive by the neon cactus sign next to the dry cleaners in a strip mall in Minnesota. Luckily for the Hungry Cowboy, customers are ready to assign familiar terms like "family," "friends," and "home" to the restaurant. Creating an atmosphere that allows customers to lay down roots and stake a claim is a lucrative practice that inspires loyalty among customers.

Each group of actors is interested in perpetuating the sense of belonging made possible at the Hungry Cowboy. Richard encourages customers to feel entitled because their loyalty contributes to the culture of investment. Similarly, regular customers tell good stories, offer praise, and proclaim "This is our place!" because they are invested, and they want their place to keep going. They do not want to see the Hungry Cowboy close its doors. What about this place inspires this kind of loyalty among its regular customers? What do customers get in return for being regular?

THE WORK OF RECOGNITION

For customers, one of the pleasures of being regular is that servers remember what they like, including food, drink, and sometimes even style of service. When I asked them to describe their favorite aspect of the restaurant, customers said things like, "She knows what we want and always remembers us," "They know what I want and how to make a drink," and, "She is always friendly, always takes care of us."

The work of recognition that servers perform is highly valued by the customers who appreciate being "known" by the people who serve them. Even when servers do not know customers' names, they develop means of recognizing them. Most servers can identify an array of guests in such a way that other servers also know whom they're talking about by simply referring to their food or drink orders. Meg demonstrates this practice when she says during the interview, "There's these people who come in on Friday nights, you know who I'm talking about, they each have whiskey and Diet Coke and two sandwiches and they have a DMC[14] [coupon] card." Patricia knows her regulars so well that their orders flash across her mind even when she sees the customers out of context, "Oh, I'll see them [shopping] with their kids and I'll think, oh, they get no olives on their salad with bleu cheese on the side. I'll be shopping on a Sunday afternoon and be like, that's the lady that always complains about her margaritas."

Customers' preferences and significant stories are passed down to new employees for entertainment or in the course of "filling in" new servers about the regular customers they will be waiting on. An experienced server will say something like, "OK, that's Bob. He comes in on Wednesdays for an early dinner. He likes the ribs and politics, but he's a little shady. He'll get touchy if you leave him an opening, so watch out for that." Customers are "handed down" to new servers with stories wrapped around them: how they behave, what they like, and what they do not is often remembered and shared with other workers.

When I asked customers what they like about the Hungry Cowboy, many replied with what I call the *Cheers* response. *Cheers* was a 1980s sitcom that took place in a friendly neighborhood bar "where everybody knows your name."[15] The repeated references to this TV show suggest that it describes what comfort and recognition a public place can provide. One customer wrote, "I always know someone, like *Cheers*." Another said, "You always know someone."[16] Referring to *Cheers* reflects the desire of customers to go somewhere they feel recognized and where their presence also affects the ambience. There are nights when the Hungry Cowboy definitely fits the bill, when most if not all customers who walk through the door are greeted by name, or remembered by their last visit, their favorite food, or their choice of table.

Cheers operates as a metaphor in a cultural realm that often evades careful definition.[17] One customer actually said, "It feels like *Cheers*." Another said, "I enjoy the familiar faces, and like it when people know and recognize me." The promise of *Cheers*, after all, is recognition, a place where "everybody knows your name." Some customers use *Cheers* as a way of explaining what they like about being there and in doing so single out the Hungry Cowboy as a special kind of public space.

The loose community of regulars is relatively easy to observe during an average day. Customers are greeted by both staff and other regulars as they walk into the bar; customers in the restaurant often pause on their way to being seated to stop and talk with other customers; and many customers gather in the entryway after their meals to chat with servers, managers, or other customers before leaving for the night. One customer nicknamed Union Joe always gets a hug or a pat on the back from every server in addition to the cold beer that awaits him. Like the character Norm from *Cheers*, Union Joe can be depended upon to come in every night. Like Norm, he has become an important part of the ambience. Servers can tell what time it is from checking to see if Joe is in his spot at the bar or not. Joe's presence is so routine that he lets the bartenders know if he is not going to be able to come in for a day or two, just so that no one worries.

It seems that the primary reward for being regular is that customers can be confident that they will be acknowledged as insiders and that the service they receive will be personalized. For customers who take pleasure in being regulars, the food and drink appear to be vehicles that communicate belonging. As Christine Yano explains, "The food is part and parcel of a social relationship (if sealed through an economic transaction)."[18] When customers say, "She knows how to make my drink," "They know what I like," or "She makes us feel welcome," the food, drink, and even the payment temporarily disappear behind the pleasure of feeling welcomed and remembered.

ONE OF THE GANG
Knowing and Being Known

"Membership" in the Hungry Cowboy is shared with friends, proudly proclaimed, and sometimes jealously guarded. Regular customers claim credit for bringing in new customers and proudly claim how long they have been dining at the restaurant. Customers attempt to train new workers into "how things are done" and even used the survey I distributed as an opportunity to demonstrate their historical knowledge of the restaurant.

Proof that membership is jealously guarded can be found in the frequent debates among regulars, servers and managers about the accurate recollection of the past. Regulars and servers will ponder how long it has been since a favorite bartender or server left the Hungry Cowboy. Together, they will recollect how awful life was before Richard became general manager, or they will laugh at the memory of really disastrous nights when someone was very drunk, the power went out, or the kitchen was slow. The telling and retelling of such stories is proof of membership, and discussion with the purpose of getting the memories "right" is a common pastime. Perhaps the best example of attempts to define one's "membership" is that almost every night at least one customer will explain to a newer server that the chips used to be free. Many customers really enjoy the homemade tortilla chips and salsa. For $1.69 customers can get a bottomless basket of chips and salsa. When I started working at the Hungry Cowboy in the early 1990s chips and salsa cost less than a dollar. But, as it turns out, the chips were never free. Yet at least once a night a new server will be confronted with a regular's imagined "insider" knowledge that indeed the chips used to be free. What is important about this knowledge is not so much whether the chips ever were free but that customers as well as servers gain a sense of authority derived from a shared experience. Even if it is a fabricated memory, the idea of free food at a restaurant allows customers and servers alike to deny that profit is the bottom line; rather, it suggests a homelike environment that customers "remember."

Some customers routinely reveal a great deal about their personal lives to their servers, and many regulars are eager to share their stories. When a new server asks them how long they have been coming to the Hungry Cowboy, many customers respond with pride that they have been coming "since the beginning" and "forever." In this way, customers are not only claiming tacit knowledge and authority regarding "how things are done," but they are also announcing a sense of ownership and involvement. Customers' answers on the survey reinforced what often happens in daily practice. If a server asks customers if they have any questions about the menu or if they know about our happy hour, they often smile knowingly and say, "We've been coming here forever." Often customers offer up their history of patronage without prompting, saying, "We've been coming here since our kids were little" or "since before we were married."

By situating their routine patronage at the restaurant in the larger history of their lives, regulars reveal a certain fondness or affection for the way that this place has fit into their own private history. For example, several couples have become engaged at the restaurant. One couple always comes in on their wedding anniversary because they came to the Hungry Cowboy for their first date eight years ago. In some cases, the history of the institution is intimately tied to customers' memories. For example, several years ago, a woman lost her wedding ring in a booth. She was panicked about the loss, and many workers gathered to help her search. No one could find the ring. Later that night, after his shift was over, her server went out back and dug through bags of garbage in the dumpster until he found it. The woman was so grateful she paid the server who found the ring a sizable reward. She often recounts the story of how she lost and found her wedding ring at the Hungry Cowboy. One of the pleasures of being regular is the practice of sharing stories, of laughing together, or the more simple pleasure of recognition, being able to say, "Yes, I remember that! Doug [a former server] was in the dumpster looking for that ring for hours!"

In contrast to McDonalidized service routines that "assume that people are largely interchangeable, that they are not deserving of sincerity, [and] possibly that they can easily be duped,"[19] customers at this restaurant get to feel recognized, remembered, and memorable. Often, customers return the favor. Asked who his or her favorite server was, one customer listed ten servers by name, dating back more than five years. The ability to list a series of servers represents bona fide knowledge of the Hungry Cowboy over time. It requires repetitive service interactions for customers to remember the people who serve them, sometimes recalling workers years after they have left the restaurant.

Knowing about others and being known by others is valued as evidence of ongoing participation and even something that looks like "membership" within the Hungry Cowboy. Customers who try to get to know servers and other regulars sometimes use knowledge of servers' private lives as currency. For instance, one regular customer might brag to another, "Well, I talked to Betsy last night, and she said that her husband does not want her to go back to working nights . . ." Paying attention to habits, changing tastes, and moods of other actors in the exchange of service—what I call recognition work—is primarily the work of servers and managers, but sometimes customers participate too.

ONE OF A KIND
The Appeal of a Unique Place

Along with references to *Cheers*, customers cited the small size of the restaurant and the fact that it is not a chain as some of the key aspects they value. Frequenting a restaurant that is one of a kind allows customers to feel that they have discovered a place where they too can feel unique. Several customers describe the Hungry Cowboy as both "unique" and "authentic." The "authentic" label is particularly ironic given that the watered-down, cheesed-up Tex-Mex fare is certainly not known for its authenticity. Rather, authenticity seems to be code for reliability and consistency provided in a "one-of-a-kind" setting. Another way to make sense of the use of the term "authentic" to describe the Hungry Cowboy is that it is an independent restaurant, not part of a corporate chain.

At a time when the number of chain restaurants is exploding both locally and nationally, both workers and customers point to the "independent" status of the restaurant as part of the appeal.[20] In her study of okazuya (side-dish shops) in Hawaii, Christine Yano discovered similar attachment to shops that customers considered to be one-of-a-kind and that they frequented as a form of resistance against the spread of corporate chains. "The imagery of this kind of nostalgized account is based in part on size, with its implications of power, temporality, and location. . . . This becomes a battle of the global versus the local, the industrial giant versus the little guy, fast food versus home-cooked food."[21] At the Hungry Cowboy, customers identified as an attractive attribute the fact that it was independently owned and managed, not part of a chain or franchise. In surveys, customers reported that they like to come to the Hungry Cowboy because "there's no place else like it." Given the disparate contexts of the side-dish shops in Hawaii and a Tex-Mex restaurant and bar in Minnesota, it is interesting that customers at both locations *want* to describe each place as both "one of a kind" and "authentic."

The fact that customers conceived of the Hungry Cowboy as both "local" and "unique"—less market-driven and more personalized—influences how customers play their roles as consumers of service there. Customers have come to expect that their experience will be personalized, sometimes in accordance with very specific requests. One customer said, "I like that I can alter the menu to fit my preferences." One infamous customer orders "supreme nachos with no olives, no onions, no tomatoes, extra jalapenos, beans on the side, four salsas, two sour creams, and a side of guacamole." This customer breaks the meal down into parts, picking which ingredients she wants and reassembling the ingredients into a different dish.

Customers also expect to personalize their interactions in the restaurant. Children often draw pictures and make art not only for their favorite server but sometimes for the cooks—even though children do not directly interact with the cooks—as thanks for making their food. Many regular customers not only expect to be recognized by their server but also hope to talk with Richard during their visit. As such, customers, especially regulars, make demands and draw from the ambience—for example, by expecting recognition—and also contribute to the production of that ambience, by drawing pictures for staff and walking through the restaurant greeting other regulars.

Customers implicitly compare this restaurant to other types of establishments. For instance, one customer said she liked that it wasn't a meat market. Liking the restaurant for what it is *not* points to the challenge of explaining preferences in the marketplace. Despite the nuances of their behavior at the Hungry Cowboy—behaviors that exhibit a high degree of comfort—customers search for the right words to describe their connection to the place. Customers may know that they feel comfortable in one place and not comfortable in another, but they often may struggle to point to the one feature that makes the difference.

THIS IS MINE
Naming Favorites

Customers contribute to the familiar "feel" that makes this restaurant such a desirable place to dine and drink. Customers tend to associate the Hungry Cowboy with ideas derived from private life: family, neighborhood, home. These associations are all ways of marking it as a special place. Loyal customers are key ingredients to the production of ambience.

I argue that customers contribute to the production of ambience at the Hungry Cowboy. But what is really meant by ambience? To encourage customers to describe the ambience, I asked customers, "How would you describe the Hungry Cowboy to a friend who had not been here?" The most common response was to describe it as a "neighborhood" bar and restaurant. "Neighborhood" is an interesting response because it is not really an adjective; it's a noun. What does "neighborhood" mean in this context? Further descriptions provide some insight. Other descriptions include comfortable, friendly, fun, cozy, homey, welcoming, good people, good crowd, intimate, and family-oriented. What is most telling about these responses is that, when asked to describe ambience, very few customers talk about the cactuses or the chili peppers; instead they emphasize the social aspects of the Hungry Cowboy. One customer says, "It's a mixer. All ages are welcome." Another customer is very specific about how service and food interact to produce a feeling of satisfaction. He explains, "The food is good, but what sets it apart from other places with good food is the people." Another customer replies, "The servers always know how to treat their customers right. And that's why the customers come back." While many sounds, sights, and materials go into the production of ambience, customers focus on the social aspects of their experience. They identify who is there and how the workers and customers act rather than the colors, sounds, or smells. Customers seem to be going out to dine, not just to eat and drink but to participate in a particular social milieu.

Customers know that their loyal business and willingness to recommend the restaurant is also a powerful recruiting mechanism. One customer writes, "I have done a lot of PR for you over the years!" and another writes, "I love this place. I tell all my friends about the HC!" Claiming the Hungry Cowboy as "my place," telling friends and family to eat there, bringing in friends and family, and introducing it as "my favorite place" are practices that contribute to the ambience of satisfaction and that indeed do grant customers power. According to *Customer Service for Dummies*, "When we receive good service, we tell 9 to 12 people on average. When we receive poor service, we tell up to 20 people."[22] The kind of loyalty professed by customers is hard to come by and invaluable to the ongoing success of the restaurant. This favorite status gets passed on to friends and families whom regulars bring in to acquaint with their favorite place.

There is a satisfaction in having a favorite, in being in the place you call your favorite place. Many customers wrote, "the Hungry Cowboy is our family's favorite" or "we come here all the time." We humans appear to derive pleasure from expecting something and getting it. While Ritzer presumes that the predictability established by large chains like McDonald's will flatten out cultural differences and homogenize consumer experiences, customers at the Hungry Cowboy describe predictability with fondness. "The HC never changes, we love it!" "Good to see that things have not changed here, it's good to be back." It seems this restaurant cashes in on the predictably pleasant nature of its food, its service, and the mood that is created by a clientele and staff who know their roles well.

Claiming this restaurant as their favorite allows customers to put their stamp on it, to say this is a place where I like to be and choose to be. As Derek Pardue explains, "People associate familiar experiences with places, i.e. locality and community, and thus tend to choose one restaurant over another based on such feelings."[23] Naming the Hungry Cowboy "a neighborhood place" and "a family favorite" are both ways of claiming it as their own, as part of their home territory. In fact, many regular customers who move away come back to "visit" as often as possible.[24] Young customers who grow up and move away or go off to college also come back to the restaurant as part of their visit home. The value of having a favorite is also expressed by children, who ask to come in and who choose it to host their birthday celebrations or graduation parties. In fact, the Hungry Cowboy has employed several teenagers who, once they were old enough, wanted to work at their "favorite" restaurant.

Developing favorites is part of how Americans make their way through the complicated American economy. Faced with an almost endless array of dining options, having one or several "favorites" helps individuals choose where to spend their time and money. Naming a restaurant "my favorite" or "our family's favorite" can provide an antidote to or at least a resting place within an economy marked by impersonal and dehumanizing efficiency.

AFFORDABLE INTIMACY

The particular mix of belonging, recognition, cheap appetizers, stuffed cactuses, and talented servers inspire a remarkably loyal customer base. Here, customers express loyalty to a particular location but also to an idea about a place. When customers talk about the Hungry Cowboy, they associate it with the fulfillment of certain desires: feeling welcome, comfortable, appreciated, and known. These ideas have taken root more easily here than, for example, the deli across the street that went out of business, or the restaurant two doors down in the same strip mall that has changed names and owners at least three times in the last decade.

Customers' connections to staff and to one another are limited but reliable. This place allows for a fluid kind of membership that is rewarding and also affordable. I describe the interactions that take place here as an example of affordable intimacy in the marketplace. Customers can experience the pleasures of feeling included, with very few of the social costs that ordinarily accompany other forms of intimacy over time. Here, someone always knows your name, but they also know what kind of tequila you like. When you walk in the door you can listen for the familiar sound of the ice as it clinks on the glass just right. Lisa sets your drink in "your" spot at the bar. Maybe Betsy coasts past and asks, "So are you up for some hot wings today or not?" Billy slips around the bar to light your smoke. Then perhaps Jessica remembers to ask how the game went last weekend, or Beth says she saw your daughter in the school play. These are exchanges that in private life we refer to as "pleasantries": light-hearted exchanges of mutual consideration. In general, pleasantries are enjoyable and do not "cost" much socially. For customers, they get to feel the warm rush of being welcomed, mixed in with good flavors, smells, drinks, and food, without having to put out very much effort to sustain their participation.

Customers borrow ideas from private life to describe their experience of the Hungry Cowboy, calling it a neighborhood, a community, and a family. Performing a feeling of family in the marketplace can offer an appealing mix of rights and responsibilities in comparison to the demands of real families. These routine associations are also affordable because paying to belong somewhere erases some of the more costly aspects of being connected with others. Limited exchanges and minimal obligations can be valuable. When asked, customers say they come in to "see who's there" or to "visit with friends," but even customers who have been coming for years do not necessarily have to pay the same social dues one might in a real family.

Writer Joan Mulcahy describes the comforts of belonging at the restaurant where she waited tables.

> Regulars wanted their orders placed as they approached. They expected inquiries about the health of their wives and mothers. Above all, they wanted to be known, called by name, pampered and nurtured. In return, they marked the seasons with flowers and Christmas gifts and unexpected surprises. They might send cards to the owner, but it was the waitresses who triggered the real sense of the familial. People came for comfort, for advice, for the assurance that there are predictable arenas of meaning in daily life. The wait-resses were family and religion and community, the only source of continuity in the lives of many regulars. It was a world in which we all knew our place.

Like the restaurant where Mulcahy worked, the Hungry Cowboy offers a feeling of family to its clientele. But if the restaurant is a community, it is one in which everyone knows their place and where responsibilities to one another are carefully and narrowly defined.

Although customers liken their experience at the Hungry Cowboy to relations in private, they do not have to pay the same social dues that actual families and even neighborhoods often demand. Here customers can take advantage of a belonging that does not cost them much and also does not demand as much as actual families. Here, no one has to put up with Cousin Susan, who is a pain, or Brother Bob, who has not showed up on time for a meal since 1992. Customers can also decide not to "show up" at all if they are ornery or sad, or they can show up in a cross mood, anticipating that it is someone's job to cheer them up, or at least tolerate their mood.

The social rules governing exchange in noncommercial relationships do not necessarily apply in the restaurant, and some customers may abuse that opportunity or, worse yet, start to expect similar asymmetrical rights in their noncommercial relations. For example, while customers might come in to cheer up or forget their bad day at work, they are not obligated to concern themselves with how their server is feeling that day.[25] Robin Leidner consid-ers this one of the real risks of interactive service work.

Through participation in encounters that violate the norms of social interaction even as they exploit those norms, service-recipients learn not to take for granted that the ground rules that govern interaction will be respected. As they adjust their expectations and behavior accordingly, the ceremonial forms that bolster individual identity and social cohesion tend to be treated as indulgences rather than obligations.[26]

For Leidner, because the market allows customers to suspend the ground rules of social interaction, it chips away at the individual's obligation to be decent to others and to contribute to social cohesion. Certainly, the risks she identifies happen frequently in service work. The appearance of someone paid to say, "How may I help you?" calls out some truly outrageous behavior from some customers. But it is also possible to reverse the equation that Leidner sets up here. What about those instances in commercial exchanges when customers, servers, or both decide to give a little extra? If expectations regarding what is required in service interactions are low, then it becomes easier to be pleasantly surprised by exchanges that raise those standards.

I call the interactions at the Hungry Cowboy affordable intimacy because I think that is how they operate. In an arena where kindness and mutual recognition is *not* required, customers get to feel magnanimous and included when they engage with servers and each other as acquaintances and maybe even as friends. For example, customers often help rearrange furniture to accommodate new arrivals, change the radio station to improve the ambience, and even help out by delivering drinks and food to one another. Some regular customers stay late at night to put up the chairs, some show up early to help set up the restaurant and chat with the workers before food or drink can even be provided. Some regular customers brag to one another about how late they stayed after close, or how they helped out the workers. Here, the power differential between producer and consumer is reversed: customers are using the "privilege" of working for no pay alongside the paid workers as a form of social currency.

As the American Express ad proclaims, "Membership has its privileges." At the Hungry Cowboy, membership includes two types of privilege: first, the opportunity to receive recognition and care, and second, the chance to contribute to the perpetuation of sociability and mutual concern. Being a regular provides customers with opportunities to go above and beyond, to play an active role in the creation of something like a community in the marketplace and to be involved in the satisfying intersubjective performance of sociability.

CUSTOMER INCLUSION AND CUSTOMER INTRUSION

Despite the significant rewards—both economic and social—of developing a loyal customer base, customer involvement can have a downside as well. Managers have to find ways to invite customers' feedback without losing control over the work process. Allowing customers to feel included and entitled to an opinion without giving customers too much power is a central challenge for managers. One of the downsides of a high degree of customer involvement is that occasionally customers overstep their limits and instead of simply being included, they are actually intrusive. For example, consider the cases of Karl and Bridget.

In the Spring of 2003, I walked into the bar to pick up a drink order and observed Richard in an excited, angry conversation with a regular customer. Richard often talks with regular customers. He emphasizes the importance of recognition as part of management and also takes very seriously what he learns in his conversations with customers about the business. On this particular evening, a regular, named Karl, had engaged Richard in a heated debate. The conversation began with Karl suggesting that Richard have a "boy's night" at the Hungry Cowboy, with male bartenders working and a focus on men's culture, sports on the TV, video golf championships, and drink specials. Richard said he was not interested in encouraging that sort of culture. Somehow the conversation devolved, with Karl intensifying his claims: he began to argue that the male bartenders were simply better and that one of the female bartenders should not even be allowed to work at the Hungry Cowboy. Richard took offense when Karl started to criticize employees and told Karl that he would decide how to run his business. Karl then took offense, raising his voice and claiming that he knew what the restaurant needed, that he came in almost every night, and spent a lot of money, and that Richard should listen to what he said, because the customer is always right. The verbal conflict continued for quite some time, attracting the attention of other customers and staff members.

At another time, a regular named Bridget told a waitress named Betsy that she "really needed to talk to her." It was a Friday night, and Betsy was very busy. Bridget proceeded to stand in the service preparation area, directly in Betsy's path, until she agreed to actually sit down with her and hear out her concerns. After several urgent requests, the two sat down in a booth on the restaurant side, which, by that point of the evening, was closed. Bridget's urgent business involved some "serious concerns" she had about employees, regarding one of the bartenders whom she thought had been depressed lately, another bartender whom she had observed overpouring drinks, and finally, one of the servers whom she felt was not getting the shifts he deserved. In short, she felt that the best bartenders were not getting access to the best shifts and that some changes in the schedule were needed. Betsy was frustrated with having taken time out of her work and refused to validate Bridget's observations. Dissatisfied with the response she received, the next night Bridget addressed the same set of concerns to Richard.

In both these cases, the customers involved are not only regular customers but regulars who frequent the restaurant anywhere from three to seven times in a week, a rate of participation that far exceeds most regulars. Also, both of these interactions occurred after ten o'clock in the evening, when the customers in question had already been hanging out for several hours and consumed several drinks. Although both Bridget and Karl spend an inordinate amount of time at the restaurant, and their alcohol consumption might have intensified their passion or their sense of involvement, customers frequently offer opinions, suggest options, give advice, and lobby for changes at the Hungry Cowboy.

These stories demonstrate the delicate balance of the triadic power arrangement for managers. The management philosophy that encourages recognition, care, and treating customers like guests in one's home encourages a loyal regular clientele. In exchange for their loyalty, some regular customers expect to shape how the restaurant is managed and run. The two examples of Bridget and Karl explained above are representative of a longer history of invited and uninvited customer involvement in the work process. Neither of these particular contacts resulted in changes. Bridget was ignored, while Karl was asked to leave for the night when his belligerence increased, and he later apologized to Richard. What is significant about these two examples is that they demonstrate customers' desire to feel involved, and sometimes intimately involved, in work processes.

At the Hungry Cowboy, customers feel involved and even entitled to express their opinions and exert their wills, for better and for worse. Regulars especially lay claim to authority regarding restaurant management. For example, when a server named Elliot was fired after a series of errors and deceptions, several customers took up a campaign to get him back. They interrogated other servers, made appeals to Richard, and filled out a series of comment cards demanding that Elliot be rehired. Although Elliot was never rehired, sometimes customers are successful in their missions. In another example of customer advocacy, regulars relentlessly lobbied Richard for years until he finally agreed to install video games and a cash machine in the bar. However, in order to fulfill their demands, Richard had to have the bar remodeled. The arrival of the video game and the cash machine was met with great celebration by the interested parties but was much bemoaned by at least another two-dozen customers, who called Richard, complained to servers, and used the comment cards to explain that the video game had negatively altered the ambience. Despite their displeasure, the video game remains, and the customers who requested it do, as promised, spend even more time and money than before it was installed.

Sometimes regulars overestimate the privileges of membership. For example, one regular customer named Ted was laid off and continued to hang out at the restaurant as often as four nights out of the week. Two nights in a row he balked at having to pay for his drinks. It seemed he expected to continue his membership even if he could not afford to pay. Ted said that other customers had told him to come in and that they would buy him a drink, but these promises had not materialized. He subsequently verbally attacked the bartender, Lisa, claiming she was adding drinks to his tab and overcharging him. Lisa dealt with his attitude and explained his tab to him repeatedly. Even though she resolved the issue and treated him with respect throughout (despite his drunken whining), Lisa still called early the next morning to make sure Richard knew what was happening. She wanted to make sure she had "her version" on the record before Ted came back and tried to describe a sad story of injustice to Richard. Lisa protected herself because she recognized the power of customer complaints to influence not only official policy but also how Richard views and treats employees.

Lisa was careful to contain the potential damage of the event because she was aware of a long history of customers choosing to get involved.

Customers' opinions about servers are very powerful. A series of customer complaints could lead to fewer or less lucrative shifts, while a series of successes, either observed by management or reported by customers could result in better shifts. Both servers and managers have to manage the advantages and liabilities of loyal and vocal regular customers. Here, the loyalty is mutual and must be negotiated delicately.

Customers like Karl and Bridget offer business advice because they feel like they get to have a voice or a vote in how the Hungry Cowboy develops over time. Regular customers debate menu changes, discuss their reactions to physical changes like new carpeting or decorations and routinely question policies. As such, the investment that servers explained in interviews is complemented by a familiar involvement expressed by regular customers.

MEASURING SERVICE
Routinizing the Intangible

There is something enticing, even mesmerizing, about the connections that develop in this funky, aging Tex-Mex restaurant in a strip mall just outside Minneapolis. Something special about the Hungry Cowboy invites customers to invest their loyalty, energy, and, yes, dining dollars time and time again. This restaurant succeeds at making money and warming up the marketplace in ways that Ritzer and others fear will become increasingly rare. Ritzer worries McDonaldization has already "dramatically altered the nature of social relationships" and that depersonalization, homogenization, and deskilling are likely to proceed, relatively unabated.[27] In many ways, the Hungry Cowboy seems free of these concerns, safe from the forces that Ritzer describes as having dehumanizing effects. More than just being separate from the patterns that Ritzer describes, it actually seems to fuel an opposite trend. For insiders, it seems to *re-humanize* the market, providing a space that feels more authentic where consumers feel more individual. Despite these positive experiences, even the Hungry Cowboy is not free of the routinization of public life that Ritzer so elegantly defines in his scholarship. Even though the general manager, Richard, and his staff run a lucrative business that has successfully produced a loyal and growing clientele for over a decade, he still uses standard measures to evaluate success.

The standard measurement that Richard utilizes is called the secret shopper service. Secret shoppers, or mystery shoppers, are people hired to judge the restaurant against other restaurants, evaluating it based on a set standard of "good service." Secret shoppers are paid to offer an outsider's perspective of the dining experience. The terms that the service uses, however, construct that "experience" narrowly, by means of questions asked or omitted. Since the quality audit form secret shoppers use tells them where to direct their attention, their observations analyze the elements of a restaurant that influence a customer by means of a formula of "good service."

In some ways, secret shoppers offer a less biased viewpoint on service than that offered by regulars. Secret shoppers offer a window into what the Hungry Cowboy feels like without the veneer of inclusion. Yet, Richard's reliance on secret shoppers presents a paradox. The Hungry Cowboy management and staff downplay the very features of "experience" that secret shoppers are trained to measure. In terms of service, the shoppers are asked to look for a predictable script, one recognizing not just efficiency but demanding specific actions in a particular order like introducing oneself, welcoming the guest to the restaurant, offering certain drinks, appetizers, entrees, desserts, and after-dinner drinks. At Hungry Cowboy, however, servers are not trained into a particular script and do not necessarily use easily identifiable techniques of getting to know their customers.

Not surprisingly, servers hate secret shoppers, mainly because these outside evaluators set up a uniform quality service standard that servers believe does not apply to their work. Workers may not mind being answerable to regular customers who insure the success of the restaurant, but they object to being accountable to secret shoppers. Specifically, servers at the Hungry Cowboy resent the secret shoppers because they almost always receive low scores on upselling techniques. To receive a high score on the overall report, servers must mention specials, offer side dishes and additions to what is ordered, and encourage customers to have three courses: appetizers, dinner, and dessert. But the peer training at the Hungry Cowboy does not emphasize upselling.[28]

In fact, upselling breaks one of the key assumptions underlying waiting tables at the Hungry Cowboy. New employees are encouraged to assume that customers have been to the restaurant before. In fact, new servers may face reproach when they fail to assume repeat business and instead treat all customers equally, by introducing them to the menu or trying to upgrade selections, for example by asking, "Would you like some Patron Silver in your Margarita?" Such attempts to encourage people to change their orders challenge the membership status that so many customers claim. Upselling undercuts the widely recognized authority of regular customers. More important, selling strategies reintroduce money-driven behavior into service interactions. Emphasizing selling is in direct contrast to the feeling of belonging that many servers and customers use to describe what they enjoy.

Interestingly, the insistence in quality audits that upselling constitutes good service is even contested by the secret shoppers themselves. One shopper writes, "She didn't try to upgrade our items but this to us is the better approach; we like the more personal service rather than the pushy programmed service." Another secret shopper similarly debated the value of a "hard sell": "He met our needs and made our dining experience fun. He fit our restaurant style. He joked with us and poked fun at my husband. He did not sell us. However, I don't appreciate a hard sell at a relaxing dinner." Similarly, servers who get bad scores for failing to upsell to secret shoppers are quick to remind Richard that an aggressive hard sell is not part of the training, and not part of the ambience offered. What is interesting is that despite Richard's attention to the individual needs of customers and employees, he still pays a monthly fee to the quality audit service, and when the reports come in the mail, he pores over them. Servers are wise to remind him that they are being "tested" on a standard that differs from the one they have been trained into, because Richard takes the reports seriously. Richard recognizes that, for the most part, customers know what they want, they have already developed their favorites over time and are paying in part for the pleasure of the familiar. Yet, Richard's attention to the quality audits as realistic measures of the Hungry Cowboy's standard of service violates much of what he professes to his customers and teaches to his employees.[29] Despite setting up this successful ambience, Richard does not really trust it; instead, he uses standardized measures that do not do justice to the intangible ambience the Hungry Cowboy produces.

Secret shopper services take the "personal" out of personal service interactions because this measure expects the secret shoppers to look for more of the same wherever they go. The measure of "quality" in the audit reports is inflexible. The forms they use to describe their experience confine their responses and ignore the differences that exist between what individual customers want by offering one universal definition of service and then testing against that. As Robin Leidner explains, inflexible and rigid standards risk alienating both workers and customers.

The danger in routinizing human interactions is that if workers do not or are not allowed to respond flexibly, form may come to supersede meaning, thus increasing the likelihood of failure on both levels. In other words, rigid routines strictly enforced can actually prevent workers from doing an adequate job, harming both customer satisfaction and employee morale.[30]

At casual restaurants like this one, sometimes customers seem to get more attached to the meaning than the form of service. If secret shopper services helped restaurants to raise their service to a level that scores high on their forms, customers could count on receiving predictable, formulaic, and routine service. Undoubtedly, under these conditions, poor, uninterested service would be less common, but so would personal, surprising, and engaging service. Evaluation by secret shopper services threatens to decide for customers what it is they want and produce it. It flattens out the individual needs of customers and the individual skills of service workers by establishing one standard of service for all.

Use of secret shopper services is growing, not just locally but across the country as new quality audit companies crop up to evaluate service.[31] The role of secret shoppers, however, goes relatively unquestioned by managers.[32] One possibility of the growing reliance on secret shopper services is that more restaurants will shape their service delivery in keeping with that universal definition of "quality service."[33] Shopper services can influence how restaurants design, train, and perform service, and their opinions may outweigh those of the regular customers.

The increasing reliance on "pretend customers" looking for easily identified service scripts displaces the opinions of regular customers, servers, and even managers by measuring all locales against a universal standard for

service. This process encourages and reinforces McDonaldization of service interactions in a variety of eating contexts. The social moments in the
Hungry Cowboy and the "extras" of service work, however, happen between
the cracks, fissures, and inconsistencies of service. The messy moments are
sometimes the best moments: when a customer's humanity breaks through
the routine of dining, or when a server truly tries to meet the needs of the
individual in front of him or her. Delivering service that fulfills the secret
shopper formula runs the risk of stripping service interactions of some of
the richness of exchange.

MESSY MOMENTS AT THE HUNGRY COWBOY

Over the years, I have observed many customers relax into a booth, kick their
feet up, and sigh deeply. I have also observed daily reminders of the messy
moments of service work at the Hungry Cowboy, when behaviors, words, or
emotional intensity spill out in a service environment. Messy moments are
when, as Robin Leidner describes, "the boundaries separating production,
consumption and sociability" break down.[34] Sometimes those moments that
connect people one to another are quite happy, as when a waiter and his
guests laugh wholeheartedly at a joke. At other times the unscripted connections that happen within the restaurant space reflect longing and loss.
Restaurants are supposed to be public spaces, but life does not always follow
the careful distinction of public and private. Take for example, the stories of
three elderly men and a dog.

   *The first elderly man was not recognized by anyone when he sat waiting
on a busy Friday night for a table. He was restless and kept asking the hostess
if she had a table for him. After fifteen minutes or so, he wandered toward the
restrooms but then pulled up a chair and sat down at a table already occupied
by a young couple. One of the hostesses noticed the event and hurried over to try
to resolve the situation. The young man at the table said that it was OK, and
even stood up to help the old man into his seat. The young couple ate dinner with
the man, and helped him, as he departed, to get to his car. The young man told
Richard that he had cared for his ailing grandfather and he knew how hard it
was, getting older. Richard paid for the young man and his wife's bill due to their
generous willingness to sit with a stranger.*

The second elderly man was a regular. He came in often enough with his daughter that he had a nickname among the staff. He was particularly fond of Richard, who sat talking with him one October evening. His daughter confessed that her father was feeling quite ill, and shortly after Richard got up from the table, the man hobbled toward the bathroom, with feces rolling down his leg and onto the carpeting. That night, Richard bought dinner for the customers nearby who felt ill, he comforted the daughter and the man on their way out to the car, and he cleaned the carpeting quickly, so that the evening could continue. The body and the mind both give out over time, and we can't always decide where that will be.

Sometimes both crisis and joy play out in the restaurants we frequent. More than one regular customer has used the Hungry Cowboy to mourn or to say goodbye to an old friend. Even River the dog and his owner are not as unique as one might think.

Since River died in 2000, I talked with another man who was calling, crying, to order a burger to put his dog to sleep. He described what she looked like as she lay dying and explained that he would come pick up the burger when his dog was calm enough for him to leave the house briefly. So we charged the burger and had it waiting and paid for when he rushed over to pick it up.

Using the familiarity of a commercial restaurant to soothe one of life's difficult moments, saying goodbye to a pet, is surprising. What's more remarkable is that sometimes regular customers even use the Hungry Cowboy to help them mourn each other. Sometimes the restaurant cannot put a price on what a customer needs.

The last elderly gentleman came in during a rainy afternoon in search of candles. I was managing at the time, and a server came to get me since the man was hanging around up front looking sort of lost. I asked him if I could help him. At first he didn't make a lot of sense. I couldn't tell what he was after, but he was obviously upset. I eventually came to understand that his wife was very ill. They had been regular customers. This restaurant was her favorite place to go out, and she had always liked the small gold and glass candles that sat on each table. Now his wife was dying. She was in and out of consciousness and somewhat delusional even when she was conscious. But she had mentioned the Hungry Cowboy and had talked about the candles there repeatedly. In his grief, he hoped it would bring her some comfort if he could have the table candle she was longing for to put by her bed. I gave him several of the candle lamps, with my best wishes. I put my

arm around his shoulders and walked him out. I heard later, that he continued to
come in once in a while by himself, after she passed.

As a participant observer, I struggled to make sense of these moments.
Despite my affinity for dining out, I could not imagine replicating the customer behaviors that I observed. My research forced me to pay heed to the
range of needs with which customers approach the service encounter. I came
to appreciate that the ultimate privilege of being a regular was the chance to
experience a sense of belonging in public.

BELONGING IN PUBLIC

The success at the Hungry Cowboy seems to be a strange brew of smart
management, dedicated workers, and customers who are seeking a place in
the marketplace where they feel recognized. It succeeds at offering a scene
of attachment,[35] offering its members the opportunity to belong in public. As E. E. LeMasters observed in his study of a blue-collar bar called
the Oasis, belonging in public can help mitigate some of the costs of late
capitalism: "In mass society, one of the crucial needs of the individual is to
defend himself against the impersonal world around him: to feel that he
belongs, that people know who he is, that somebody cares about him. For
its regular patrons, at least the inner circle, The Oasis performs this function quite well."[36]

If both servers and customers can be encouraged to participate in the
exchange of pleasantries, recognition, and sociability within the space of the
restaurant, then their mutual emotional engagement reproduces the labor
process while simultaneously producing a controlled community where
anonymity is mitigated and participants feel at home. Food is at the center
of this hominess. But comfort, pleasure, and recognition are also feelings;
they refer to the experience, or the feel of a place, not only what happens
there. In *The Managed Heart*, Hochschild reflects on the "crucial steadying
effect of emotional labor."[37]

> For these workers, emotion work, feeling rules, and social
> exchange have been removed from the private domain and placed in a
> public one, where they are processed, standardized, and subjected to
> hierarchical control. Taken as a whole, these emotional laborers make

possible a public life in which millions of people daily have fairly trust-
ing and pleasant transactions with total or nearly total strangers. Were
our goodwill strictly confined to persons we know in private life, were
our offering of civility or empathy not so widely spread out and our
feelings not professionalized, surely public life would be profoundly
different.[38]

Certainly the Hungry Cowboy is not immune to customers who take
out their bad feelings on service workers, or the disorderly drunk, or the
night when a server refuses to keep pace with customers' needs; however, the
main quality it offers its customers, the prevailing characteristic agreed upon
by customers, managers, and servers alike, is that it is comfortable. Comfort,
pleasure, and recognition—the mutual appreciation of these qualities not
only highlights the unique ambience, it also tells us something about the
culture we live in. Customers seem to stake a claim to "belonging" at the
Hungry Cowboy because it provides these qualities that are missing from
huge sections of the American marketplace, and by extension, the experience of consumers as they go about their days and nights.

Customers, workers, and managers are all quick to apply ideas ordinarily reserved for private life to the public realm of the workplace. In a
recent dissertation, Maria Poarch comments on the tendency for work to
absorb additional needs or wants, "as Americans spend more of their time at
work, work gradually ... assumes more of the concerns and activities of both
private (family) and public (social and political) life."[39] I would add to her
observations that the growing service sector invites Americans to turn to
the marketplace to fulfill desires that were previously understood as private
concerns. In her study of bars, Madelon Powers discovered that the local
saloon "answered a need felt by most residents of modern American cities
for sociability and a sense of connections with others."[40] At the Hungry
Cowboy, customers, managers, and servers all agree to emphasize sociability,
but their successful collaboration must be contextualized within the culture
outside those four walls that makes a "cozy, familiar" place to work and dine
so attractive to so many people.

This story of connection that is told by many members of the Hungry
Cowboy is not particular to one place. As consumers, many of us locate
these pockets of sociability within the marketplace. Some observers of

social life have identified similar connections in a range of public, for-profit locations. In *Slim's Table*, Mitchell Duneier reflects on how the cafeteria he studied shortened the spaces and weakened the divides that separate people on the street outside. Then, he explains, "during a time when the socially erected barriers between cliques" were shifting, "it was evident that many patrons derived a particular satisfaction from the reduction of social distance. Rather than attempting to remain among their own groups, in their places, they seized the opportunity to get to know members of the larger collectivity a little better. They obviously felt gratified to have contact with other habitués in the larger group and the feeling was mutual."[41] In his study, Duneier observed social cliques that were divided by race merge over time at the cafeteria. What is striking here is how customers derive a "particular satisfaction from the reduction of social distance." Individuals who often move seamlessly past one another, on the street, in the grocery store, here find an opening, a chance to connect. This impulse—this reaching across difference and shortening up the social distance—is a compelling finding about public spaces. Like the servers who invest, customers' behaviors reveal a desire to connect with others in the marketplace. After all, customers can get good service, cheap appetizers, and strong drinks without chatting up other customers and servers; their choice to reach out to one another appears to fulfill additional desires for meaningful interaction and connection in public.

Customers not only bother to make contact with one another, they express loyalty to places that foster connections in the marketplace. Many scholars who worry about American culture would have us believe that we are too far removed, too individualized, too divided by wealth, culture, racism, and sexism to be bothered to make connections—we are, in the words of Robert Putnam, "bowling alone." Others would say that Americans are now successfully atomized. We move through a world of machines and routinized human interactions, procuring what we need in a sanitized, individualized service society characterized by a drive-through window.[42]

The pleasures of making contact at places like the cafeteria featured in *Slim's Table* or the Hungry Cowboy do not undo many of these larger cultural patterns, but consumers' desire to make a home in the marketplace certainly contradicts concerns about a nation of strangers. The language Duneier uses reflects the underlying feelings made possible by connections in public spaces: people at the cafeteria "seized the opportunity" and "felt gratified to have contact," and "the feeling was mutual." These desires conflict with the picture of a population that has given up on the possibility or even extinguished the need to meet with one another, make contact, establish rapport, and get to know one another.

There is no question that, because these contacts take place within an odd, nostalgic Tex-Mex restaurant, they are less tidy, less "pure" than block parties and backyard fences. These fleeting connections, what I call compensatory economies of pleasure, are not perfect, nor do they replace other forms of affiliation, but they certainly speak to the potential of consumers and producers of service to dig the humanity out from beneath the anonymity of service exchanges.

4

MANAGING SERVICE

◆◆◆◆◆◆◆◆◆◆◆◆◆◆◆◆◆◆◆◆◆◆◆◆

TRAINING AND THE PRODUCTION OF AMBIENCE

Well, the restaurant business is totally different, because it's about personality. You're dealing with people, which is the hugest variable you can ever have in a business. No business deals with the "X factor" that we do, where you have people coming in and sitting down and who knows what kind of day they've had. 'Cause it's all about the people; it's not necessarily about the products we're selling. It's about the interaction that you receive between server and guest, and server and manager, and manager and guest that really matters. There's tons of places that have good food, but if you get good food and you get a personable experience, you're gonna go back. And corporations are really bad at addressing that issue; to me, all they want is their people to stand there.

I'm so not a corporate guy. I am the shoot from the hip and go for whatever works at the time. And the corporate approach—I've always felt that corporations don't belong in the restaurant industry; it's a bad thing. One thing that blows me away, and we had to deal with briefly at a chain [where I worked] is that they give you a script to read at the tables, which I am so totally against. I am so adamantly against it; I would say everything opposite to it. I'm like, you know what, fire me for it, but I'm a good goddamn server, better than anyone who is reading the script. It so takes away from the personality; the way I make my money is my personality. Developing a rapport with people, people dig that. Scripts limit you, and in a lot of ways, I think they lower the expectations of what an individual brings to an establishment. It looks at people like groups, not like individuals, which, of course, corporations are notorious for.

The attitude of the company slides down from the top, and when you've got a top man that's got the attitude Richard's got, it makes the whole place enjoyable to be at. It's why the clientele is there; it's why [workers] have stayed as long as they have. The way Richard operates his business, he's always about the guest and that's the most important fact. That's why the Hungry Cowboy has succeeded, and it really breaks all the rules of the restaurant industry. It's set in an off-the-beaten-path strip mall. C'mon! It should not have survived, even in its inception. Places like this don't usually get the following we have. You walk in the place, eat the food, get the service, and you're blown away. It's an anomaly. It shouldn't be there. And Richard is pretty much the reason, I would say, that it's still here, because the owners know nothing about the business. It's about Richard and about the way he's conducted the business, and the way he's taken care of his people and taken care of his guests that keeps people coming back.

When you're walking into a little local restaurant and whether you know it's independently owned or corporate or not, you kind of get the feel when you walk in that it's not a corporate shop, it's one of a kind. You can tell from the carpet, the paint, everything else, you can tell it's the Hungry Cowboy; there's nothing else like it. It doesn't have that cookie-cutter feel, which so many places have. When you walk into [a chain restaurant] there's a cookie-cutter feel, there's a plan. Anytime you see a moose head on a wall—there's a pretty good chance it's not chained out.

As Trevor explains, management in the service sector involves three sets of relationships: between customer and server; server and manager; and manager and customer. This triadic arrangement of power complicates the traditional, dyadic model by which most businesses train workers.

In the traditional dyadic model, two groups of actors interact in the labor process: managers or bosses who give the orders and workers who react to manager directives. Dyadic models rely on a model of the work process that sees it as rational; that is, the model assumes that if the worker correctly follows steps one through twelve, the process will be completed successfully. Such rationalization involves using mathematical calculations and abstract rules to order and organize human behavior and movement in order to fulfill specific goals.[1] Work structures like industrial manufacturing or even data processing are relatively easy to routinize using such principles of scientific management.

Scientific management is the systematic ordering of labor processes to insure maximum efficiency and output. Sometimes referred to as Taylorism, after Frederick Winslow Taylor who first introduced the idea in 1911, scientific management breaks the labor process down into parts and establishes specific procedures designed to complete each portion of the process.[2] Each part of the process is therefore narrowly defined in order to make the production process predictable and efficient. This process was made famous by the Ford company's automobile plants. Principles of scientific management have been widely applied in fast-food contexts like McDonald's, where management narrowly defines workers' jobs by imposing strict behaviors and even using timers and alarms that keep the production of food consistent and fast. Unlike these more predictable tasks in fast-food restaurants, service interactions in full-service restaurants resist such routinization.

In the triadic model, managers incorporate flexibility into the work process. In this model, since customer satisfaction is the ultimate goal of the work process, all rules must be subject to change depending on context and the needs of individual customers. Labor regimes in service work must be flexible enough to take into consideration personalities, moods, and spontaneous needs of customers. If servers are inflexible, service can seem unfriendly, feigned, and unconcerned with customer satisfaction. In short, you can't feed two hundred people in the same planned and regimented way that you assemble two hundred parts. Because workers are allowed to be flexible, they have more autonomy and can make spontaneous adjustments to context and customer.[3]

The behavior of customers cannot ever be completely predicted because customers are not interchangeable pieces of machinery nor are they reliably the same from day to day. This variability is the "X factor" that Trevor refers to in his narrative. Managers in the service sector must direct employees as to how they are expected to cope with the messy moments that occur between the "steps" provided in service work. For example, most full-service training regimes include the following necessary steps: greeting the table, taking the order, placing the order, bringing drinks, delivering appetizers, refilling drinks, serving dinner, offering dessert, and clearing plates. But these steps do not direct servers as to what to do when a family moves to another server's section between the greeting and the drinks. These rules do not establish a policy for whether a server should wait for a customer talking on a cell phone to finish their phone call or move on to another table that is ready to order. Servers can instinctually solve some problems not outlined by the rules. For example, when a child dumps all the drinks from the table onto the floor, the server cleans them up. But when two customers at a table will not answer their server's questions because they are giving each other the "silent treatment" and will not break it to answer if they want dessert or not, their behavior disrupts the work process.

Managers also have to allow for some flexibility for workers because the labor structure in the restaurant does not allow managers to monitor the behavior of their employees consistently. The architecture of restaurants also limits and occasionally prevents surveillance by managers. Imagine a server rushing from table to table with a manager one step behind, simply observing the employee's behavior. Such an arrangement would undermine the ambience of the server "getting to know" the customer, would undo the feigned effortlessness of service, and would make painfully clear the labor structure into which the customer had entered. This violation of performance is not the goal of restaurants. Consequently, frontline service workers have to be trained in a way that enables them to react and respond without the immediate assistance or even knowledge of their managers.

Since managers recognize the customer/worker interaction as the primary source of profitability, they cannot afford to disrupt service workers' autonomy by imposing inflexible control mechanisms or rules. For example, a manager from another restaurant in Minneapolis called Neighbor's explained that his restaurant encourages service workers to sell certain "featured" menu items, like a top-shelf mixed drink or an appetizer sampler, each week, and monitors their monthly sales. A "top-shelf" drink refers to any drink that uses expensive liquor. In many bars, the available liquors are arranged from least expensive at the bottom, to the most expensive liquors on the top shelf. The manager from Neighbor's was pleased during my interview with him to find out that my server had indeed offered me the drink of the month. "He did offer you one? All right! Yes, we need every customer who walks in to be offered a drink of the month." His comment reflects his limited ability to monitor his employees' behavior continuously. He encourages his employees to "push" certain featured items, but he cannot hover behind them at each table, checking to see if they follow through. Only at the end of the day or week can he assess how many featured items were sold and by whom. Electronic monitoring of numbers of sales tells only part of the story, however; it conveys the number of transactions but not the quality of the interaction. Measuring human interactions is much more difficult. Given these challenges, how can the social interactions necessary to food service in restaurants be trained and managed?

To answer that question, I interviewed managers from eight restaurants that compete with the Hungry Cowboy. For this part of my research, I drew a three-mile circle around the Hungry Cowboy and contacted all twenty-seven of the full-service restaurants in that circle. In addition to the managers at the Hungry Cowboy, I interviewed managers from eight competing restaurants. Six of the nine were chain restaurants: Rosie's, All-Star, Peppers, Fiesta, Neighbor's, and Fisherman's.[4] Three of the nine were independent restaurants: Hometown Bar and Grill, Jefferson's Restaurant, and of course, the Hungry Cowboy. My research reveals that chain restaurants and independent restaurants differ in patterns of training and in hiring and management philosophies. Chain restaurants tend to use routinized scripts, themed packaging, and carefully defined training practices, an approach I call Total Quality Service. In contrast, independent restaurants tend to rely on specialized systems of management that grow out of the operation of individual companies, an approach I define as the Cut and Paste method.

Whether customers know it or not, when they choose a restaurant they are choosing between at least two distinct approaches to training workers: the Total Quality Service approach, which attempts to predict all possible situations and lay out rules prescribing appropriate behavior, and the Cut and Paste approach, which arises in a much less organized or predictable manner, developing out of the idiosyncrasies of the particular workplace culture. Sites that use Total Quality Service have lengthy training materials, evaluate employees frequently, and impose a totalizing mission statement by weaving it throughout training materials, daily pre-shift meetings, and reward systems, often using the same mission statement in communication with customers.[5] Training regimes are uniformly implemented at restaurants all across the country and even internationally.[6] Although in practice, workers and managers alike are often forced to make judgment calls and accommodations on the spot, Total Quality Service restaurants ideally keep to a set of rules outlined in training and operating manuals.

While in Total Quality Service direction flows down, in Cut and Paste management schemes, information flows up. Cut and Paste management often emerges out of a weak or nonexistent central training and management philosophy. "How things are done" becomes an approach that develops organically over time and then is slowly but unevenly institutionalized through practice and occasionally through minimal written materials and rules. In Cut and Paste management schemes, frontline service workers have responsibilities that include knowing and learning from their customers and conveying what they know to managers when policies are determined, menus are changed, or marketing strategies designed. Rather than written materials, a Cut and Paste approach relies on informal indoctrination into a workplace culture that the workers themselves reproduce and maintain.

Both Total Quality Service and the Cut and Paste method suffer from some constraints. While Total Quality Service procedures may limit human discretion and worker autonomy, the Cut and Paste method of adapting to spontaneous demands in the moment results in a variegated mixing of the social world of the restaurant with the needs of business and makes it difficult for servers to address inconsistencies, hierarchies, and biases. In what follows, I compare Rosie's with the Hungry Cowboy in order to scrutinize the attendant advantages and limitations of each management approach.

TOTAL QUALITY SERVICE AND TOTALIZING PHILOSOPHIES IN CHAIN RESTAURANTS

Al runs a franchise of a national chain restaurant called Rosie's. He is forty, lumbering in his movements, but clear and snappy in his speech.[7] In the past, Al owned his own restaurant, but when he and his partners disagreed and dismantled their partnership, he was hired as a general manager at Rosie's. He is quick to offer me time to talk but frequently defines the information he shares with me as a "protected formula." If he isn't a true believer, then Al is a great performer. Never does a sliver of uncertainty enter his descriptions of their "formula 4 success." The formula 4 success is pretty self-explanatory: 1) cocktails and wine, 2) appetizers, 3) entrees, and 4) desserts. In fact, though much of the internal training and promotion literature for Rosie's is self-explanatory, the training literature and Al speak of its concepts as if they were exceedingly complex. For example, he says, "OK, so then there's 4-star level. 4-star is the next level after 3-star level." He often pauses dramatically before announcing something taken for granted in restaurant work. For example, he says, "And the key here is—and we make sure no Rosie's worker forgets—happy customers are how we make money." His pontificating tone demonstrates how seriously he takes Rosie's motto, rules, and job categories; it also likely reflects his approach to indoctrinating new workers.

Al's dramatic, patronizing tone is matched in Rosie's training materials. For example, the Rosie's "Steps of Service" are 1) Seal the Deal, 2) Check Back Within 2 Bites, 3) Table Maintenance, Refills and Team Work, 4) Desserts, Coffee, and After-dinner Drinks, 5) Drop the check, 6) The Rapid Return. All of the restaurants I studied have their own sequence of service; what varies is how the tone and language highlight the steps, that is, how they "package" the sequence.

The packaging of the training materials at Rosie's is remarkably succinct, and compelling, but a little excessive when you consider what it is designed to do. All of the training materials are marked with military allusions like dog tags, compasses, and binoculars. The opening message sets the tone. "It's a War! For almost ____ years, Rosie's has fought the battle well. Our plan has been strong and our execution courageous. We've learned from the battles we have won—and from those that we have lost, and . . . . now is the time for the Battle Plan." This language reveals that the war is not internal; rather, the restaurant faces a foe not contained in the four walls of the restaurant. The battle being waged is with the competing restaurants in the area. In this formulation, servers are soldiers, and customers are either the ammunition used to beat the enemy or the resources over which the two enemies fight.

The catchphrases and symbols of the restaurant are laced throughout the training materials in a process called theming.[8] What's significant here is that employees are subject to the same marketing strategies as customers.

As Leidner discovered in her analysis of training regimes, training materials imagine both customers and workers as highly programmable: "Collectively, these excerpts tell us that no detail is too trivial, no relationship too personal, no experience too individual, no manipulation too cynical for some organization or person, in a spirit of helpfulness or efficiency, to try to provide a standard, replicable routine for it."[9]

While Rosie's uses "battlefield" imagery, another chain restaurant called All-Star's uses a winning sports team approach, and Fiesta uses a party theme. Restaurant management structure messages to workers in the same symbolic framework they use to package the menu, the decorations on the walls, and the uniforms workers wear. For example, the same fish-focused ambience provided to customers at Fisherman's appears throughout the training materials, where scripted lines are referred to as "hooks" that "catch" the customers' dollars. Theming of this type does not differentiate between customers and workers; it targets both groups with similarly themed messages, practices, and even slogans.

Rosie's training materials instruct servers to battle an enemy they do not see, making use of their interactions with customers to win a war. "The Battle Plan" is described as a state of emergency where the critical edge is being lost, the enemy is closing in: "The three mile ring is getting crowded, the enemy is better trained and better armed, business and development costs continue to escalate, and the consumer is changing more rapidly, is more dining sophisticated with higher expectations, and has more choices than ever before." The Rosie's plan is described as the new offensive: "We must develop a crystal vision of each of our roles and of what will be required of our troops. The war has escalated! Success depends on the unwavering commitment to our mission, strategies and care processes/tactics, that is our blueprint for success. Now, more than ever before, there is no room for error. No room for misunderstanding. Our plan must be clear. Our commitment must be strong."

What does it mean to mix war metaphors with service work? The contradictions between service and war are clear in the training materials. For example, the irreconcilability of war strategies with service reverberate in the clumsy joining of "care processes/tactics." Framing training materials within a war model also creates soldiers out of service workers. The borrowed drama of a war introduces an intensity into the training regime that inevitably affects the ambience available to customers: in this case, the metaphor produces an aggressive, heavily packaged environment intent on selling customers more than they thought they wanted.

The tension between the desire of the chain owners to make lots of money and beat out the competition contradicts the concerned, friendly service attitude managers hope their workers display as they approach a table in their restaurant. If the war model seems to be an uncomfortable fit, the question remains, can customers be comfortable if waited on by servers indoctrinated into a fear of losing the "war"? The contradictions of "The Battle Plan" point to the challenge of top-down Total Quality Service management schemes and raise larger questions about the challenge of training frontline service workers. How are desired qualities like sincerity and fun produced and reproduced across the country, in different towns, by different people? How are such qualities defined, trained, evaluated, and converted into charts and graphs that track success and situate individual restaurants in the larger chain against one another?

WE HIRE PERSONALITIES

When I ask Al what Rosie's is looking for in servers, he replies, "We hire personalities. I don't care if they have any experience. We hire personalities; we're looking for people who are energetic, friendly, like to smile. As long as they like people and they can do those things, I can teach them everything else." Although Al is enthusiastic about Rosie's training program, the militaristic training does not seem to coincide with his descriptions of the service the restaurant aims for. Al's explanation of Rosie's goals highlights one of the central tensions in service training:

> We don't want the server to say, [imitating a robot] "Hi, my name is Bob. I am your server tonight. Our special is." We try our hardest to keep away from that; that's real important when you come in that we offer you a specific cocktail, that we offer you an add-on salad bar with your entree because by doing that we increase our sales, we make more money. And again, we're real selfish about that; we're trying to increase our PPA—Per Person Average—but we don't care that they ask every

customer about a specific drink, or that they introduce themselves in a real specific manner. Because it gets so tough, to do it at that table and then turning around and going to another table like this, and doing the exact same spiel, I think it becomes phoney. So yeah, we want them to know about the guest; we want them to know their wants, needs, and desires, and how to get more money from them.

Al's description reveals ambiguities and tensions central to training service workers. Somehow Al reconciles the idea of hiring personalities with that of Per Person Averages. He discusses servers' ability to seem sincere, to perform a script that does not sound rehearsed, to reproduce a smile again and again without ever losing the sparkle. On the one hand, he is aware that scripted routines can seem stale to customers. On the other hand, for Al, getting to know customers is a purely instrumental activity in that a connection with customers might provide servers with insights into how to get more money out of customers. Robin Leidner describes some of the tensions that arise when companies attempt to "speed up" human interactions.

> Organizations that routinize service interactions are acting on contradictory impulses. They want to treat customers as interchangeable units, but they also want to make the customers feel that they are receiving personal service. The tension inherent in this project was apparent when I asked one of the trainers at Hamburger University about McDonald's goals for customer service. He told me quite sincerely, "We want to treat each customer as an individual, in sixty seconds or less."[10]

Similarly, even though Al says he's "hiring people, hiring personalities," the didactic, almost ideological nature of the training materials encourages staff members to streamline their selves in the process of becoming certified servers.[11]

What Al reports enjoying most of all about his job is that "everything has been set up." He feels freed up by the availability of an all-inclusive, thorough, deliberate model for training, hiring, and promoting. Even the hiring process is succinctly routinized, beginning with a "thirty-second interview" in which Al "sizes up" the potential hire, followed by psychological tests, and then concluding with a situational interview with two managers. I ask

Al if he feels that this extensive pretesting helped prevent turnover.[12] Turnover is an industry term for the proportion of employees quitting or getting fired to the total number of employees needed to run the restaurant. For example, if a restaurant has twenty servers, a 200 percent turnover means that they would need to hire forty people in one year to keep the restaurant fully staffed.

Al cannot confirm that Rosie's extensive hiring process lowers turnover, which in his store is over 170 percent annually, but he feels that it gives employees an opportunity to imagine themselves into the job, to see if they really want to work at Rosie's before management invests in training new workers. He says, "We're not looking to hire anyone for six days or sixty days; we want to hire them for six years, six months, whatever; long-term is what works for us." His verbal adjustment from the fairly long-term "six years" to the much shorter "six months" points to a tension between his ideal of hiring long-term employees and the reality of the employment situation in which he operates. Most restaurants turn over at least 100 percent of their staff per year and turnover rates up to 300 percent are not uncommon, meaning that many of the "soldiers" he is training will not survive the battle for very long.

Al's description of selling aggressively without inflicting "the same spiel" at every table vibrates along that fine line of managing people without turning them into robots. Al is clear about his ultimate objective; his concern is not that the "robots" will feel bad or be unhappy but rather that the robot routine will not sell with customers. The need to sell runs throughout Rosie's training materials. For example, the job description of "server" is "suggests and sells food and drinks to guests in dining room." "Suggestively sell" is also number one in a list of "essential functions." The only listed function that acknowledges the human, unpredictable nature of service work is the requirement to "observe guest and respond to additional requests to determine when meal has been completed." Observing and responding are mentioned only once, in comparison to the overriding requirement to "Suggestively Sell, Every Guest, Every Time!" Consistency, not personalization, is the rule. For example, Al firmly believes that the training system virtually guarantees personal service; however, it does so not by allowing servers to develop their own style but rather by insisting on the "pivot point order system," which requires servers to write orders in a particular fashion so that any server can deliver the food without "auctioning off" food. Auctioning off food refers to when a server calls out the meal name when they deliver the food because they don't know or don't remember who ordered what. At Rosie's, management avoids this process by providing workers with specific rules for how to write down the order and enter it in the computer. Presumably, auctioning off food would reveal that food is being delivered to customers whom the server does not recognize. The pivot point system is designed to prevent customers from realizing that their server doesn't remember or know them. Another outcome of Rosie's pivot point process is that it encourages servers to follow company policy for which customer at the table or booth places their order first, rather than reacting to customers' prompts, or social customs that dictate, for example, that women or children order first.

PACKAGING SERVICE

Scripting Interactions

Like all of the chain restaurants I studied, Rosie's provides scripted lines and key words that employees should use to introduce customers to "the Rosie's way." Scripts, which provide key terms and also specific sentences and questions, serve two purposes for management. First, scripts produce uniform service interactions, because all employees are directed to say the same things; second, they strengthen the themed packaging at the restaurant. One example of scripting is Rosie's menu guide. It directs servers how to upsell by offering a "pairing" for every food item. For example, servers are taught to suggest a glass of Chardonnay with fried cheese sticks and to recommend adding a small Caeser salad to the fried shrimp platter. The training materials do not simply offer "pairings" but also teach servers the words they should use to sell. For a seafood platter, the selling line is: "A meal fit for a king deserves to be washed down with the Silver Bullet!" Ice cold beers are also suggested with all spicy items to "tame the fire!" Salads can be upsold by saying, "Don't forget you have an opportunity to add grilled chicken to this salad!" All sandwiches should be upgraded by saying to the customer, "Adding a platter to this can round out the WOW for just $1.99!"

Such training materials highlight the negotiations of language, metaphor, and expectations that attempt to balance business needs with consumer desires. Frontline service workers perform their jobs in a precarious position, accountable to both management and customers. The delicate process of producing and reproducing quality service shows up in the training literature that schizophrenically fluctuates between "sell, sell, sell" and "personalize, personalize, personalize." New employees must be encouraged to do both simultaneously. Leidner reveals how routinization diminishes the very values the restaurant may claim it is upholding:

> For although the routinization of interactive service work challenges the values of authenticity, autonomy, sincerity, and individuality, service organizations often draw on these and other widely shared values to bolster the legitimacy of their control efforts. In the process, the values themselves may be diminished. For example, the line "We want to treat every customer as an individual in sixty seconds or less" . . . draws [its] meaning from the values of individualism and authenticity, yet [it is] embedded in processes that flatly contravene those ideals, using them only instrumentally.[13]

At Rosie's, management seizes upon ideas like family, friendship, and belonging because these values increase connections between customers and servers so that customers will spend more money. In these cases, the use of these ideas is entirely instrumental. But management also offers these same values to employees, as a means to make sense of their labor. For example, Rosie's literature includes statements like "We are committed to 100% guest satisfaction. You will be amazed at how much you enjoy treating guests like family." This attempt to define delivering burgers and fries as analogous to family relationships seems on its face just as outlandish as the war metaphor. How might an individual employee, a nineteen-year-old server, reconcile the encouragement to imagine guests as family with the inducement to win the war? These conflicting directives reveal the tension between the profit-motive and inducing workers to produce something like care for their customers. A manager named William from Jefferson's explains his own struggle between an instrumental approach to service and a more relational one.

It's hard to find someone [managers] who can sustain that focus on the guest, when for a lot of companies, the focus is going to be on the managers and showing certain results, which can keep many managers lost in the office. [This] . . . has been happening to me a lot lately; it's the last place I want to be. Since I've been in the business and I'm really trying to get people to behave in a caring way, I find it's very difficult to teach. People can develop, but most people start out having it; they really have the desire to give of themselves and to care for someone doing that job, whereas there are a lot of people who try their best to minimize any sort of giving.

This conflict, between relational needs of customers and even servers with the more instrumental need to keep profits up and compete with other restaurants shows up in the mixed metaphors Rosie's mobilizes to train new workers.

Another challenge to the Rosie's formula for success is the sheer messiness of human behavior. Tightly organized service regimes do not prepare workers well for the range of customer behaviors that they will encounter. For example, Rosie's encourages workers to treat children as important guests in their own right, which includes bringing them supplies like a high chair or booster, crayons, games, wet wipes, and napkins. Servers are told to greet children with an enthusiastic smile, ask their names, write their names on their menus, bring out their meal first, and make sure their plates are cool to the touch. Serving children is one site where directives to workers, workers' desires, and company profits can potentially all come together. A server might benefit from paying special attention to children, who then may behave better and become easier to deal with. At the same time, servers are conforming to company policies, while also investing in future sales to a family pleased by their experience at Rosie's. While this situation is ideal, such a confluence of objectives is rare. The messiness of human behavior continually challenges servers' ability to stick to the rules. What if the children are unpleasant, unhappy, or unwilling to interact? What if the parents resent the server's involvement with their children? What if interactions with children, who don't follow timetables, slows a server's ability to serve another table?

Training materials are designed to inspire workers to cater their performances to the goals of the company. But training materials also strategically limit server behavior. For example, Rosie's trains new workers to memorize the "Forbidden words poster": a list of words not tolerated on the floor of the restaurant. This list includes the standard profanity considered inappropriate in many workplaces, but it also includes sanctions against negativity of any kind. For example, servers are forbidden to say "no" or "I can't." Such directives are impractical. Obviously, servers cannot reasonably make it through a shift without saying "no." This careful laying down of expectations also infantilizes the employee; directives like these assume a certain nonthinking, programmable worker.

Rosie's message to new workers is alternately empowering and infantilizing. For example, training materials encourage workers to feel empowered and optimistic about their future at Rosie's. The training manual introduces new workers to the "Career Pathway Mountain," which offers a visual metaphor for workers' ability to climb in the ranks of the company by equipping themselves with the compass, dogtags, backpack, and binocular tools highlighted in the training manual. Despite this encouragement, the language and visual clues included in the training materials simultaneously envision a worker who cannot be trusted to learn even the smallest skills on the job. Everything must be laid out, reviewed, and tested before the server can be "released" onto the floor of the restaurant. For example, the training manual provides a list of restaurant lingo including: "upsell," "garnish," and "on the fly." By providing a lexicon in advance, the training at Rosie's leaves nothing for on-the-job learning.[14] Such training materials seek to simplify the occupational learning curve, leaving nothing to the server, or to chance.

CUT AND PASTE MANAGEMENT AT THE HUNGRY COWBOY

Cut and Paste management is marked by less formality, less consistency, and more personalized, rather than streamlined, approaches to training new workers. For example, at the Hungry Cowboy, training is informal and changes over time, sometimes from trainee to trainee. Training is also less common at the Hungry Cowboy than at many comparable restaurants because the staff consists of only twenty servers at a time, and turnover is very low. Turnover remains below 100 percent annually, with a core group of servers who have worked there for over five years. The presence of this core group contrasts sharply with Al's unfulfilled wish to hire "permanent" workers at Rosie's for "six years, six months, whatever." As a result of Hungry Cowboy's comparatively low demand for new workers, servers are ordinarily hired one at a time, and their training fluctuates with both the priorities of the management at the time of hire and the proclivities of the server assigned to train them.[15]

These two approaches to managing service differ in four key aspects. First, in Cut and Paste management schemes, once hired, rookie servers receive training that recognizes the relevant experience of the person hired and supplements the hiree's preexisting skills. As a result, the training period varies according to the trainees' previous work experience and speed at which the rookie server picks up knowledge while on the job. Second, in comparison to chain stores, rules and policies are rarely, if ever, written down, but are most often conveyed verbally by both managers and coworkers, and occasionally even by customers. Third, Cut and Paste management tends to rely on peer training.[16] Trusted long-term employees are responsible for training new employees into the workplace culture. Fourth and finally, rather than exhaustive documentation of the company philosophy and theme, rookie servers are orientated into the workplace culture through storytelling. These practices result in a work culture in which social inclusion and occupational socialization are synonymous.[17]

At the Hungry Cowboy, all new servers follow and then are followed by trainers before they are given their own shift. The duration and content of training varies dramatically depending on the person doing the training and the experience level of the new server. By contrast, Al insists that Rosie's five-day training period is nonnegotiable. "We're absolutely committed to five days. You come in, you've got ten years experience—and I've had that happen—too bad. You have to learn our language, you have to learn our processes, our six steps, things like that." I asked Al if he had observed any resistance to the training from new employees who already had service work experience. He replied, "Typically not. You know how to serve, I'm not going to be able to teach you much about serving, but somewhere else they have four points of service, we have six steps. It's important that you know what our expectations are." It's clear from this comment, and throughout our interview, that Al takes the training very seriously. So seriously in fact that he does not consider general skills to be transferable from other jobs, as if Rosie's culture is so complex, so different, that nothing but the specific training can prepare a new hire.

Unlike Al, servers at the Hungry Cowboy describe the adaptable training as key to recognizing new servers' existing skills and to reproducing the particular ambience of the Hungry Cowboy. Like some regular customers, servers credit the Hungry Cowboy with a feeling of "authenticity" because the place has not yet been replicated or "chained out." In interviews, workers explain that, as an independent company, the Hungry Cowboy is more directly influenced by the personality, desires, and decisions of individuals than are other types of public establishments. Four of the servers I interviewed contrasted their experience at the Hungry Cowboy with "attempting" to work at a chain or franchise establishment, where they resented having to be retrained and where they felt constrained by the rules dictating how they should perform their work.

Rather than front-loading training by providing new workers with exhaustive directives, at the Hungry Cowboy, coworkers indoctrinate workers into the workplace culture of the restaurant. Peer training moves new servers into the occupational community. In peer training, servers socialize each other into the work culture of the restaurant by modeling their approach to their work, telling stories about the history of the restaurant and the people there, and sharing strategies for dealing with regular and new customers.

The lack of official training documents or practices means that inclusion into the inner circle of workers becomes the mechanism through which new servers are trained to do their jobs. In other words, if servers do not make it into the inner circle socially, they rarely last long at the Hungry Cowboy. At first glance, this situation would seem to limit the power of managers; after all, servers appear to have a high degree of control over each other's training. Instead, peer training masks the directives of management beneath the veneer of workplace culture and peer inclusion. When learning "how things are done," rookie servers are being socialized into the behaviors that are encouraged and permitted by managers, without the managers "dirtying" their hands. Peers indirectly convey management authority.

Since new servers have a trainer who "shows them the ropes" in an informal manner, much of how they perform their job is truly left up to them. In the absence of specific guidelines, tests and measures of accountability, the "style" of service is informally reproduced as long as both trainer and trainee choose to cooperate with the norms that others understand and describe to them. The result is a standard of service that evolves over time. Long-term servers train new workers who eventually may take on the mantle of reproducing service by training in a new generation of servers. This method of peer training communicates the style of service and sanctioned behaviors to new workers, but the new workers themselves can adapt and pass these on in a slightly altered form to the next group of workers.

After the official training period has ended, the now more seasoned rookie server is subject to the same kind of occasional rewards and punishments as any other. In other words, unlike the chain restaurants in this study, new servers at the Hungry Cowboy don't "graduate" but instead they can mark their success through a series of informal promotions: better shifts, inclusion in banter and gossip behind the scenes, and, eventually, full inclusion in the inner circle, which includes the ability to tell stories and indoctrinate the next round of rookies.

Vicki Smith's research on flexible models of management in the new economy suggests that some businesses are moving away from the formulaic training and management regimes employed by many chain restaurants. Her research is a useful litmus test for how Cut and Paste management measures up, both in terms of achieving company goals and producing ambience. In "Institutionalizing Flexibility in a Service Firm," Vicki Smith argues that, in response to widespread retooling of production processes, companies are increasingly moving away from "hierarchical, mass-production work systems"[18] and have moved toward one of two models she identifies. The first she labels the "enabling approach," which relies on peer training and high levels of investment in technology. It then creates ongoing training, encourages worker participation and teamwork, and results in high levels of worker attachment and commitment. This results in a "core" workforce that stays at the company and contributes to peer training of new employees. The second she labels the "restrictive approach," which externalizes workers by relying on temporary staffing agencies and which decreases the firm's commitment to the workers: such firms offer lower benefits, provide less on-the-job training, and tend to lay off workers during downturns in business.

Smith's categories of "restrictive" and "enabling" are useful for thinking through how the management dilemma in service work parallels larger questions in labor management. In her estimation, workers who are enabled feel a greater commitment to work, while those who are restricted tend to be less loyal and less attached to the company. The ironic tension that seems to prevail at the Hungry Cowboy is that workers are enabled in terms of their participation in the work process but restricted in terms of the structure of their employment. Here, workers are expected to train one another, enforce standards, and actively participate in how work is organized and performed, yet workers receive no benefits, no training of new skills, and little assurance that they will not be fired if business takes a downturn. Servers' narratives reveal high levels of commitment to their work in the absence of formal organizational support. At the Hungry Cowboy, the core group of servers successfully reproduces a committed wait staff without the company offering the incentives Smith defines as "enabling" to workers.

Smith identifies two groups of workers; what she calls the "core" workforce and the temporary, low-prestige positions that are staffed and then eliminated in keeping with a company's needs. While she studies a business in which the use of temporary workers is made explicit, at the Hungry Cowboy, the existence of a core and periphery of workers is not official policy. Although the existence of a two-tiered hierarchy of workers is not defined by company policy, in practice such a hierarchy exists and has powerful influence. While the core workers work the greatest number of hours, and negotiate for the busy closing night shifts, the less lucrative lunch shift functions as a training and sorting ground for second-tier, often temporary workers.[19] New employees are required to work low-volume lunch shifts during the first few months of their employment. Lunch shifts operate as a testing ground of new workers' commitment. Lunch workers do the grunt work of the restaurant, completing a disproportionate amount of prep work to prepare the restaurant for the night shift, from which they do not benefit economically; they hope eventually to be promoted to the lucrative night shifts and perhaps even to the core of workers.

While the Hungry Cowboy has been more successful than many restaurants in keeping long-term staff members and thus maintaining a more stable core, the process of using some shifts to audition workers is not at all uncommon. Of course, most work is structured in this way: when workers are gradually given increasing opportunity, challenge, responsibility and autonomy, their commitment and investment consequently grows. In restaurant work, however, servers can step up only by raising their reputation in the eyes of the managers and thereby gaining access to more lucrative shifts. Liz refers to the two-tier system as "A team" and "B team": "I'm going to be the best server I can be. I'm back on the A team actually, so I'm very proud. [Laughs] I got kicked off for a while because I was not keeping my tables clean enough. On weekend days, I wish I could just close my eyes, and the dishes would go away, but they never do, so I got demoted for a while when I was not hurrying to get those dishes bussed."

The only measurable incentive is access to better shifts. Managers use this hook deliberately, as a promise; they also use it as a threat, when they perceive workers to be slacking or not "worthy" of working the busy, profitable shifts.

Once servers break out of the lunch shift and start working dinner shifts, they work alongside the "core" of servers; at this point, distinctions between the core and periphery are based not just on ability but also on social markers. Both coworkers and managers evaluate workers in terms of "fit" with the Hungry Cowboy, which means attitude, work ethic, and personality. In a job that makes use of personal characteristics, judging on personality is fair game.[20] From the point of view of the rookie servers, however, the absence of official training materials makes it difficult to differentiate between fitting in socially and performing their jobs in a way that earns them access to better shifts and more money.

Despite the lack of an official promotion structure, rookie servers are eager to put in the necessary time and develop the necessary attitude to garner the manager's favor and also to achieve membership in what they refer to as the "inner circle" of servers. Although the two-tier hierarchy is unofficial, servers are aware of this structure. Meg reports that social inclusion is necessary to keep her job: "If you're not accepted at the Hungry Cowboy, you're not going to work there." Julia remembers working to gain membership in the inner circle: "At this restaurant, there's this group that you have to be 'in' with in order to come into work and not worry about what she's gonna say or he's gonna say, and it's sort of like in high school, you have to be accepted into the group. You know what? I really kind of worked at being accepted into the group."

This two-tier system influences who can work and, particularly, who can survive over time at the Hungry Cowboy. Since experienced workers train new workers, the rookies look to their coworkers for cues and approval. Surviving training and succeeding at the work of waiting tables is synonymous with fitting in socially. Billy says, "It's such a small, tight-knit family that you have to get into the family or you're out. And even if someone likes you, they're not just going to [cross the family]; instead they say, I don't have any room for you, my family's already full." Clearly, the conflation of inclusion in the social world with job success is a powerful force for indoctrinating new workers into the "Hungry Cowboy Philosophy." For example, when servers explain processes verbally, it appears that they are in charge of structuring the workplace. They teach both formal and informal rules at once, verbally. When new workers choose to reproduce the work culture, it feels like gaining membership, or achieving social status, not submitting to work rules.

Compared to the exhaustive sophistication of the themed training at chain restaurants, Cut and Paste management seems to offer few external incentives to workers to internalize organizational goals and manage their own performance. By intertwining the social world with the goals of the business, however, the Hungry Cowboy is able to disguise occupational socialization under the guise of peer training and social inclusion. Peer training appears to put all the power into servers' hands to indoctrinate one another, and yet servers are promoting a style of service that is lucrative for the restaurant and is in alignment with management goals. When servers reproduce the work culture, they often pass on the same practices and advice that Richard would promote. Rather than having less power over workers, managers', and especially Richard's, power is successfully masked by the peer training process.

These two distinct approaches to training reveal several patterns. While the Cut and Paste management style of the Hungry Cowboy initially appears to be spotty and to weaken management power by relying on peer training, workers are trained and socialized simultaneously, resulting in a faster and perhaps more enduring indoctrination of new workers. What's striking about these findings is that, like the customers who respond favorably to personalized service, workers are also responsive to personalized training. These findings suggest that corporate attempts to script and then reproduce "quality service" are not necessarily the most compelling or even the most effective approach to producing ambience in restaurants.

HERDING SQUIRRELS
Instrumental Versus Relational Management

Of the many building blocks of sociability that make up a particular ambience, training is often one of the least visible; yet training is the first and often a defining step on the way to building an ambience and workplace culture. Phil from Neighbor's points out the connection between training and atmosphere: "It's interesting to think about how you train that friendly atmosphere. Well, it's hard to train, but it's also infectious; it's creating the culture more than anything. That's what we really work on, creating the culture in the restaurant, and you can walk into the restaurant and you can feel it. But you can walk into another restaurant and know it's not there. It's creating that culture and I think it starts with the management team, how they take care of their people. So we really work on that."

Finding the right people, who then treat customers right, compelling them to come back, is a central goal of all restaurants. What challenges management is trying to produce just the right mix of control and freedom for workers to produce quality service. As Al explains, sometimes the challenge of managing workers can feel like "herding squirrels, trying to get them all going in the same direction at once." Training regimes are meant to indoctrinate new workers into the rules and practices of the workplace and to get them, as Al suggests, all going in the same direction. William, the manager from Jefferson's explains, "Much of a manager's job is to get other people to do something, to get something done through people." Training is often the

first step to getting "something done through people" and, as such, influences
the ambience available to customers and the workplace culture that develops. The disparate approaches of Rosie's and the Hungry Cowboy touch on
larger questions about service interactions and social life.

One of the questions raised by this case study is "Can personalized service be produced in a routinized work culture?" In their study of service
work, Linda Fuller and Vicki Smith determine that "quality service requires
that workers rely on an inner arsenal of affective and interpersonal skills,
capabilities that cannot be successfully codified, standardized, or dissected
into discrete components and set forth in a company handbook."[21] While
Smith and Fuller are certain that the necessary skills cannot be successfully routinized, many restaurants—and particularly chain restaurants—do
attempt to define and enact an exhaustive set of rules and practices. These
questions matter because, as the National Restaurant Association points
out, routinization is spreading: "Recently, bureaucratic control of workers
who wait on tables and greater routinization of the provisions of service
is spreading with the increase of franchise restaurants, in all but the most
expensive restaurants, throughout the industry."[22] Can a regularized "formula
4 success" coexist with personalized, satisfying, social interactions? How can
managers train workers to be "sincere" or "really care" about their customers?
These questions are very much on the minds of managers.

In interviews, managers regularly express ambivalence about what can
be achieved through routinized training processes. For example, William
from Jefferson's seeks to construct a work culture that will entice and keep
"the right kind of people" to produce a friendly atmosphere.[23] William wres-
tles with his desire to provide servers with tools that will help them give
good service and with his concerns about how too many management directives can produce service that feels stilted and over-determined. He worries
that very systematized directions have a dehumanizing effect: "I've been a
trainer, and it's really easy to spit out stuff that people can't do. Servers are
not going to describe it like that, no matter how hard you insist, they can't
use that many descriptive adjectives or phrase it exactly that way and make
somebody feel human; it's so obviously a sales ploy." William explains that
he left a more lucrative position at a chain restaurant to come to Jefferson's
because at the chain he found himself having to focus solely on "pushing

the numbers." He explains, "I had a difficult time in training and dealing with the operators [of the chain restaurant] because they would want to see numbers jump; they want to see that we're moving a certain product, and you always end up making a choice between your short-term sales and your long-term loyalty to guests." What stands out in his explanations is his personal struggle between encouraging a relational approach to service and the more instrumental pressure to sell certain products and "push the numbers."

Al demonstrates a similar ambivalence when he fluctuates in his descriptions between "sell, sell, sell" and "personalize, personalize, personalize," and also when he talked about hiring employees "forever" or for "six months." While Al's ambivalence shows up in his narrative, he never acknowledges it. Many of the other managers I spoke with are uncertain about the effectiveness of their current approach. Perhaps owing to this uncertainty, four of the six chain restaurants I compared were revamping their hiring and training practices. Managers described detailed personality assessments used to hire and psychological profiles used to identify promising employees. Changes in these elaborate systems require retraining managers and workers, and yet these chains frequently discard the systems for new models. For example, Fiesta recently instituted a hiring and managing system that relies on four personality types. Fiesta managers carry around a card that identifies the personality type of each of the employees working during a particular shift. As Jack, the manager, explains, those cards allow the manager to consider what "type of worker he is dealing with so he knows, 'Oh, OK, this is a D4 server, so I need to approach her like this . . .'" Later, I asked Jack about the employee-of-the-month program because I had noticed a plaque posting the names of employees who received special recognition over the last few months. He replied, "Actually, that program does not exist anymore. We developed a new employee recognition club and that is called the 1 percent club." Later he continued, "Well, there's lots of programs. We have so many that sometimes it's kind of mind-boggling." Unlike Jack, some of the managers speak with great enthusiasm about the next program they are "rolling out" or about the next best thing, be it the new training formula, or the new profile a human relations firm has designed to help them identify promising new candidates for front of the house staff. Even in the face of their enthusiasm, the constant scrutiny and frequent alterations of training speak to the challenge of routinizing service work that incorporates the messiness of human workers, deals with the unpredictability of human recipients, and strives for the illusive goal of providing "good service."

Approaches to training and managing reflect ideas about what service should entail. Servers like Trevor at the Hungry Cowboy position the system they work within as different from and superior to the more corporate approach to managing people. Trevor's adamant support is not surprising considering he has worked at the Hungry Cowboy for several years. What is more striking are the philosophical and practical concerns raised by managers working *within* corporate chain restaurants. These managers have put their time and energy into executing expensive, elaborate, and often well-researched techniques for getting workers to comply with company policies and advance corporate goals. Despite the considerable effort they invest in routinizing service, they are not always certain that these processes allow their workers to seem human or to provide the kind of service experience customers want. Their concerns speak to larger cultural dilemmas about the possibilities for and limitations to connecting to others within service settings.

Some of the managers of chain restaurants believe it is indeed possible to routinize that special mix of sociability and skill that they believe customers seek. The manager at Neighbor's explains, "It starts with management, rolling out all the new systems, menus, policies, and programs. They trickle down, [and] we try to do a cascade as much as possible." What was most surprising is that right after this particular manager explained how he "cascades" policies down to the frontline service workers, he found out that I worked at the Hungry Cowboy. He smiled and said, "Yeah, places like that, sometimes you just want to go to a mom and pop, hole-in-the-wall place like that, someplace comfortable, get away from that 'chain feeling' for a while." Despite working sixty hours a week to "make it happen" for the chain restaurant he manages, he expresses a nostalgia for places like the Hungry Cowboy "where you can really hang your hat." As the preponderance of chain restaurants grows, workers, customers, and, in this case, managers express longing for those pockets in the marketplace that resist routinization, that feel like home.

5

FEELING LIKE FAMILY

◆◆◆◆◆◆◆◆◆◆◆◆◆◆◆◆◆◆◆◆◆◆◆◆◆◆

PATERNALISM, LOYALTY, AND WORK CULTURE

In March of 2002, Richard called an emergency all-staff meeting. Over the past few weeks, he had noticed that his liquor cost was skyrocketing. The liquor cost is one of the sales percentages of which managers must keep track, and on which their bonuses are based.[1] This cost had been inexplicably on the rise for weeks, so much that Richard did not receive his usual bonus. Liquor cost problems are not unusual; often a rising liquor cost can mean that employees are taking liquor home, drinking on the clock, failing to charge friends or regular customers, overpouring drinks, or drinking after hours. At any given time, restaurant servers have thousands of dollars of alcohol within reach that is delivered and sold so quickly it is hard for management to keep track of where it went. In fact, some restaurant workers start to see the restaurant's liquor as a free resource; the availability of almost-free liquor is what attracts and keeps some restaurant workers in the restaurant business.[2]

In this instance, Richard had not discovered any workers drinking for free or giving away drinks, and so his liquor cost problem remained unexplained until a week later. At that point, the bartender, Meg, started complaining that she was getting a series of voids on her printer for drinks that were served, so the voids seemed odd. She mentioned it to Richard in the random complaining that goes on during a busy night. Richard, plagued by his unsolved mystery, was curious about the discrepancies and followed up the next day.

What he found appalled and angered him. By searching the sales records from the previous night, he uncovered a series of voids all traceable to the same three individuals: an assistant manager, his girlfriend (a server), and his best friend (a bartender). In short, these three employees had conspired to ring up beverages and some food, serve them, charge for them, and then erase the record of them and pocket the cash; they had made off with fifteen hundred dollars in nine days.

This conspiracy, the most blatant theft in the Hungry Cowboy's history, resulted not only in the firing of the three employees, but also in felony charges against each of them. After having spent the weekend sleepless, ranting, and aggressively pursuing evidence to support the case against them, Richard met with a police detective to file the charges and then posted a sign informing all workers of a mandatory meeting the following Sunday morning.

The tone of the emergency meeting on that Sunday morning was one of disappointment, of loss. Richard used the moment for those of "us" who had not stolen to get together and regroup. The meeting had a very particular focus: to return to the idealized Hungry Cowboy that he believed had existed in the past. Richard felt betrayed by the three workers who had stolen from the restaurant, and his concerns about those three workers made him worry about the entire staff and fear that the Hungry Cowboy family was "in decline." He opened by saying, "People you work with side by side on a Friday night, and you support each other, you think they're your friend, but you find out they're unethical." From this opening comment, making implicit reference to the departed workers, he proceeded to outline his sources of disappointment about recent events and to suggest how he wanted employees to adjust their mindset. He asked employees to "give back to the restaurant what it has given to you."

The Hungry Cowboy is run in a paternal way: all decisions are run through Richard, the head of the restaurant.[3] While Richard is responsible for making purchasing and hiring decisions and receives part of his pay based on profit margins, he is not the owner of the restaurant. The owners are local businessmen who own the restaurant as an investment but leave the ongoing management of the business to Richard. As such, the owners are relatively invisible. Most customers assume that Richard is the owner, and they assign him both credit and blame. Richard metes out punishment, and he is the one to whom employees are expected to give loyalty.

At the meeting, Richard's tone was like that of a disappointed father of teenagers whom he has trusted until he comes home to find out that they have thrown a party in his absence. He explained that the Hungry Cowboy had never been just another job for him: "To many of you, this is not a real job; to me it's a real job. This is what puts food on my table, a roof over my head. I've dedicated twenty years of my life to this job."[4] He reminded workers of what it felt like when they first starting working at the Hungry Cowboy: "A person who is new can feel like an outsider here." He feared that if workers did not do a better job of welcoming and training new workers, the rate of turnover would increase, further damaging both the ambience and the long history of serving excellence. He spoke passionately about rebuilding the "right group of people" who would restore the Hungry Cowboy to what it used to be. He reminded servers, "We are not a chain, but we are well known. Customers know about the good staff and the quality of service."

The scandal and meeting that followed it provide one example of how management uses familial tropes to inspire and also to punish workers. When Richard chastised his staff, he was simultaneously reminding family members of their responsibilities and ordering his workers to do their work better. What stood out on that particular morning was that Richard clearly felt betrayed. He dealt with that betrayal interpersonally, as a problem in "the family" that might fester if he did not address it. Instead of being upset about the significant amount of money the workers had stolen, he mourned the loss of a mutual trust between himself and his workers. The thieves' behavior violated the operating symbolism of family at the Hungry Cowboy.

On a strictly strategic level, Richard's mournful speech inspired workers to work harder. This sort of paternal leadership sets up a structure where employees monitor themselves to make sure they are living up to Richard's standards whether he is present or not. Given this result, Richard's approach not only furthers the feeling of family but also functions as a form of control.[5] In her study of domestic workers, Judith Rollins argues that personalizing relationships between employer and employees is a form of psychological exploitation. Extending Rollins' insight, Jennifer Pierce finds that when lawyers treat their paralegals like friends "when, in fact, they are not, [that behavior] obscures the asymmetrical nature of the relationship."[6] Even if bosses make efforts to befriend their employees, the bosses still make more money and have more control. While personalizing relationships can mask exploitation, at the Hungry Cowboy, appeals to family inspire workers to work hard and to feel loyal to their workplace and to their boss.

The tone of the meeting was also nostalgic. Richard's approach to this meeting was to remind his employees of the kind of restaurant he wanted to have, by comparing it not to the competition but to an idealized Hungry Cowboy of days past. Richard began the meeting by saying he had gathered us together to "remember the Hungry Cowboy as we used to be." He concluded with a tone of longing, "It wasn't always that way here, we had parties, we used to have so much fun." His nostalgia was meant to work in two ways: to reinforce workers' sense of being part of a special community, a family of workers; and to encourage workers to return the restaurant to the former state of excellence Richard imagined. At the same time that he was asking workers to rebuild the Hungry Cowboy family, he was also asking them to reproduce that special community through their own hard work. This emergency meeting was the corrective side of a routine approach to managing: familial metaphors of belonging that both inspire workers and obscure managerial power.

In this chapter, I bring together the experiences and vantage points of all three groups of actors—servers, managers, and customers—to explore how a work culture of emotional investment combined with a "homey" ambience and paternalistic management, helps produce loyalty at the Hungry Cowboy. I consider how notions related to family shape daily practice and how, like many families, this "family" is crosscut by the often unequal costs and rewards of belonging.

LOYALTY TO THE FAMILY
Servers and Managers

As Hannah Creighton explains, work cultures reproduce by initiating new workers and by establishing the "rules of the game" in terms of how to behave, what is tolerated and what is punishable in a particular restaurant. Work culture also provides a common language to discuss the world of that particular restaurant.[7] At the Hungry Cowboy, that common language is the notion of family. During my research, managers, servers, and even customers referred to "the family" of the Hungry Cowboy.[8] Servers celebrate and bemoan their loyalty to the work culture, comparing their attachment to a family obligation. Several of the male servers referred to each other in interviews as brothers. Workers described Richard as a second father or father figure. Customers also use familial metaphors to describe their relationship to the restaurant. Customers routinely write on comment cards "I feel at home here," and "The staff is great, like family!" The salience of the idea of family suggests it must help people make sense of their roles in the restaurant and the culture that develops. Allusions to family accomplish both symbolic and practical goals.[9]

As an idea, "family" is rich in history and complicated by the expectations, desires, and behaviors that emerge in families. At first glance, it seems a stretch to imagine the complicated web of interactions that take place at the Hungry Cowboy as forming a family. As Derek Pardue reflects in his study of restaurants, "The articulation of 'family' to a public dining restaurant is a remarkable semiotic and marketing achievement."[10] Any attempt to ascribe "family" to the commercial, profit-driven context of a public dining space is circumscribed by the fact that customers and workers are brought together through a market exchange, not through blood-relations, adoption, marriage, or other forms of the familial; however, if we explore more deeply some of the possible meanings of family, we can see how imagining a family in the marketplace might be comforting, or even descriptive. Family is defined as "a household, a group of people united by shared convictions, and any of various social units different from but considered equivalent to the traditional family."[11] A family is the group of people you consider your home, even if you do not live with them; the word connotes an emotional and physical resting place.

Describing work as family is a handy and effective ideological tool because, as Nicole Woolsey Biggart explains, family is "a well understood model for interpersonal relations" that "puts [workers] in familiar interactional territory by importing the logic of one institution—the family—for use in another—business."[12] As Hochschild reflects in her study of "family-friendly" workplaces, many companies capitalize on familial metaphors. "If a family gives its members anything, we assume it is surely a sense of belonging to an ongoing community. In its engineered corporate cultures, capitalism has rediscovered communal ties and is using them to build its new version of capitalism. Many Amerco employees spoke warmly, happily, and seriously of 'belonging to the Amerco family,' and everywhere there were visible signs of this belonging."[13] At the Hungry Cowboy, the "visible signs of belonging" include easy smiles, mutual recognition, and active participation in sociability, but these signs of belonging do not include structural rewards for loyal workers. The return on loyalty does not include insurance or stability, or any of the occupational guarantees for which loyalty has traditionally been levered. The sole benefit that accumulates over time is the fact of working with people with whom one feels close, whom one views as "family." Despite this limited reward, many servers are insistent about their loyalty to the Hungry Cowboy and describe the group of regulars and servers who come together there as a family.

Customers, servers, and managers all explain that they are loyal to the Hungry Cowboy. But it is difficult to maintain loyalty to a place alone. Despite a stable core of long-term workers and regular customers, the participation of temporary workers and less-regular customers guarantees that the community of people who gather there changes all the time. Since the restaurant is a public space, the specific faces of the people who inhabit it change from hour to hour, and from month to month. Despite the shifting composition of this family, workers, managers, and customers root their loyalty to the Hungry Cowboy and to one another.

When I asked about the source of the loyalty, customers and servers replied that their loyalty stemmed from an attachment to the general manager, Richard. Customers prove their loyalty by citing the length of time they have been patrons, while servers note their years of service as evidence of a "fierce loyalty" that keeps them in place, sometimes longer than they like. For example, when I asked Meg what kept her at the Hungry Cowboy, she explained that her commitment to Richard made it difficult for her to "get out": "I feel like I have some loyalty to him; I feel like it would be wrong of me to leave because there's no reason. I mean, I would probably hate serving anywhere." Meg's allegiance reflects the politics of families, in which members are expected to make individual sacrifices for the sake of the whole. In *The Velvet Glove*, Mary Jackman explains that families often demand that the needs of the group subsume the needs of the whole. "Children owed allegiance to their families: their personal interests were defined, at best, as inseparable from those of their families, and in the event of a conflict, personal interests were subjugated to the financial, status, or political interests of the family."[14] Meg reluctantly sacrifices her desire to "get out" because she feels an obligation to Richard. Her commitment to the place is therefore mediated through loyalty to Richard, as the head of the family.

Working within the framework of the family, Richard clearly models loyalty in a paternalistic way that inspires workers not only to do their jobs well but also to actively please him. For example, Patricia describes her number one priority as not disappointing Richard: "I don't want to let Richard down. I treat him like he is on a [pedestal]. I don't want to let him down; he takes such good care of the employees. He would be the first one to help you out if you needed help. If you're struggling, [need] personal help, or whatever he would be the first one to steer you in the right direction or to offer you some help. Yeah, not to screw up and not to disappoint him." In fact, Patricia says she would follow Richard if he ever left the Hungry Cowboy.

Servers' loyalty to Richard, as the head of the symbolic family, is premised on his own loyalty, commitment, and wisdom. He is a source of inspiration. Jackman explains that "paternalistic actors [are] distinguished by two characteristics: an un-self interested, benevolent intent, and a presumption of greater moral competence than the subject of his or her intervention." Richard's paternalistic management style softens demands and punishments by making such interactions seem interpersonal, not instrumental. Servers and customers alike believe they have developed a personal relationship with Richard that elides his power in the restaurant. Servers often explain their willingness to give their all to their work as a mirror of Richard's own commitment to the work; they follow where he leads. For example, Patricia explains that Richard "doesn't lead like a dictator like [another manager] did": "I totally look up to him and respect what he says, and he's the best manager. He's a good person, he's a caring person. He cares about his employees, he bends over backwards, like he doesn't have to be as nice as he is to employees, he doesn't have to do half the stuff he does." These examples reflect a consensus among servers that Richard is unique, that he works very hard, and that they "owe" him the same kind of loyalty and commitment he exhibits.[15]

At the Hungry Cowboy, paternalism works to secure workers' loyalty. Servers report being happy to produce high-quality work because the Hungry Cowboy is a family and the head of that family needs their cooperation. On a theoretical level, Jackman explains that paternal rule creates conditions in which allegiance is gained without force: "To that end, their unequal relationship is swathed in a morality that identifies subordinates' worth and value within the terms of that relationship. Such an orientation must rest on persuasion rather than on force and can only be really effective in the circumstance of mutual affection between the groups. With affection comes the ability of those in command to shape the needs and aspirations of subordinates and to portray discriminatory arrangements as being in the best interests of all concerned." As Patricia's admiring tone reveals, at the same time that Richard is being a role model and a friend, he is also very successfully inspiring loyalty among his staff and customers.

Charles explains his first impression of Richard, situating him as the head of the metaphoric family. "And when I talked to him, it was just his attitude, it was less the sterile corporate side of restaurants, more involved, so it intrigued me, the restaurant intrigued me in that way. So when I got to know him, his example of leadership, my first impression was one of, not dividing yourself but to be involved; it's like family to him. He's involved, it's not just a business." As the head of this particular family, Richard's behavior sets the tone for his employees.

Richard's intense commitment to work also alarms many of his employees because Richard is challenged by several health problems, including diabetes. For example, Julia wonders about the costs of Richard's own commitment to his work. "I think Richard appreciates the loyalty of the people who work there. I guess Richard's the kind of manager—I admire him so much, but I think that he lives at the Hungry Cowboy. He puts every ounce of energy he has into the Hungry Cowboy and that's really good, but it's kinda bad for him." Julia worries that Richard is at times overcommitted to the Hungry Cowboy. One of the ways his commitment is costly to him is that he often forgets or fails to eat, with frightening health consequences.

It is not unusual for him to get light-headed or approach a blackout. Once he was found passed out in the cooler in the back of the house because of a crash in blood sugar. The employees deal with Richard's very real health concerns within the paternal structure: the workers keep track of his health, urge him to take care of himself, and focus significant energy on monitoring his health.

Certainly the admiration and respect that servers express for Richard are relatively uncommon in other restaurants or workplaces. In theory and often in practice, managers and workers are pitted against each other. For workers, a feeling of family helps explain their commitment and long tenure at the Hungry Cowboy. Their loyalty to Richard motivates them not only to stay but to work hard to make him proud, to avoid disappointing him, and to keep him from working too hard himself, much as children might do to protect a parent in a "real" family.

INTIMACY AND AMBIGUITY
The Family of Customers

Not only do Richard and the servers reinforce the family metaphor but customers also subscribe to the belief that the Hungry Cowboy is "like family." Take for example a letter the restaurant received in the spring of 2002. The letter is from a regular customer who had subsequently moved to California.

> Greetings friends, How are you all doing? I'm doing just fine out here. So far (ask Dan-) it's been an extremely wet winter and spring. The past couple weeks it's been back to normal tho,' [sic] thank goodness. It was 89 degrees today. Talk about perfect weather. I just can't wait 'til summer hits. It won't be much longer. So when is someone from there going to come visit? There would be no regrets. Guaranteed. This time of year is the best time to visit. It's amazing, all the rain we've had this year so far has actually turned the desert green! Yes, desert green! It's actually quite awesome. I'll try to get some good pics. Maybe Dan took a few when he was here. Hopefully this is the beginning of a long life here. Richard, I just found the napkin with the cigars you wanted

me to try to find. I'll look this weekend. Maybe we can trade cigars for "Hungry Cowboy" shirts, eh? Well, take care my friends and write once in a while. Here's my address and phone number.

This letter expresses the deep desire to feel a part of something and the sense of belonging that many regular customers experience as a result of routine patronage. This particular customer's sense of being a "member" of the restaurant community is so strong that he chooses to "write home" to the Hungry Cowboy.

The tensions between intimacy and ambiguity in this letter point to the difficult-to-describe closeness among customers, servers, and managers. The author of the letter offers several pieces of evidence that establish him as an insider or member of the restaurant community. The author refers to "Dan's visit" and "Dan's pictures" because Dan is another regular customer; having had Dan visit is another sign of membership and an additional incentive for "someone from there" to make the journey to visit him in his new home. On the other hand, the salutation "Greetings friends" is at once intimate and vague: to whom is the letter actually written? He mentions Richard by name later in the letter, promising to find his cigars so that he can trade them for Hungry Cowboy paraphernalia. Naming Richard points to Richard's prominence in the Hungry Cowboy family. While Richard is the head of the family, he is not the person with whom this customer would have had the most contact. As frontline service workers, the servers had much more direct contact with this customer over the years, and yet he addresses them as a group, not as individuals.

While he feels he is writing to a friendly audience and that someone will want to read the letter and maybe even visit him, the author of the letter is not certain enough of his membership to direct the letter toward specific recipients. The same vague sense of missing an unnamed group of people recurs when he writes, "So when is someone from there going to come visit?" Again, although he misses the place and the faces that people it enough to sit down and write a letter, he expresses only a generalized hope that "someone from there" will come to stay with him.[16]

Despite the incomplete intimacy of the letter, it's still striking that a customer could feel so attached to a particular restaurant that he would want to continue corresponding, continue wearing the insignia of the place, and invite workers to come stay with him in another state. The final detail of the letter is perhaps the most telling of the familial nature of the place: he signs it with his Hungry Cowboy nickname. Nicknames serve a very important function within the restaurant: by designating regular customers as recognizable, they provide a badge of "membership." Lisa describes how she plays up the nicknames of her regular customers as a means of acknowledging and playing with these unusual associations.[17] She even types regulars' nicknames into the computer, so that their order and their bill are personalized.

> LISA: We've got this deal now, we've got Lawnmower Mike—'cause everyone has their own nicknames—who I can't stand, but Joy can't stand worse, so I said I would wait on Lawnmower Mike if she waits on Fat Ass Nick. (laughs) So that's the deal.
> KE: Do all regulars have nicknames?
> LISA: (Laughs) Well, the nasty ones get nasty nicknames and the nice ones get nice nicknames. Sometimes with Nick, you know Fat Ass Nick? I'll put his name—'cause you know we type in names for the regulars—I'll leave off the N and just put "ick," it's just my own little deal.

The fact that the author of the letter from California marks himself as a member of the Hungry Cowboy community by signing with his nickname means that he is included enough in the "family" to be aware of the nickname originally given to him by servers. As Lisa explains, the "icky" customers probably are not aware of their nicknames; only the nice customers who have nice nicknames are privy to the names that servers give them. For example, Karl, the customer who once argued with Richard about having a "boys' night" is referred to as TooTan Karl because he is very tan all year round. "TooTan" is not complimentary, and the name also captures the flavor of how workers feel about Karl. He spends too much time at the Hungry Cowboy for their liking, but he's there to stay, inescapable. His presence is like his tan; it never fades. The process of granting special names demonstrates that the restaurant produces difficult-to-define associations among regular customers, servers, and managers. The letter mailed to the Hungry

Cowboy also demonstrates the lengths that some customers will go to sustain the associations that begin in the restaurant.

RELATIONSHIPS WITHOUT A NAME

The ways that people seek associations in public places under the auspices of eating provides one example of what I call affordable intimacy in the marketplace. Feeling recognized and remembered as we move through the marketplace can be extremely comforting. While this role of restaurants in people's lives is rarely acknowledged, most of us recognize an island of familiarity when we see it. Consumers know what it's like to walk into a restaurant cold: you have to figure out the ground rules, the way that things are run, how the exchange will play out, and what kinds of connections are possible. The experience of walking into a place one knows and where one is known is entirely different.

As consumers move through consumer spaces, they relate differently to the ambience and to the people who play a role in the delivery of goods and services. Some places facilitate and encourage ongoing connections while others do not. Consumers can potentially develop relationships with a range of service providers: barbers, dry cleaners, nursing aides, mail carriers, or food servers, to name just a few. The point of contact between server and customer provides interesting insights into the ways that people make contact in our society and how they occasionally build on the fleeting connections in the service exchange to form more intimate relationships. Yet despite routine and sometimes very rewarding interactions with people through service, it can be challenging to talk about the nature of these relationships or points of contact in the marketplace.

Part of the challenge of addressing this phenomenon is a linguistic one. For example, although she regularly participates in both momentary and ongoing associations, as Jessica explains, they are difficult to describe.

> KE: So, what would you call them, are any of your customers friends?
> JESSICA: No, my customers are not friends, and how I separate that
> is that I don't do anything outside of work with those customers,
> so how can they be my friends? However, I do care about a lot of

them and what's going on with their families and all of that, so I don't know what you would call that, but we don't have an outside work relationship, so I can't really say it's a friendship.

Because Jessica's guests are so utterly devoted to her—many refuse to be waited on by anyone else—I paid particular attention to her connections with customers in my participant observation. As it turns out, Jessica does have contact with some customers outside of work. She emails with at least four regular customers; she refers some customers to her regulars for legal advice, loans, counseling, and salon services; and she receives references in return from her regular customers, who send friends and families to the Hungry Cowboy to be waited on by her and also to contribute to her customer base in her day, or "real," job. Jessica even goes on sport outings with one group of regular customers. Even though Jessica actively invests in her connections with customers and even though some of those points of contact do include activities associated with friendship, Jessica does not claim these relationships as friendships.

Although these points of contact can be sustained over years, these interpersonal exchanges do not follow the same rules as relationships that originate in other ways. For example, servers can wait on people for years without knowing basic facts about them, like what work they do or even their real names. Toward the end of my research, a series of events reminded me how situational the work of recognition can be. In the fall of 2003, I put in my final notice and worked my last shift at the Hungry Cowboy. A couple months later, I stopped in to chat with my former coworkers and Richard. Richard ran back to the office to get a comment card that a customer left for me. The comment card said, "Have Karla call me, we miss her." At the bottom of the card, the customer wrote her home phone number. This exchange demonstrates the degree to which Richard encourages his employees to foster and maintain personal relationships with their customers; after all, he had saved the card for me for several weeks. It also exemplifies the close but contingent connections between server and served.

Leaving me a note with a request to call was a rather intimate gesture from this customer, but the sad fact was that I did not know who wrote it. When I could not figure out whom the note was from, Richard seemed disappointed and started listing off customers who liked to be waited on by me. When he described one particular couple that came in late on Friday nights after bowling, I realized that the note was from the woman in this couple. As it turned out, I was really fond of the couple. In addition to sharing in weekly conversations, she had brought her extended family to the restaurant to meet and be served by me, and she had even brought me a Christmas present the previous year. Despite these points of contact, I struggled to make sense of the note because when I talked to her, I called her not by name but by her Hungry Cowboy nickname. Of course I would have recognized her immediately in person, and particularly if she sat at a table in my section, but when she signed her real name, I drew a blank. Richard's investment in reconnecting me to customers even after I had quit demonstrates the degree of his involvement in perpetuating the "family" of the Hungry Cowboy. This customer's note, like the one from the regular who wrote "home" after he moved away, demonstrates the intricacies of identification and recognition that arise in service-based relations.

The work of recognition and the labor of memorizing and responding to other people's needs and wishes can produce a real but often unarticulated pleasure for customers, and sometimes even for servers. Having one's needs recognized and fulfilled is a privilege. Who else knows our individual needs so precisely? As waitress and poet Suzanne Matson writes, "This was years ago, / I could still serve them to perfection, / remembering every stubborn taste like a harried mother, / and though I don't miss them I could make them happy, / knowing their happiness consisted of / not changing, ever."[18] In private relationships when someone knows us well enough to predict our needs, we perceive that as a sign of intimacy and care. By contrast, as Jeff Weinstein explains, we frequently fail to acknowledge the relationship that is created by being served. "The trust implicit in eating is similar to that in sex, opening your inside to the outside, your self to the other. None of this should surprise anyone, but sometimes I am amazed that we enter a restaurant, or even someone else's home, and assume that no bond of trust is being formed, or is even necessary."[19] In short, the associations that form under the auspices of serving and being served defy conventional patterns of sociability. Over the years of my waiting on her, I probably spent hours in conversation with the customer who later left me her phone number. I know how she special orders her salad, some of her fears related to aging, and what her grandchildren do for a living, but I do not know her first name. The conversations we had were always interrupted by my need to leave the table because I was at work. I had to walk away to serve other customers in between maintaining a lively conversation with her and her husband. She has never seen me without an apron on, but she still bought me a Christmas present. Considering the complexities of these relationships, it is not surprising that members of the Hungry Cowboy "family" struggle to define the relationships that develop within the restaurant.

INEQUALITY WITHIN THE FAMILY

Relationships that begin within service exchanges are made more complicated by the fact that workers are paid to recognize and welcome customers.[20] The asymmetrical nature of their relationship influences how customers and servers play their roles in the "family."

The exchange of money, even when it is obscured by sociability, practically guarantees that customers will be treated like welcomed guests, even if servers do not enjoy their company. Servers and managers do not have the same guarantees. Arlie Russell Hochschild describes a similarly uneven right to deference, courtesy, and recognition in the work of flight attendants and their passengers. She explains that "high-status people tend to enjoy the privilege of having their feelings noticed and considered important. The lower one's status, the more one's feelings are not noticed or treated as inconsequential."[21] Between servers and customers, the uneven right to feeling clearly works in customers' favor. Workers can and do exclude other workers, but since customers are related through commercial interaction, servers and even managers are not at liberty to deny customers outright the privilege of feeling recognized and included.

The family metaphor is more lucrative for customers than for workers; workers have to build and maintain the family even if a customer is rude or refuses to reciprocate. Customers have the upper hand in that they get to choose how involved to become in the restaurant community, while servers, for the most part, must react to their choices. For workers, reassuring customers becomes a means of making money: welcoming them, appearing happy to see them, remembering their likes and dislikes, asking questions, displaying wit, and expressing a desire for them to return. When the interaction, including the tip, goes well, servers feel appreciated for their skill. Customers get to take or leave the sociability that servers offer because they pay the money, a relationship of control that grants them additional power and influence in this particular "family." Regular customers' greater entitlement to recognition and welcome provides them "membership" in a commercial site; such paid-for membership may in fact be more reliable than that offered by groups or families to which they belong in the private sphere.

Commercial communities that are "like family" can afford to be more predictable than real families, because these are families for pay. This family has opening and closing hours, and it reproduces itself even in the absence of key members. As long as the Hungry Cowboy stays in business, customers and servers alike can be assured that every day of the year—except Christmas and Easter—someone will be waiting at the "backyard fence"— or in this case, the bar—to chat with them. The Hungry Cowboy offers an always-open door that regulars can walk through to feel recognized and included.

The Hungry Cowboy family is less messy than real families because it has more limits. It is also defined more narrowly than real families and, as such, seems to guard some of its members against disappointments. As a business that benefits from a veneer of the familial, the Hungry Cowboy is invariably available and welcoming to its members. Customers and staff members get to interact in ways that are familiar without taking on many of the responsibilities associated with family.[22]

Restaurants like this one that bank on the work of recognition succeed because they respond to culturally produced needs for experiencing a sense of belonging. Some spaces in the marketplace invite customers to feel attached to a place and to experience "membership" within a culture that can leave individuals feeling rootless or lost. At the Hungry Cowboy, customers discover a kind of extended family that they can pay for and that they can visit when they want to, because the door is always open.

INTERACTION AND CONNECTION
The Paradox of Service

My experiences at the Hungry Cowboy have led me to think of service as a kind of paradox. Service is both economic and social; it is both relational and instrumental. Even though the Hungry Cowboy tries to emphasize the social milieu rather than the bottom line, the relationships that emerge are influenced by the material conditions out of which they arise. Even if all three groups cooperate to perform equality, this family is still crosscut by power differentials that originate in the exchange of cash for recognition. In fact, among the multiple violations committed by the three workers who stole from the restaurant, one of the major transgressions was that their act exposed just how thinly the veneer of family operates to obscure the economic utility of the restaurant. In nine days, the thieves stripped the res-taurant of fifteen hundred dollars and exposed the fact that the restaurant is not only a social world but also a lucrative business. What is striking here is not that family fails to describe accurately what takes place at the Hungry Cowboy but rather that workers, customers, and managers all want it to be a family. All these participants use the term "family" to mark a particular kind of closeness that is hard to describe and yet is experienced by many self-proclaimed "members" of the Hungry Cowboy.

The paradox of service was always difficult for me to reconcile when I worked at the Hungry Cowboy. On days when the work of waiting tables was particularly difficult for me, I would quickly get fed up with the performance of family. At times, I wanted to yell out, "We are being paid to be here!" But even on those difficult days, it was hard for me to ignore the "extras" of ser-vice work: the events, conversations, and occurrences that blur the lines of power and temporarily even out the divisions in the Hungry Cowboy family. For example, customers reverse the serving equation by bringing food (which communicates care) to the people who serve them. Customers attend work-ers' weddings, graduation ceremonies, and birthday parties, acting as guests of a different type by celebrating workers' joys with them far away from the restaurant. Customers also help servers set up and close down the restaurant. By voluntarily working to maintain the restaurant, customers give up the leisure of being served, choosing instead to work where they dine. Customers who choose to perform voluntary labor temporarily blur the lines designating who serves whom. Being allowed to "stay after" and help also marks regulars as "insiders" because they get to share in the camaraderie of the staff after hours. Feeding workers, celebrating with them, and helping them do their jobs are just some examples of customer behaviors that extend beyond the role functions of worker, manager, or customer.

Another way in which the culture of the Hungry Cowboy blurs the consumer/producer divide is that customers attend the annual employee party. Every year, Richard invites a handful of regular customers; most of the servers are not only willing but even happy to share a celebration of their work with the people they serve. Certainly the fact that all three groups of actors considered it appropriate for regulars to be invited to a (free) employee party points to how well "the family" blurs distinctions between server and served.

At the Hungry Cowboy, behaviors that symbolically support the idea of "family" are quite common. Perhaps part of what is so enticing about being a member of the Hungry Cowboy family is the possibility of sticking together. Patricia Hill Collins identifies this kind of "commonality of interests" as one of the promises of an idealized family: "By definition, families stick together against outsiders. Within idealized notions of family, family units protect and balance the interests of all of their members—the strong care for the weak, and members contribute to and benefit from family membership in proportion to their capacities. Though there may be differentiation within the family, family members share a common origin through blood and a commonality of interests.[23] "For a long time, I suspected that the commonality of interests among customers and servers ended when the bill was delivered and paid. I assumed that the asymmetries of power between consumers and producers foreclosed the possibility of actual reciprocity between the two parties. Despite having observed and participated in these points of contact at the Hungry Cowboy, I was skeptical that the bond between servers and served could ever truly morph beyond the origins of the relationship. In my view, the naked inequality between customers and workers, the fact that half of the family spent a lot of their time sitting around getting served by the other half of the family, made the claims of "family" hollow. Much of my disbelief melted, however, when customers and servers rallied around one of its members without hesitation and with rather remarkable results.

One January morning, Billy and his girlfriend awoke to a fire in their apartment. In the middle of the night, a huge icicle had dropped from the roof and punctured a gas line. Instantly, a ball of fire blew out the front door of the apartment complex, and all the residents ran out into the snow. The fire had left them literally out in the cold with no clothes or coats, so Billy and his girlfriend—who lived only a mile or so from the Hungry Cowboy—took refuge in the restaurant. The couple also did not have renter's insurance, so they had no immediate way of replacing all of their possessions that had burned in the fire. Since they both worked for tips, they had also lost several weeks' worth of pay when their piles of one-dollar and five-dollar bills went up in flames.

At the Hungry Cowboy, the response to this misfortune was immediate. The story of Billy's loss spread quickly. At the time, Billy was no longer working at the Hungry Cowboy, although he later returned. He had left to try working at an upscale downtown bar. The fact that he no longer worked at the restaurant seemed to make no difference in the communal response to his situation. Regular customers wanted to do something to help Billy. The staff and regulars worked together to raise a relief fund, not only at the Hungry Cowboy but also at the surrounding establishments where Billy was well known as a customer. All told, they raised over two thousand dollars in cash in under two weeks.

Broke, with no insurance, Billy and his girlfriend saw the "family" of the Hungry Cowboy step up to protect and, in this case, clothe them. For Billy and his girlfriend, the family of the Hungry Cowboy did not disappoint. Even though he was a former member of the staff, Billy received money and support that emerged solely out of commonality of interests. For the two weeks that workers, managers, and customers "passed the jar around" to collect money to help Billy, I was also struck by just how much pleasure and pride customers took in playing a part in Billy's recovery. When the jar was full, everyone celebrated together. Like the posting of the epitaph to River the dog, this relief effort was one of those moments that defies a clear distinction between work and play, public and private, server and served. These occurrences represent moments that are irreconcilable with job requirements, when the division between "real" and commodified relationships melts away.

FEELING AT HOME AT THE HUNGRY COWBOY

I began my account of the Hungry Cowboy with a reference to how the sociological imagination provides scholars with the tools to "make the familiar strange." Conducting research at the restaurant allowed me to see the space and the routine interactions that take place there with new eyes. I learned more about my boss, my coworkers, my customers, and myself. My studies also dramatically altered how I think about service in our culture. And yet, for all the surprises I encountered along the way in my research regarding how attached people are to the Hungry Cowboy and the family of people who gather there, I feel that I should have known better, because the restaurant also means something to me. After my research concluded, I spent more than a year away from the Hungry Cowboy. I returned recently with my dad, a member of my "real" family. As I walked through the door, I experienced a momentary panic: Would the Hungry Cowboy that I remembered be there? Would it be there for me? Would I be recognized as having played a role in its history? Perhaps peoples' attachment to these special places, including my own, is as simple as what I call "the Norm effect." Perhaps we all want to experience the pleasure that Norm, the character from Cheers, must have felt when he walked through the door and people shouted his name. Perhaps, as we each make our way through an accelerating market economy where we are so often processed by machines, and where we participate in processes that are detached from place, this increasingly globalized world causes us to wonder if we matter at all. Perhaps many of us are willing to play a part in perpetuating a place where, when our foot crosses the doorstop, a smiling face turns to greet us, and calls us by name.

The passionate participation of customers, workers, and managers in the Hungry Cowboy "family" demonstrates their desire to be a part of something, to experience a sense of belonging within the market economy. They stake a claim to the Hungry Cowboy by labeling it their "favorite." Both workers and customers say, "This is my place" and "We're like family here." Having agreed to cooperate in social exchanges that obscure the profit motive, all three of the groups of actors in service interactions benefit from their participation because it provides them with a way to feel at home in the marketplace.

Many "members" of the Hungry Cowboy family will say to a server who is leaving for a different job, or a customer who is moving out of the state, "You can't leave; this place will never be the same without you." And yet, like most places, the Hungry Cowboy manages to stay the same even when members depart. Once ambience is established, it can carry forward, sustained despite changes. The feel of a place has a life of its own, recreating itself with a new "generation" of customers and workers.

Together, customers, servers, and Richard have created a warm pocket of sociability at the Hungry Cowboy for a decade. Whether or for how long this particular place will continue to provide the benefits described by members remains to be seen. My analysis of the Hungry Cowboy has focused on identifying what I call the building blocks of sociability. Staff, customers, management schemes, food, and spatial arrangements all contribute to the unique "feel" of a place. While the structure that houses the Hungry Cowboy will continue to stand for many years, the social world made available to customers and servers can be more easily destroyed. This social world is a coproduction by three groups of actors who have decided to focus on the social aspects of service. Servers, customers, and managers have to agree to perform sociability. The departure of key actors might disrupt the reproduction of this community. In particular, given how unusual Richard's approach to management has become, his departure might make it impossible to reproduce or even sustain the qualities that servers, customers, and Richard himself currently value and protect.[24]

The Hungry Cowboy is one place where workers, customers, and managers all try to build a home of sorts in the marketplace. When I present papers at conferences or I tell my friends what my study uncovered at the Hungry Cowboy, many people are eager to tell their own consumer stories of places that allow them to, as one of the managers put it, "hang your hat." Hang your hat, kick up your feet, let your hair down—all of these phrases come up when people try to describe their favorite locations in the marketplace. Yet, at the very same moment that someone fondly refers to a homey place, a marketing firm somewhere is devising a new campaign to package that feeling and sell it back to them. Are we all duped, or is there something different about these places in the marketplace, the places that we name with a smile?

I view the Hungry Cowboy as one example of a range of places where customers go to rehumanize the market economy. I understand this place as one of many gathering places that people use to connect in an ever-expanding marketplace.[25] While many chain stores rush to create better formulas to insure that customers feel cared for, shabby little places like the Hungry Cowboy that allow customers to feel involved and recognized flourish in a marketplace that can feel dehumanizing and cold.

Increasingly, these special places in the marketplace that customers name with a smile are not family owned. Sometimes the stories I hear of fond memories when customers were remembered, welcomed, and made to feel at home even take place in chains, not in one-of-a-kind shops. There is no rule that says Cut and Paste management makes this ambience available while Total Quality Service does not. While I argue that management style is one of the building blocks of sociability, I do not think it is absolute. What is noteworthy is the way that consumers and producers share a desire to have service interactions that feel real, that over time grow, and that allow us to connect with each other.

At the Hungry Cowboy, servers are drawn into emotional performances through multiple routes—not only managerial strategies but also their own sense of craft and the collaborative construction of a sense of community.[26] Despite the precariousness of their jobs and the low status afforded the work they do, they manage to "emotionally triumph" and bring dignity to their own work.[27] In doing so, they shape the ambience made available to guests. Their emotional performances are the equivalent of rolling out the welcome mat.

Servers' approaches to their jobs also challenge views that service work is not necessarily meaningful work. In *Working*, Studs Terkel explains that meaningful work is a privilege enjoyed by few. "Work is about a search, too, for daily meaning as well as daily bread, for recognition as well as cash, for astonishment rather than torpor; in short, for a sort of life rather than a Monday through Friday sort of dying . . . There are, of course, the happy few who find a salve in their daily job: the Indiana stonemason, who looks upon his work and sees that it is good: the Chicago piano tuner, who seeks and finds the sound that delights."[28] Like Terkel, early into my research, I was distracted by common perceptions of what "counts" as meaningful work—what sorts of jobs might offer fulfillment or a satisfying work role. I routinely looked for evidence of servers being exploited or being "falsely conscious" in the Marxist sense, which is really just another way of saying that they were duped.[29] Perhaps having grown up in the middle class, I was convinced that enjoying one's work and developing an identity through it was the privilege of professionals or artists, not all workers.[30]

Despite my own misgivings about the paradox of service, my early interviews quickly challenged my outlook: I found that customers were not being duped by employees who were encouraged by management to act pleasant; rather, servers repeatedly reported that they felt affection for their customers and that they enjoyed the ability to be caring and compassionate through their jobs. Servers' investment in their labor counters assumptions that work is by its very nature alienating.[31] Tim Hallett discovered similar patterns in his study of food servers: "Rather than becoming alienated servers at TD's manage to triumph emotionally, despite their location in a low status occupation."[32] Despite the negative connotations of waiting tables, many of the servers at the Hungry Cowboy take pride in their jobs and their ability to do them well. On good days, their pride and investment creates an oasis in the marketplace that extends the predictable arenas of meaning in daily life.[33]

Servers' approaches to their jobs reveal the potential rewards of giving and receiving service in the marketplace. In some locations, customers are quick to cooperate, seizing on service interactions as a means to experience feelings of belonging, membership, ownership, and mutual recognition that are often in short supply. Customers may begin by searching out a warm meal, but regular customers end up returning for what I have coined the "extras" of service exchanges: the sociability and shared camaraderie that develops between producers and consumers of service. The communities that arise in restaurants are testaments to how, given the least encouragement, associations can flourish. The interactions I have recounted from the Hungry Cowboy draw attention to the way that individuals make the most of living in a service society, finding opportunities within the confines of capital to give and receive pleasantries, recognition, and a feeling of being at home. Some days, it's enough to make you want to hang your hat, and stay a while.

CONCLUSION

◆◆◆◆◆◆◆◆◆◆◆◆◆◆◆◆◆◆◆◆◆◆◆

REFLECTIONS ON THE HUNGRY COWBOY

On good days when I worked as a waitress, I would be filled with admiration for people's desire to know and be known, talk and connect, even across a little thing like food. On bad days, I would hear a repeated joke or opening line from a regular in the bar and think, "Seriously, can't you get a 'real' life?" As I became increasingly aware of the paradox of service, I started to think about the cultural impact of service interactions. What if we imagine these funky, fun, sometimes sad interactions that happen at the Hungry Cowboy happening simultaneously at the twenty-seven restaurants that surround it, in the thousands of restaurants in this city, in the thousands of cities across this country? What do people's interactions in restaurants tell us about the culture in which we live?

As consumers, we help shape the production and reproduction of ambience, and, in turn, we are also affected by the consumer spaces we inhabit. Our choices and behaviors as producers and consumers of service are culturally significant. It is imperative that we think critically about living and working in a service society. Gutek and Welsh raise questions about the consequences of service environments, arguing that they sheer volume of such interactions requires close scrutiny. "Do customers benefit from service being delivered in a standardized way through large organizations? It is an important question because Americans spend a large part of their time and income being customers. The average household spends 45 percent of its income on services. We all play the role of customer over and over at work and in our personal life."¹ Our behaviors within service exchanges have implications for how we feel about ourselves, about other people, and about the culture in which we live and move, as people and as consumers.

Consumer groups talk about politicizing consumption in terms of buying products that are environmentally friendly, or that are made in the United States, or that are produced under fair trade standards. Such purchasing decisions are indeed political, and well-informed and strategic choices can help customers feel empowered to influence the economy. I want to advocate a similar politics of consumption but one that focuses on how the human qualities of our service interactions have both political and cultural consequences. That is, I am interested in what might be called a political economy of emotion. This approach ties our feelings as we move through the marketplace to larger political and ideological issues. Rather than focusing on the environmental impact of consumption, I am interested in an affective analysis of living and working in a service economy. How do we feel as we move through the marketplace? How do our affective experiences of consumption shape our future choices and inform how we treat one another?

My analysis of the Hungry Cowboy suggests global cultural implications of service work and service interactions for both consumers and producers. In this final chapter, I want to spin out from what I observe at the Hungry Cowboy and ask the reader to think with me about some of the implications of service interactions on our emotions, our relations, and our selves. These are unfinished musings; my hope here is to suggest possible directions for future research for ethnographers, labor scholars, and students of social life. The Hungry Cowboy could inspire us to explore questions about dining out, or about social investment in other service work, or even about the global spread of American chain restaurants. Of the many possible directions that could arise out of this study, I am most interested in how we make creative use of the marketplace, and in the social, emotional, and cultural implications of our decisions and behaviors in consumer realms. Specifically, I want to take a closer look at three patterns

I observe at the Hungry Cowboy: the feminization of social investment, the production of "home," and gathering in public. Here, I want to begin to extrapolate the cultural, social and affective consequences of each of these three patterns of behavior.

THE FEMINIZATION OF SOCIAL INVESTMENT

As one locale in the exponentially expanding global economy, the Hungry Cowboy offers a particular snapshot of how the service economy combines labor and leisure, consumption and production, pleasure and coercion. The behaviors, rationales, and identities made available through interactions at the Hungry Cowboy occur against the backdrop of global transformations in labor.[2] Shifts in the global arrangement of labor are deeply gendered, as paid services increasingly replace work that women once did in homes for free.[3] From giving massages to walking dogs; from shopping for groceries to picking out gifts; from planning parties to serving a hot meal, our culture is outsourcing many tasks to the marketplace.

As these tasks move from the home to the marketplace, they are distributed along "predictable" lines of who has the right to purchase and consume service and who will be paid, although poorly, to produce it. Service work tends to solidify rather than transform dominant power relations. Even when this work is done for pay, recent immigrants, men and women of color, and white women continue to be overrepresented in these underpaid and low-status service jobs. As Chandra Mohanty explains, these transformations in the work of social reproduction build succinctly on "gender, race and ethnic hierarchies already historically anchored in the U.S."[4]

One example of how service work solidifies dominant social relations and makes use of existing social hierarchies is how gender has shaped the distribution and practice of service work. Gender informs how individuals negotiate their roles in the new economy. Gendered logic works to structure service work in two specific ways; first, by influencing ideas about who should do what, and, second, by influencing ideas about how women and men should perform their jobs. This first gendered logic influences women's and men's ideas about who should hold positions in the service economy. Gendered ideas influence how comfortable men and women are providing and receiving paid service. As the service sector grows, women will continue to be ghettoized in the job market if the work of serving others continues to be viewed as the "proper" type of work for women.[5]

Next, even when men and women hold similar positions, gender can and does influence how workers approach the necessary tasks that make up their job. For example, at the Hungry Cowboy, I observe a "feminization of social investment."[6] Women appear to invest more deeply in their labor but also explain their work as extensions of their feminine, female, and emotional selves. At the Hungry Cowboy, the majority of women invest in their work roles through gendered idioms of being "more caring," and "more nurturing." Servers who invest articulate their decision to invest in terms of care, concern, and a feeling of family—all terms that are more closely associated with femininity.[7] It seems that the narrative of caring about customers as if they were family is more appealing for women to adopt than men.

Gendered logics inform how workers express loyalty, protect their emotions and construct work identities.[8] At the Hungry Cowboy, most of the male servers achieve distance from customers' demands (or at least claim to) by emphasizing their masculine privilege not to "have" to care about their work. At least at the Hungry Cowboy, the majority of men detach, an interesting finding considering that, traditionally, men have been under more pressure to root their self-concept in their job. Of course, only certain types of jobs have been considered appropriate for developing a masculine work identity.[9] Service work, which requires deferring to others, entails emotional labor, relies on teamwork, and has traditionally been considered women's work, does not offer what men have traditionally been encouraged to pursue: autonomy, room for ambition, and opportunity for career building.

This study raises two central concerns about the gendering of service work: first, the potential for women's skilled emotional labor to be exploited in the service sector and, second, the potential for men to struggle to develop satisfying work identities through service work in feminized work cultures.[10] Some jobs encourage some workers to embrace their work as a gender-affirming performance, while other jobs encourage workers to distance themselves from their work roles to protect their gender identity. If women willingly invest themselves emotionally at work, this tendency reinforces gendered assumptions that women are naturally more skilled at serving others.

As customers move through the service society, they can become accustomed to being the recipients of women's paid emotional labor. For customers, the preponderance of women in service work and the feminization of social investment reinforce expectations that women will offer up more of their emotional wares in the service interaction. Leidner discovered similar patterns in the interactive service jobs she studied. "Because interactive service work by definition involves non-employees in the work process, the implications of the gender constructions of the routines extend beyond the workers. When service jobs are done predominantly by women, the gender segregation provides confirming 'evidence' to the public that men and women have different natures and capabilities."[11] Preferences for women's more "sincere" work risk producing an emotional proletariat that isolates women and increasingly excludes men.

Historically, men have been absolved of equal responsibility for the work of social reproduction in the home. Similarly, not only are fewer men working in the service sector, but my study suggests that when men do labor in emotional labor settings, they are not expected to perform emotional labor in the same way as women. M. V. Lee Badgett and Nancy Folbre argue that focusing on emotional labor draws attention to "the gendered character of social norms that shape the division of labor in both the family and the market. Women are expected, even required, to provide more care than men."[12] The feminization of social investment continues when women are expected to invest because of their gender and men are excused from emotionally engaging with their work because of their gender.

Initially, the feminization of social investment seems to maintain men's hegemonic power in American culture;[13] however, taking into account the fast expansion of service work, accompanied by the decline in manufacturing work, more men and women will need to seek paid employment in the service sector. Dramatic changes in the availability of secure lifelong employment and the decline of what was once called the blue-collar aristocracy have meant that more men and women will find themselves serving others in exchange for a paycheck.[14] The salience of traditional gender roles and subsequent expectations about how men and women can and should behave toward others creates a situation in which women have greater incentives to embrace the emotionally demanding aspects of waiting tables than men do.[15]

Whereas women can benefit from their "choice to enter an occupation where one is allowed to be human, sensitive and nurturing," men must defend their choice to work in a job that seems to be in conflict with their gender identity.[16] Men's emotional socialization does not prepare them as well as women's to earn a living serving others. As Hochschild explains, "When the emotional skills that children learn and practice at home move into the marketplace, the emotional labor of women becomes more prominent because men in general have not been trained to make their emotions a resource and are therefore less likely to develop their capacity for managing feeling."[17] These norms run the risk of creating an emotional proletariat of female service workers, while subsequently devaluing women's skills and making it difficult for men to comfortably inhabit service jobs.[18]

As dining out plays an increasingly important role in the social fabric of the United States, perpetuating the idea that women are the best workers to be paid to provide "service with a smile" will not only influence how people interact in the restaurant but also reinforce assumptions about gender roles and the value of social reproduction. As Joan Acker first explained, gender is a performance that individuals bring with them when they come to work, but gender is also constructed through worker's performances, interactions within the workplace and the distribution and evaluation of work.[19] As Badgett and Folbre conclude, concerns about worker exploitation and women's disproportionate emotional labor "converge on a set of questions and concerns about the future quality of life in a capitalist marketplace in which paid care services are playing an increasingly important role."[20] Leaving the emotion work of our culture disproportionately to women not only devalues women but also devalues emotional labor more generally.[21]

THE PRODUCTION OF HOME

Women's changing roles have shifted the expectation that women must know how to cook. As gender roles and educational systems have changed, women are no longer routinely taught how to cook by older relatives or by the public school system through home economics courses. Many cooking skills are not being passed down to either female or male children, resulting in a generational divide in cooking know-how. What happens when women stop doing the feeding work they have done in the past? Rather than the work of feeding being distributed equally between women and men, particularly in the middle class, individuals and families rely on the marketplace to supplement and supplant the cooking women once provided in the home.[22]

Knowing how to cook may be viewed as an individual idiosyncrasy, not a larger historical pattern. But restaurants, knowing that cooking is time-consuming and stress-producing, play upon people's insecurities about not wanting to or not knowing how to cook. For restaurants, the greater the dependency customers develop on the marketplace to eat, the better the business environment

Restaurants were not always an appealing substitute for home cooking. Up until the 1920s many Americans considered restaurant food a sorry substitute for food made at home. In the 1930s, the "home cooking" campaign was launched by the National Restaurant Association to "woo customers by promising to revive traditional middle-class domesticity."[23] As Samantha Barbas explains, restaurants banded together "to lure patrons with promises of family harmony, female subservience, and the feasibility of domestic bliss."[24]

The industry-wide home-cooking campaign played specifically on ideas about home that had a special resonance during a time of quickly transforming gender roles. It marketed domestic technologies as a way to free women from household drudgeries; yet these same changes produced widespread anxieties about how gender, family, and home were changing. One of the ways to ease anxieties about changes at home was to promise personalized service from someone (usually a woman) who remembered customers' likes and dislikes.

At one Portland, Oregon, cafeteria, noted for its exceptionally "home-like" atmosphere, "waitresses remember [patrons'] particular wants; whether their tea shall be green or black, whether they shall have French or mayonnaise dressing on their combination salad." Like "home cooking" "home atmosphere" became a code word for the customized service that was fast disappearing in an age of mass production. To feel at home, suggested industry leaders, was to feel the increasingly elusive "personal touch."[25]

Service interactions that included remembering customers and recalling their favorite foods became important practices in providing a "home-like" atmosphere in public dining establishments.

Having promised "home" to millions, the challenge was then to find ways to regularize it. As Barbas argues, streamlining home risked undermining the "home sweet home" feeling. "If the essence of home was its individuality and intimacy, how could it be packaged and sold? As they attempted, awkwardly, to define 'home'—and more difficult yet, to reproduce and market it—restauranteurs found themselves mired in formidable contradictions."[26] The situation today presents similar contradictions: companies search out ways to routinize personalization and make people feel at home because "home" is a lucrative promise.

Home then and home now. Some ideas remain appealing even during vastly different time periods.[27] Clearly the campaign in the 1930s was successful, encouraging millions of middle-class families to carry their socializing out of the house and into the marketplace. Indeed, the home-cooking campaign marketed a cultural approach to eating that was being destroyed by technological innovations. As Barbas explains, the 1930s campaign very intentionally picked up on cultural anxieties and feelings of loss and promised to reproduce or restore in the marketplace what was missing at home. "In one of the great ironies of the modern social experience, restaurants have lured middle-class Americans by promising to restore the very traditions they helped to destroy."[28] Indeed, this transformation is part of what fuels capitalism: the marketplace devises means to sell back to us what the economy has undone. As capitalism offers more alternatives to eating at home, consumers make use of them and in the process rely less on their own knowledge and competence.

Today, the promise of home continues to resonate. As the experience of home changes, the promise of home remains tantalizing. Again, the marketplace is offering (or at least promising to offer) experiences that are valuable precisely because social life has been altered by the expansion of the marketplace. Today, being recognized and welcomed in a service setting can help to ease loneliness or dislocation experienced elsewhere. In this case, customers' and servers' service interactions and social connections take place within a culture that is changing quickly, in which, as Robert Putnam explores, voluntary associations, civic participation, and the social capital that emerges out of people connecting with one another are on the decline.

Putnam's title, *Bowling Alone*, captures the cultural shift from dense networks of voluntary association in the last century to an increasingly individualized, privatized lifestyle experienced by many Americans today. Putnam views this shift as costly because it decreases the available reserves of social capital from which people can draw. Social capital refers to "connections among individuals—social networks and the norms of reciprocity and trustworthiness that arise from them."[29] Social capital is the trust and connectedness that arises out of being in relation to others as neighbors, coworkers, members of the same bowling league, or volunteers at the same church. While you cannot touch social capital like you can a dollar bill, social capital can be saved up, spent, and traded. Perhaps the best example of social capital generated at the Hungry Cowboy was when the customers and workers came together to raise economic capital for Billy and his girlfriend. Putnam would label that as a return on the social capital Billy had built up through his connections with others. What is interesting about that instance is that the social connections at the Hungry Cowboy arise out of economic relations and eventually give rise to not only money, in the form of tips, but, over time, social capital as well. In Putnam's words, social capital makes us "healthy, wealthy and wise."[30] Customers, managers, and servers at the Hungry Cowboy all experience rewards arising out of connecting with people within the marketplace. These exchanges are not "free" or "voluntary" like bowling leagues, but they do speak to the very real benefits of structured relationships.

This practice of building social connections out of service interactions challenges the common distinction between public and private relationships. The dichotomy between the public and the private often infuses our thinking, and yet, it does not correspond to the reality of most people who cannot or at least do not separate their emotions and desires for social relations from "rational market" transactions.[31] The relationships that develop at the Hungry Cowboy remind us that, in the words of Jim Farrell, "it is possible to have real feelings in a structured, commercial and 'artificial' setting."[32]

GATHERING IN PUBLIC

In the late 1990s, as the new century approached and cultural anxieties increased, I was fascinated by a particular trajectory in American social thought that positioned America as always on the edge of decline. At the same time that I was studying this American tradition of bemoaning increasing apathy, growing social isolation, and lost community, I was working my way through graduate school by earning tips at the Hungry Cowboy. The discourse of an America divided, where people did not talk to each other anymore and where neighborhoods were disappearing, directly conflicted with the exchanges I witnessed every day at work. During that same time, I often used other restaurants as my study area, to read, write, and observe. I recorded the following notes in the spring of 2000.

I completed much of the work of this study in bars and restaurants. I carried my transcripts to greasy spoons on rainy mornings, made sense of my notes in local diners on sunny afternoons and tossed around interpretations and memories of service work with friends over a cold beer in dimly lit taverns. At a time when many Americans feel anxious and isolated, restaurants and bars occasionally provide a soothing familiarity in what can feel like an increasingly indifferent world. As I write this, I am perched in a booth of an aging Northeast sandwich shop where eight of the last ten customers were greeted by name. Despite the perpetual motion of the hurried waitress, she took time out to patiently escort an elderly woman with a walker to the restroom. One customer actually walked in and announced, "Is anyone important here?" Clearly customers come here for more than food and hot coffee.

A couple weeks later I was taking notes at a nearby bar, when the woman in the booth next to me said, "I feel ripped off when I go to church. All they want is my money." Many of the customers sitting on stools nodded in agreement, and a couple started up a discussion with her. Many cultural critics worry over the decline of associational participation. They say that Americans are living increasingly atomized existences, but here, on the northeast side of Minneapolis in this smoky, funky bar on the corner between gentrified condominiums and 1950s track houses, people gather all the time for the pleasure of being together.[33] Sometimes they tell stories about the old neighborhood, and sometimes they talk about how disappointing church can be. Some of the locations we frequent in the marketplace seem to operate like the proverbial backyard fence, where neighbors gather just to "shoot the breeze."

Perhaps, as Robert Putnam worries, we do "bowl alone" now, or not at all, but if we look around there are plenty of commercial locations that operate like gathering places. Places like the Hungry Cowboy or this smoky little bar in northeast Minneapolis continue the tradition of belonging in public made famous in workingman's saloons and the British pub. Today, these "watering holes"—as customers sometimes refer to them—also include women, children, and men of all ages. No longer are these exclusionary places where men are the customers who come to be served by women. As Richard Sennett explains, feeling a sense of belonging to a place is valuable:

> One of the unintended consequences of modern capitalism is that it has strengthened the value of place, aroused a longing for community. All the emotional conditions we have explored in the workplace animate that desire: the uncertainties of flexibility; the absence of deeply rooted trust and commitment; the superficiality of teamwork; most of all, the specter of failing to make something of oneself in the world, to "get a life" through one's work. All these conditions *impel people to look for some other scene of attachment and depth.*[34]

It seems that what Sennett calls "scenes of attachment and depth" or what I call gathering places are valuable because they offer an alternative or a temporary antidote to a commercial economy that threatens to detach us from place and from each other. As Phillip Crang argues, making our way through an economy in which "social relations themselves are increasingly commodified"[35] can challenge our dignity and connections to others. Leidner issues a warning about the potentially dehumanizing consequences of service regimes that seek to streamline human interactions. "These scripts and instructions make various kinds of assumptions, some more morally problematic than others, about the actor and the target audience, but they raise interconnected questions about the status of the self and the treatment to which others are entitled."[36] While I have directed attention to places like the Hungry Cowboy that provide a place to gather for both workers and customers, it is certainly not my goal to induce complacency regarding the increasing protrusion of the marketplace into social life. I share other scholars' concerns about the potential harm of becoming accustomed to using each other not as people but as service delivery systems. In fact, I worry about much of the contemporary marketplace.

Navigating the service economy can be challenging, and even nerve-wracking. Recently, I've noticed how nervous I get in McDonaldized settings. Trying to cram my own extras into efficient exchanges with workers who are not, after all, machines, but people, makes me uncomfortable. I don't want to feel "processed," and I don't want to interact with other people in routinized settings that encourage me not to acknowledge them, and that devalue the services I consume, rendering other people's labor invisible to me.

For the most part, I don't have a choice. None of us can entirely evade McDonaldized processes; they have invaded the fabric of our daily lives. We learn quickly in our culture to make ourselves efficient when we are being processed and, better yet, to process ourselves. For example, I might walk past the young woman working as a teller at the bank to use the cash machine located fifteen feet away from her. I wait in line for the self-service checkout at the grocery store and bag my own groceries rather than having to talk, ever so briefly, with the checkout clerk. Why bother? Next month she may be replaced by the machine and by me. When she is deskilled right out of a job, I'll service myself, and she'll go looking for a new job. Perhaps one or both of us will situate that small change in a far greater cultural shift toward streamlining human interactions, but more likely, we'll both find ways to keep moving through the marketplace. For my part, I'll probably comfort myself by hiding out in my home and the compensatory "homes" I've made for myself in the marketplace: my favorite bookstore, a yoga studio that feels friendly and peaceful, a smoky, loud corner bar in my old neighborhood where I meet my friends. And when I feel particularly adrift, I'll drive the extra distance to get to the Hungry Cowboy, because there people know me.

The marketplace encourages us in a host of ways to treat each other like any other cog in the machine, deprive other people of their basic dignity, and deny them the courtesy of being recognized. Despite these tendencies, not all consumer experiences entail affectless consumption and production

of service. Efforts to routinize human interactions, to shape and mold sociability like any other raw material are imperfect and incomplete. We often
find ways of enriching even the most controlled exchanges. And sometimes,
despite the frumpy appearance of the taxidermic animals and dusty cactuses
at places like the Hungry Cowboy, customers, managers, and workers there
cooperate to create a warm little spot where people come together for food,
fun, relaxation, and the pleasure of being together. For me, this is one of
the central contradictions of late capitalism: how we make a "home" in the
marketplace, against all the odds.

APPENDIX

CHARACTERISTICS OF SERVERS INTERVIEWED					
NAME	AGE	YEARS AT HC	YEARS SERVING	DETACH/ INVEST	CHARACTERISTICS
Julia	21	4	5	I	Student, married to bartender, enjoys serving, full-time server
Meg	21	3	3	D ⟶ I	Recent college graduate, upper-middle class, resents serving, full-time server
Jessica	32	9	11	I	College graduate, single mom of two daughters, part-time "real" job and full-time server
Patricia	29	10	11	I	College graduate, married, two children, left full-time serving at Hungry Cowboy to start her own business
Lisa	39	10	18	I	College graduate, waits tables as second job and way to meet people, sales manager at "real" job
Alex	n/a	10	12	I	College graduate, divorced, over a decade at the Hungry Cowboy, "real job" now is interior designer, waits tables part-time
Beth	28	4	12	I	Student, married, recently had first child, full-time server
Betsy	30	2	13	I	Raised teenaged son on her own, working serving and office jobs, newly married, new mom

NAME	AGE	YEARS AT HC	YEARS SERVING	DETACH/ INVEST	CHARACTERISTICS
Tammy	20	2	2	I	Student, left full-time serving at Hungry Cowboy to work in an office, serving is "not for her"
Liz	21	2	2	I	Student, former bank teller, left in order to get insurance for pregnancy
Joey	30	3	5	D	Odd jobs his whole life, left several times but keeps coming back to Hungry Cowboy
Billy	29	8	8	D ➔ I	Graduated from technical college, disillusioned with music industry, now plans to continue serving
Trevor	29	6	15	D	Used restaurant work to get out of small town, degree in restaurant management, fluctuates between serving and managing
Ralph	33	1	15	D	Family involved in service work, never tried anything else, provides mobility as he moves from place to place
Charles	37	1	20	I	Enjoys the food, smells and warmth of the industry, fluctuates between serving and managing

NOTES

1. Spaces in the Marketplace

1. Merriam Webster Dictionary. http://www.m-w.com/dictionary/sociability. Accessed on July 19, 2007.

2. Renato Rosaldo labels this cultural longing "imperialist nostalgia" ("Imperialist Nostalgia," 112).

3. Rachel Sherman first used this phrase in her dissertation research. See *Class Acts*.

4. *Great Good Place*, 64.

5. On comment cards customers reported traveling up to two hours to come to the Hungry Cowboy.

6. Thanks to my colleague, David Gray, for suggesting this term.

7. For more on commodification, see for example, Hochschild, *Commercialization of Intimate Life*, and Kuttner, *Everything for Sale*, 356.

8. *Time Bind*, 230–35.

9. As Phillip Crang explains, "thus in the performances of these staff and in the spaces of the stage in which they are set paid labour is not just surrounded by but fused with a number of social relations often understood as its exclusions; communicative understanding, performances of sexuality, gender, age, and social class" ("It's Showtime," 699).

10. Foucault, *Discipline and Punish*.

11. Goffman examines how the potential for "contamination" is negotiated in public, with social distance often expressed through spatial difference. "There is ecological placement of the body relative to a claimed territory. The model here is classical Indian caste relations, with its conception of measurable distances which mark a safe approach between persons of different castes, the ranking person serving as the center of a personal space and the other as a source of contamination, the potency of which depends on the social distance between the castes" (*Relations in Public*, 44).

12. At the time of the study, seven of the servers I interviewed worked primarily in the bar, and eight worked primarily in the restaurant. However, all but two of the interviewees had worked in both areas at some point. Servers perceive working in the bar as a promotion because bartenders earn up to twice what servers on the restaurant side earn. Although bartenders pour more drinks and sell less food than waiters and waitresses in the restaurant, all servers, whether they work primarily in the bar or restaurant, wait tables.

13. In keeping with changes in the law regarding smoking in Hennepin County, Minnesota, the Hungry Cowboy later made the entire space nonsmoking.

14. Goffman, *Presentation of Self*.

15. Russell Muirhead calls this "visible deference" through which social divisions are maintained. Habits of subservience and segregated entrances and work spaces symbolized a general inferiority by virtue of which servants were thought not to need or deserve the same attention to their health, the same rest, or the same leisure as the families they served" (*Just Work*, 82).

16. See also Bolton, *Emotion Management in the Workplace*, 140–50.

17. I use "backstage" in keeping with Erving Goffman's theorizing of backstage/frontstage personas (*Presentation of Self in Everyday Life*).

18. I refer to the men from Mexico who work in the kitchen as either "Mexican," "Mexican and Mexican-American," or "Latino." To the best of my knowledge all but one of the men referred to by these titles moved to the United States from Mexico. One of the men had attained American citizenship. The rest of the men remained Mexican citizens. Some were seeking to remain in the United States, but most were temporarily in Minnesota to earn money (sometimes for a year or two at a time) to send back to their families. Their goal was to return to their homes in Mexico. So "Mexican" almost captures the characteristics of the group; however, because the term "the Mexicans" was used in a derogatory way within the workplace, I have avoided using that term throughout. In addition, because I set up a comparison between the white female front of the house workers and the men who work in back, I want to avoid equating "Mexican men" with "white women," as if Mexican is a racial category, and to avoid the assumption that white can stand in for American in this context. Having said that, in my discussion of raced identities at the Hungry Cowboy, I do not directly take up the issue of the social construction of race. Here, I am interested in how race is produced in part through work. Such an analysis assumes that race is a social construct that is created and maintained through discourse and practice. To acknowledge that race is not real is not to say that race is not powerful: race continues to be one of the primary avenues through which opportunity, privilege, discrimination, and disadvantage are filtered. For more on the social construction of race, see, for example, Omi and Winant, *Racial Formation in the United States*; Morrison, *Playing in the Dark*, and Williams, *Alchemy of Race and Rights*.

19. During the time that I worked at the Hungry Cowboy, only one woman worked in the kitchen.

20. For more on occupational typing, see for example, Cohn, *Race, Gender, and Discrimination at Work*, 23.

21. Foucault, *Discipline and Punish*.

22. LeDuff, "At a Slaughterhouse."

23. Mohanty, "Women Workers and Capitalist Scripts."

24. Ibid., 17.

25. Whyte, *Human Relations in the Restaurant Industry*, 19.

26. Ibid., 33.

27. Ibid., 174.

28. For more on intersubjectivity, see Husserl, *Cartesian Mediations*; McNay, "Situated Intersubjectivity"; Prus, *Symbolic Interaction and Ethnographic Research*; Crossley, *Intersubjectivity* and *Key Concepts in Critical Social Theory*.

29. *World of Waiters*, 132–33.

30. Leidner, *Fast Food, Fast Talk*, 8.

31. For more on social territories, see Goffman, *Relations in Public*; and Duneier, *Slim's Table*.

32. For more on occupational myth and stories, see Trice and Beyer, *Cultures of Work Organizations*, 78–83.

33. Mills, *Sociological Imagination*, 6.

2. Producing Familiarity

1. This phrase is taken from Studs Terkel's book *Working*, in which a server named Dolores Dante reports that one customer said to her, "You're great, how come you're just a waitress?" (391).

2. With notable exceptions. See, for example, Hallett, "Emotional Feedback and Amplificiation in Social Interaction," and Tolich "Alienating and Liberating Emotions at Work."

3. One of the servers was born in Russia and immigrated early in life. To say who that was would destroy any anonymity provided by the pseudonyms.

4. *Stigma*, 3.

5. See Bureau of Labor Statistics (www.bls.org) for occupational descriptions.

6. *Waiting*, 73.

7. See Bureau of Labor Statistics (www.bls.org).

8. For more on tipping, see Crang, "It's Showtime," and Sutton, "Tipping."

9. "Tipping," 191.

10. As Tim Edwards explains, while the supposedly "open shop" of the consumer democracy does not really differentiate among gender, race, or class, as long as you have money in your pocket, in practice, the capitalist marketplace "leads precisely to the trade-off of style and taste that then tends to form a reinstatement of the hidden social divisions of class, race and gender in particular" (*Contradictions of Consumption*, 102).

11. *Managed Heart*.

12. Ibid., 7.

13. *Where the Action Is*.

14. *Managed Heart*, 8.

15. Goffman, "Nature of Deference and Demeanor." In her book, *Gender Trials*, Jennifer L. Pierce then goes on to apply the notion of "doing gender" as a performance, to talk about how deference is also raced and gendered. Black men might be expected to defer to white men but not the reverse, while women are advised to do deference when looking for a spouse. Pierce explains that "deference, then, implies not only a relationship between subordinate and superior, but a power relationship with a gendered and racialized character" (90).

16. *Managed Heart*.

17. "Alienated Labor."

18. Thanks to anonymous reviewer #2 from Cornell Press for this phrasing.

19. *Encounters*, 125.

20. Ibid., 77.

21. Servers and bartenders are held accountable for serving alcohol to customers on two levels: company policy and state law. Workers who are convicted of selling alcohol to a minor

as a result of a sting operation or a lawsuit are immediately terminated. Both in the law and in the state-mandated training, the focus is on proper carding and on cutting customers off before they have "had too much." This onerous burden—of being responsible for cutting off customers whose tips constitute the primary source of a server or bartender's income—was referred to in several interviews.

22. Merriam Webster Online dictionary: http://mw1.merriam-webster.com/dictionary/ rationalization. Accessed on June 26, 2007. See also, Trice and Beyer, *Cultures of Work Organizations*, 63, and Illouz, *Cold Intimacies*.

23. Merriam Webster online dictionary: http://www.m-w.com/dictionary/rationality Accessed June 29, 2007.

24. Joey strikes what Richard Majors and Janet Mancini Bilson would call "the cool pose" (*Cool* Pose). As Majors and Bilson explain, black men put on airs of being impervious to hurt in order to protect their dignity and masculinity; this is the cool pose.

25. See Trice and Beyer, *Cultures of Work Organizations*, 10, for more on the prevalence of these shared symbolic meanings in workplaces.

26. Paules, *Dishing It Out*, 286.

27. Ibid., 286.

28. *Blue-Collar Aristocrats*, 24.

29. *Corrosion of Character*, 30.

30. Bartlett and Lorenzini, "What are you waiting for?" 46.

31. *Presentation of Self*, 141.

32. *Emotion Management in the Workplace*, 161.

33. Linda Fuller and Vicki Smith give the example of an emotional labor slowdown. "A manager in a large hotel reported that her desk clerks had been so angry about the prospect of being anonymously observed by shoppers that one shift staged a 'smile strike,' treating each and every customer that day in a rapid, affect-less fashion" ("Consumers' Reports," 12).

34. Martin B. Tolich suggests that rather than assuming that emotional labor is inherently alienating, scholars should instead make analytical distinctions between autonomous and regulated emotion management ("Alienating and Liberating Emotions at Work").

35. *Emotion Management in the Workplace*, 52.

36. For more on the influence of coworkers on work attitude, see Leidner, *Fast Food*, 47.

37. Benson, *Counter Cultures*, 228.

38. In his study of emotional feedback and amplification, Tim Hallett also discovers that workers' increased emotional involvement arises out of their interactions with coworkers. In other words, there may be a cyclical process at work in which workers form relationships through a shared approach to the job and support that approach or performance through interactions with one another ("Emotional Feedback and Amplification in Social Interaction").

39. Robert Putnam describes this as the bystander benefits that arise out of the production of social capital. See *Bowling Alone*, 20.

40. Thanks to anonymous reviewer #2 from Cornell University Press for this description of my work.

3. Consuming Belonging

1. *Enchanting a Disenchanted World*.

2. Ibid., 89.

3. Ibid., 3.

4. For a dramatic example of fast food's effects, see *Super Size Me*, a documentary by Morgan Spurlock on the physical effects of eating fast food.

5. "Sameness of Things."

6. Ginsberg, *Waiting*, 131.

7. *Emotion Management in the Workplace*, 121.

8. Bolton observes workers extending "extras" to their customers as well: "an organizational actor may not only follow organizational prescription but may decide to give that 'little extra' during a social exchange in the workplace" (ibid., 291). To create an alternative to what Hochschild conceptualizes as emotional labor, Bolton creates a typology that recognizes four types of emotion management performances. In this typology Bolton considers multiple instances of how what Hochschild calls the "transmutation of feeling" is incomplete. Bolton describes a series of ways that emotions play out within the space of the corporation without being financially motivated or secured by the company for organizational ends. Amid these examples, Bolton also explains that "there are some occupations where actors are not only financially motivated but abide by prescriptive feeling rules due to status or altruistic motivations or, quite simply, they enjoy the social nature of their work" (297).

9. I used a multifaceted approach to gathering information regarding customers' experiences at the Hungry Cowboy. First, in the spring of 2002, I surveyed one hundred customers with the help of several staff members, particularly Beth. Only 10 percent of the customers invited to participate declined, while an additional 10 percent expressed interest in or even demanded to be included in the survey before they were even approached. The survey is therefore not a random sample but rather primarily representative of a cross-section of regular customers. The survey is biased toward the experience of regulars who were more likely to be present during the three days the survey was administered and who were more likely to be tuned in enough to the activities in the restaurant to request inclusion. Regulars' desire to have their opinions represented in the survey is another example of how customers seek out opportunities to increase their involvement in the Hungry Cowboy. I also gathered five hundred comment cards collected over two years and quantified customers' comments from that larger sample. Comment cards tend to reflect the highs and lows of service (Fuller and Smith, *Consumers' Reports*). Customers tend to use comment cards to offer praise or to complain; rarely do customers report mediocre experiences. To balance the full range of customer experience, I collected all of the secret shopper reports since 1999.

10. In her study of Sagara Shop in Hawaii, Christine Yano discovered intergenerational patterns of patronage. "Each owner I interviewed proudly mentioned 'regulars'—customers who have frequented their establishment for years, exhibiting loyalty that often extends to succeeding generations" ("Side-Dish Kitchen," 54).

11. There are several outstanding studies of regulars. See for example, Duneier, *Slim's Table*; Powers, *Faces Along the Bar*; and also "24 Hours at the Golden Apple." For more information go to: http://www.thislife.org/

12. Similarly, Tolich discovered in his study that restaurants customers can "enliven otherwise monotonous tasks" ("Alienating and Liberating Emotions at Work," 370).

13. To give a sense of just how informal that commercial was, my sister and I were featured in it. Neither of us have any training or particular onscreen talent.

14. DMC cards are evidence of membership in a diner's club, for which members get five

dollars off once a month. Servers don't like the DMCs much because they take money off the bill, and consequently, usually off the tip too.

15. Song lyrics from "Where Everybody Knows Your Name" © 1983 Gary Portnoy, performed by Gary Portnoy and Judy Hart Angelo.

16. *Cheers* indoctrinated a whole generation of viewers into the sociability available in public spaces. Diane, Sam, Coach, Carla, Frasier, and Woody all became household names. Because my name is Karla, I cannot calculate the number of times that customers have made a wisecrack or a joke about "Carla the waitress, like *Cheers*" even though I look nothing like Rita Pearlman and my serving style is markedly different than hers.

17. Here, I am referring to the television show *Cheers*. Not only is Cheers a metaphor, there are bars named Cheers. In customers' answers, however, the term refers mainly to an idealized space, not an actual place.

18. "Side-Dish Kitchen," 65.

19. Leidner, *Fast Food*, 11.

20. See for example, Schlosser, *Fast Food Nation*, 7–8, and Hurley, *Diners, Bowling Alleys and Trailer Parks*, 45.

21. "Side-Dish Kitchen," 63.

22. Leland and Bailey, 17.

23. "Familiarity, Ambience, and Intentionality," 69.

24. LeMasters observed a similar pattern at the Oasis. "(The proprietor) knew the wives and children of his regular customers, and also many of their relatives because it was customary to bring family visitors to the tavern 'to meet the gang'" (*Blue-Collar Aristocrats*, 11).

25. As LeMasters explains, commercial relationships can also be more tolerant of quirks and faults because, after all, you are paying. "The tavern offers more or less uncritical acceptance of the individual—within broad limits. If your spouse doesn't like you, or your children reject you, a person can usually find a tavern where the customers are friendly. This feature should not be discounted in considering the function of the tavern in modern America" (*Blue-Collar Aristocrats*, 145).

26. Leidner, *Fast Food*, 21.

27. *Enchanting a Disenchanted World*, 182.

28. In her study of scripting, Leidner found that when it came naturally, some workers did not mind upselling; at other times, upselling tended "to heighten the sense of distance between scripted interactions and ordinary conversations" (*Fast Food*, 140).

29. Like his employees, Richard's loyalties within his job are complex and at times conflicted. For more on the identity of managers, see Vicki Smith, *Managing in the Corporate Interest*.

30. Leidner, *Fast Food*, 18.

31. Most service industries have some version of mystery shoppers; for example, Bolton and Boyd describe the ghost fliers: "Passenger surveys and 'ghost fliers' also act as control mechanisms to ensure cabin crew compliance in the absence of a base manager during flights" (Bolton and Boyd, "Trolley Dolly or Skilled Emotion Manager?" 301).

32. One of the ads for the Sights on Service Performance Monitoring System explains that customers tell you different things than they tell their customers and friends. Sights on Services promotes its auditing service by referring to research that suggest 96 percent of unhappy customers do not complain and 90 percent do not return. Further, unhappy

customers tell up to nine friends about their experience (source: White House Office of Consumer Affairs TARP study). The literature promises that it "maintains an extensive pool of carefully screened and trained shoppers, selected because they are detail-oriented and good communicators." To test this claim, I applied to be a secret shopper. The whole process was completed online, I wrote a couple of sample answers to questions about restaurants and received notice the next day that I was now qualified to accept audit assignments. The word "trained" here is sort of a stretch.

33. As Bolton explains, the idea of quantifying intangible qualities is appealing—"the greatest appeal, however, lies in its package as a science. Relational qualities that are deemed to be valuable work based attributes, frequently referred to as 'people skills,' have been given a scientific credibility with the claim that they can be reliably measured" (*Emotion Management in the Workplace*, 35).

34. Leidner, *Fast Food*, 230.

35. Sennett, *Corrosion of Character*, 138.

36. LeMasters, *Blue-Collar Aristocrats*, 23.

37. Hochschild, *Managed Heart*, 17.

38. Ibid., 153.

39. *Civic Life and Work*, 86.

40. Powers, *Faces along the Bar*, 227.

41. 89.

42. See, for example, Baudrillard, *America*.

4. Managing Service

1. See also Leidner, *Fast Food*, 2.

2. *Principles of Scientific Management*.

3. See Cobble, *Dishing it Out*, 338.

4. All of these names are pseudonyms. To protect the identity of the restaurants I studied, I have given each restaurant a pseudonym and disguised or omitted details that would make it recognizable.

5. Like many scholars, anthropologist John Van Maanen is suspicious of total quality systems: "The roaring success of the American comic strip Dilbert reminds us of the mocking contempt many employees have for their bosses and the popular management theories they import willy-nilly into the workplace. Such theories often come christened with silly acronyms, tarted-up in fancy scientific language, and so fast do they rise and fall, written in disappearing ink. Much high-flying and mass-marketed management theory is thin gruel indeed. Full of vapid rationalization and superficial fad, more than a few best-selling management books offer little more than an intellectual, if not ideological, justification for the foolhardy, flavor-of-the-month notions top executives rain down on lower- and mid-level employees. Airport bookstores are today stuffed with organizational salvation texts preaching the latest gospel of business process re-engineering, downsizing (or, as some say, rightsizing), knowledge-based organizational design, economic value-added analysis (EVA) and (fading fast) total quality management" ("Afterword," 243).

6. For example, servers might help decide which specials to offer in Cut and Paste, whereas corporate headquarters decide which items to feature under Total Quality Service.

7. Training materials include drink and menu descriptions, employee tests, mission statements, rule and procedure manuals, and manuals detailing the roles and promotional structure of an organization.

8. Bryman, "Disneyization of Society," 52–60.

9. Leidner, *Fast Food*, 10.

10. Ibid., 179.

11. A scene from the movie *Office Space* has now become shorthand for irrational demands for workers' to "be themselves" by complying with company ideology. *Office Space*, as the title suggests, is a movie about work. The conditions of one office branch of a technology corporation is juxtaposed with the work conditions of the main character's love interest, Joanna (played by Jennifer Aniston), who works at a T. G. I. Friday's look-alike restaurant called Chauchkie's. The viewer first encounters Chauchkie's when the bored-to-death cubicle workers go for a coffee break after just thirty minutes of work. They are waited on by Brian, who epitomizes the ideal server Chauchkie's seeks to mold. He is aggressive, tries to sell them dessert at 9 A.M., and portrays an enthusiasm that is both sickeningly sweet and impossible within the confines of his role. By contrast, Joanna is portrayed as resisting the character-shaping demands of her work. In a conversation with her manager, she debates the necessity of "speeding up" the personality demands of her job. Her manager asks her to have more "flair." Flair consists of the "funny" buttons and stickers (like at the real T. G. I. Friday's) that workers are forced to wear to look fun. She has the minimum, and he yells at her for doing the minimum and not expressing herself. Joanna's struggles demonstrate the central tension between individualizing and management control. The manager's task is to encourage individuals to be who the company needs them to be under the guise of "expressing themselves," but she refuses to play the game.

12. As Butler and Skipper explain, "The commitment of the dayshift is especially notable as turnover in the restaurant industry exceeds 200 percent annually" ("Working the Circuit," 20).

13. Leidner, *Fast Food*, 221.

14. For more on jargon as a means of occupational inclusion, see Trice and Beyer, *Cultures of Work Organizations*, 148–50.

15. Despite frequent alterations and modifications to training practices at the Hungry Cowboy, there are a couple of orientation processes to which all new workers are subject. Servers fill out federally mandated legal forms about sexual harassment, tax withholdings, and state-regulated safety standards. All servers—new and old—are also required to go to alcohol awareness training once a year. These formal procedures are mandated at the state or federal level. The only regular practice that is dictated from within the restaurant is that new servers are assigned to a more "seasoned" server.

16. All three of the independent restaurants I studied rely on peer training.

17. For more on occupational socialization, see Trice and Beyer, *Cultures of Work Organizations*, 129–33.

18. Smith, "Institutionalizing Flexibility in a Service Firm," 286.

19. For more on the two-tier system, see Hallett, "Emotional Feedback."

20. See also Illouz, *Cold Intimacies*, 16; and Sturdy, "Customer Care in a Consumer Society," 31.

21. Fuller and Smith, "Consumers' Reports," 3.

22. Hall, *Waiting on Tables*, 195.

23. At the time of interview, William had also recently become a regular at the Hungry Cowboy. I was his waitress for his third or fourth visit to the restaurant, and he asked me, "What's Richard's secret? Does he have a formula for finding these people or is everyone at the Hungry Cowboy just super nice?" After we talked for a while, I told him about my study, and he volunteered to be part of the research. His desire to be involved and even his question about Richard's management techniques that spurred the conversation point to the intensity of his interest in how he can, as a manager, establish a workplace culture that attracts workers who really care about their work.

5. Feeling like Family

1. "Liquor cost" is the percentage outcome of a cost worksheet that calculates what is paid each week in liquor stock and supplies against what is charged to customers. Ideally liquor cost should be at 20 percent, which means that the restaurant pays twenty cents on every dollar it charges the customer. Restaurants aim to make an 80 percent profit on alcoholic beverages and a 70 percent profit on food. The operating costs of the restaurant, everything from labor to building upkeep are subtracted from that amount to produce the monthly profit. The Hungry Cowboy maintains a high profit margin in comparison to an industry standard of 10–15 percent. The information I have gathered about the economic success of the Hungry Cowboy was collected unintentionally, when I was a bookkeeper for the restaurant, as such, it is not the focus of my study but part of the backdrop of the "success story" of the Hungry Cowboy.

2. In fact, thirteen out of fifteen servers at the Hungry Cowboy mentioned the connection between excessive drinking and drug use and the work of waiting tables. Joey said, "I think the exposure [to alcohol] is really there with this business because first of all we work in a setting with alcohol and it's so easy to get off of work and have a beer and a shot. Drugs too, that's the other thing too, restaurants don't drug test, because they'd lose a lot of their employees." Jessica was even more adamant: "Restaurants make alcoholics. It's just too easy, even if you have to pay for it, whether it's free or not, it's still right there and available, it's too easy to sit down and have a cocktail."

3. In *The Velvet Glove*, Mary Jackman defines paternalism as "a powerful ideological mold that offers the most efficient and gratifying means for the social control of relationship between unequal groups" (10–11). She explains that "some scholars have applied the concept (of paternalism) to an analysis of management-labor relations in anachronistic pockets of the developing industrial enterprise." Owing to its Cut and Paste management style, which resists McDonaldization, I imagine the Hungry Cowboy would qualify as "anachronistic" in her figuring.

4. His attitude echoes that of the proprietor in the tavern LeMasters studied. "I once heard him say to a rowdy customer:'this is my home—this is where I spend most of my life. My customers are my friends. Do you understand?'" (*Blue-Collar Aristocrats*, 11).

5. See Gamarnikow et al. *Public and the Private*.

6. Pierce, *Gender Trials*, 168.

7. "Tied by Double Apron Strings."

8. See also, Yano, "Side-Dish Kitchen," 56.

9. For more on symbolic goals, see Illouz, *Cold Intimacies*. She writes, "A discourse will keep functioning and circulating if it 'accomplishes' certain things that 'work' in people's everyday life" (67).

10. Pardue's fascinating study examines the cooptation of ideas about home and neighborhood in the marketing of corporate chains. For example, he points out the oxymoronic quality of "world's neighbors" through which "a number of locally-franchised businesses, even corporations with several thousand locations across the U.S., Europe, Asia and Latin America, advertise a 'neighborhood' feel" ("Familiarity, Ambience, and Intentionality," 74). Similarly, Richard Sennett reflects on the mobilization of "community" to motivate workers at Subaru-Isuzu: "Subaru-Isuzu uses this fiction of community at work to help justify its fierce resistance to labor unions; moreover, the fiction of community helps justify the existence of a Japanese company extracting profits in America to be sent home" (*Corrosion of Character*, 113).

11. *Merriam Webster Dictionary*. http://www.m-w.com/dictionary/family accessed on June 1, 2006.

12. Biggart, "Family, Gender and Business in Direct Selling Organizations," 171.

13. Hochschild, *Time Bind*, 44.

14. 13.

15. Richard has worked in the restaurant industry for almost thirty years and worked at the Hungry Cowboy for a decade. Many of the servers predate Richard, so their memory of the place includes the previous general manager.

16. To my knowledge, none of the workers at the HC ever went to visit him.

17. Goffman, *Relations in Public*, 190.

18. Weinstein, *Learning to Eat*, 217.

19. Ibid., 218.

20. Recognition does not go both ways. Patricia told the story about seeing the people in the mall and remembering their order, I asked if she talked to them. She replied, "Oh no! Most [customers] walk by me and stare at me, I know them from the Hungry Cowboy, but they don't know how they know me." Lisa told a similar story about when four of the waitresses from the Hungry Cowboy went out to a nearby community festival. "So by the end of the night, we would walk by people and they would do the double take and we'd be like 'Hungry Cowboy' and they'd be like 'Oh! That's where we know you from!' We just started telling people. Just to see all four servers hanging out together. People were just shocked." These stories of customers being unable to "place" servers outside the Hungry Cowboy context were extremely common in interviews. Some servers used them as examples of how customers perceive servers as inferior to them. Considering how often servers offered stories of being unrecognizable outside the service context, it suggests that servers' recognition is not a two-way street.

21. Hochschild, *Managed Heart*, 172.

22. Sociologist Morris Janowitz refers to these as "communities of limited liability" (*Community Press in an Urban Setting*, xvii).

23. Patricia Hill Collins, *Fighting Words: Black Women and the Search for Justice* (Minneapolis: University of Minnesota, 1998), 74.

24. For more on the reproduction of workplace cultures, see Trice and Beyer, *Cultures of Work Organizations*, 293. Trice and Beyer explain that in order for charismatic leadership to reproduce over time, it must be routinized. Because Richard's leadership style is not documented or recorded, the influence of his approach may quickly fade after his departure.

25. Tönnies, *Community and Society*.

26. Thanks to anonymous reviewer #2 from Cornell University Press for this phrasing.

27. See Hallett, "Emotional Feedback."

28. xiii.

29. False consciousness is a concept used to describe the proletariat's misplaced belief in the possibility of upward mobility within a capitalist system. While the idea arises our of Marx's thinking, the best source for direct reference to the idea is a letter from Frederick Engels to Franz Mehring written on July 14, 1983. The letter can be found in print: Mehring, *Absolutism and Revolution in Germany*. Originals can be found at the RCChIDNI, Moscow, fund 201. Copies of the letter are also available online; for example: http://www.marxists.org/archive/marx/works/1893/letters/93_07_14.htm

30. Ehrenreich reflects a similar assumption: "only in the professional middle class is work seen, and often experienced, as intrinsically rewarding, creative and important." Such assumptions automatically position service work as "just a job" (*Nickel and Dimed*, 31).

31. For other examples of low-paid workers investing in their work and enjoying emotional demands, see also Wharton, "Making People Feel Good"; Bell, "Tending Bar at Brown's"; and Sturdy, "Customer Care in a Consumer Society."

32. "Emotional Feedback," 77.

33. For example, Putnam finds that connections at work are one of the key factors that positively influence worker satisfaction, *Bowling Alone*, 20.

Conclusion

1. Gutek and Walsh, *Brave New Service Strategy*, 20.

2. See, for example, Kuttner, *Everything for Sale*, 95.

3. See also, Folgero and Fjeldstad, "From On Duty-Off Guard," 301. They write, "as people lose their self-sufficiency, due to an 'atrophy of competence,' dependence on the market increases (Glenn 1992). Health care, care of children and the elderly, food preparation and serving, overnight services, money transfers, communication services and entertainment are all growing sectors."

4. "Women Workers and Capitalist Scripts," 15.

5. See for example, England, Budig and Folbre, "Wages of Virtue."

6. Erickson and Pierce, "Farewell to the Organization Man," and Putnam, *Bowling Alone*, 94–95. Putnam notes that women tend to be more socially involved than men in voluntary organizations and civic participation. These tendencies may be connected to women's demonstrated propensity to invest socially within paid labor structures as well.

7. Erickson and Pierce, "Farewell to the Organization Man."

8. For example, see Martin, "'Said and Done' Versus 'Saying and Doing.'"

9. See for example, Milkman, *Gender at Work*; Newman, *Falling from Grace*; and Padavic and Reskin, *Women and Men at Work*.

10. See for example LeMasters, *Blue-Collar Aristocrats*; Sennett, *Corrosion of Character*; Leidner, *Fast Food*; and Erickson and Pierce, "Farewell to the Organization Man."

11. Leidner, *Fast Food*, 158–59.

12. "Assigning Care," 320.

13. See also Erickson and Pierce, "Farewell to the Organization Man."

14. See for example, Macdonald and Sirianni, "Service Society and the Changing Experience of Work."

15. In the decision whether to invest or not, gender is clearly the most salient factor; however, if gender is the superstructure through which servers' choices are filtered, social class may moderate the effect of gender. The two gender nonconformers in this study, Meg, who initially detached, and Chuck, who invested, were both raised in households with a considerably higher class standing than the majority of the workers. They lived in households that would be defined as upper middle class, their parents had college educations and at least one parent held a white collar job. Although I am not officially counted in the findings, my social class may also inform my ability to detach. Both Meg and I, the only female servers who detached, had siblings who were college educated and in white-collar positions and were expected to graduate from at least college, if not pursue an advanced degree. The sample of three servers whose strategies vary from the gendered norms is too small to conclude with certainty that social class is a mediating factor, but the similarities between the gender nonconformists is curious enough to suggest that future studies of emotional labor should consider social class in combination with race and gender.

16. Creighton, "Tied by Double Apron Strings," 61.

17. Hochschild, *Managed Heart*, 165.

18. See also Wilson, *When Work Disappears*, and Liebow, *Tally's Corner*, xxxiv.

19. Acker, "Hierarchies, Jobs, Bodies."

20. "Assigning Care," 315.

21. See for example, England and Folbre, "Cost of Caring."

22. Cancian and Oliker, *Caring and Gender*, 26. See also VanMaanen and Kunda, "Afterword," 254. Also see Halford, Savage, and Witz, *Gender, Careers and Organizations*, 194, 214–16.

23. Barbas, "Just Like Home," 43.

24. Ibid., 50.

25. Ibid., 48.

26. Ibid., 48.

27. Barbas quotes some of the industry literature. "Remember that word, 'homey.' Home style recipes, home-baked bread, homey atmosphere, homemade dinners—home, joked one restauranteur, had become the most 'abused word in the entire restaurant language'" (ibid., 47).

28. Ibid., 51.

29. 19.

30. 287.

31. Thanks to David Sutton for this observation, personal communication.

32. Thanks to James Farrell for this insight into one of the salient themes that emerges out of daily practice at the Hungry Cowboy. He shared this perspective in personal communication in July 2006.

33. In his research, Putnam discovers that the rate at which Americans go to bars, nightclubs, discos, and taverns has declined by 40–50 percent over the last two decades. He writes, "Whether we live alone or not, Americans are staying home in the evening, and *Cheers* has become a period piece" (*Bowling Alone*, 101). His research is important for contextualizing the patterns of sociability I observe at the Hungry Cowboy. On the one hand, the routine

associations seem to be in tension with the larger patterns Putnam identifies. On the other hand, it may be that the Hungry Cowboy is valued precisely because places like *Cheers*, where relations in public are reliably the same, are becoming rare.

34. Sennett, *Corrosion of Character*, 138, emphasis added.

35. Crang, "It's Showtime," 18.

36. Leidner, *Fast Food*, 10.

REFERENCES

Abel, Emily K., and Margaret K. Nelson. *Circles of Care: Work and Identity in Women Lives*. Albany: State University of New York Press, 1990.

Acker, Joan. "Hierarchies, Jobs, Bodies: A Theory of Gendered Organizations." *Gender & Society* 4, no. 2 (1990): 139–58.

Adams, Michael. "The Server's Lexicon: Preliminary Inquiries into Current Restaurant Jargon." *American Speech* 73 (Spring 1998): 57–84.

Adler, Peter, and Patti Adler. *Paradise Laborers: Hotel Work in the Global Economy*. Ithaca: Cornell University Press, 2004.

Aikau, Hokulani, Karla Erickson, and Jennifer Pierce, eds. *Feminist Waves, Feminist Generations: Life Histories of a Movement*. Minneapolis: University of Minnesota Press, 2007.

Alcoff, Linda. "The Problem of Speaking for Others." In *Who Can Speak? Authority and Critical Identity*, ed. Judith Roof and Robyn Wiegman, 97–119. Urbana: University of Illinois Press, 1995.

Anders, K. T. "Bad Sex: Who's Harassing Whom in Restaurants?" *Restaurant Business* 92, no. 2 (Jan. 1993): 46–54.

Appelbaum, Eileen, Annette Bernhardt, and Richard J. Murnane, eds. *Low-Wage America: How Employers are Reshaping Opportunity in the Workplace*. New York: Russell Sage, 2003.

Ashkanasy, Neal M., Charmine E. J. Hartel, and Wilfred J. Zerbe, eds. *Emotions in the Workplace: Research, Theory and Practice*. Westport, Conn.: Quorum Books, 2000.

Badgett, M. V. Lee, and Nancy Folbre. "Assigning Care: Gender Norms and Economic Outcomes." *International Labor Review* 138, no. 3 (1999): 312–26.

Bailyn, Lotte. *Breaking the Mold: Women, Men, and Time in the New Corporate World*. New York: Free Press, 1993.

Balzer, Harry. "Interface." *Restaurants and Institutions* 113, no. 8 (2003): 29–30.

Barbalet, J. M. *Emotion, Social Theory, and Social Structure*. New York: Cambridge University Press, 1998.

Barbas, Samantha. "Just Like Home—'Home Cooking' and the Domestication of the American Restaurant." *Gastronomica: The Journal of Food and Culture* 12, no. 4 (2002): 43–52.

Barker, Kathleen, and Kathleen Christiansen. *Contingent Work: American Employment Relations in Transition*. Ithaca, N.Y.: ILR Press, 1998.

Baron, Ava. *Work Engendered: Toward a New History of American Labor*. Ithaca, N.Y.: Cornell University Press, 1991.

Bartlett, Michael, and Beth Lorenzini. "What are you waiting for?" *Restaurants & Institutions* 105, no. 23 (1995): 42–49.

Bataille, Georges. *The Bataille Reader.* Oxford: Blackwell, 1997.

Baudrillard, Jean. *America.* New York: Verso, 1988.

Bauman, Zygmunt. *Consuming Life.* Cambridge, Mass.: Polity, 2007.

Becker, Gay. *Disrupted Lives: How People Create Meaning in a Chaotic World.* Berkeley and Los Angeles: University of California Press, 1997.

Bell, David, and Gill Valentine. *Consuming Geographies: We are Where We Eat.* London: Routledge, 1997.

Bell, Michael J. "Tending Bar at Brown's: Occupational Role as Artistic Performance." *Western Folklore* 35 no. 2 (Apr. 1976): 93–107.

Bendelow, Gillian, and Simon J. Williams, eds. *Emotions in Social Life: Critical Themes and Contemporary Issues.* London: Routledge, 1998.

Benson, Susan Porter. *Counter Cultures: Saleswomen, Managers and Customers in American Department Stores, 1890–1940.* Urbana: University of Illinois Press, 1986.

Berberoglu, Berch, ed. *The Labor Process and Control of Labor: The Changing Nature of Work Relations in the Late Twentieth Century.* Westport, Conn.: Praeger, 1993.

Bernstein, Charles. "Industry Image Ailment: Long Hours, High Turnover." *Restaurants and Institutions* 106, no. 14 (1996): 36–37.

Biggart, Nicole Woolsey. "Family, Gender and Business in Direct Selling Organizations." In *Working in the Service Society,* ed. Cameron Lynne Macdonald and Carmen Sirianni, 157–83. Philadelphia: Temple University Press, 1996.

Bills, David B. "Labor Market Information and Selection in a Local Restaurant Industry: The Tenuous Balance between Rewards, Commitments, and Costs." *Sociological Forum* 14, no. 4 (1999): 583–607.

Bird, Sharon, and Sokolofski, Leah. "Gendered Socio-Spatial Practices in Public Eating and Drinking Establishments in the Midwest United States." *Gender, Place and Culture* 12, no. 2 (2005): 213–30.

Birenbaum, Arnold, and Edward Sagarin. *People in Places: The Sociology of the Familiar.* New York: Praeger, 1973.

Blair-Loy, Mary. *Competing Devotions: Career and Family among Women Executives.* Cambridge: Harvard University Press, 2003.

Boas, Max, and Steve Chain. *Big Mac: The Unauthorized Story of McDonald's.* New York: New American Library, 1977.

Bolton, Sharon C. *Emotion Management in the Workplace.* New York: Palgrave Macmillan, 2005.

Bolton, Sharon, and Carol Boyd. "Trolley Dolly or Skilled Emotion Manager? Moving on from Hochschild's Managed Heart." *Work, Employment and Society* 17, no. 2 (2003): 289–308.

Bourdain, Anthony. *Kitchen Confidential: Adventures in the Culinary Underbelly.* New York: Ecco, 2000.

Breines, Wini. *Young, White, and Miserable: Growing Up Female in the Fifties.* Boston: Beacon, 1992.

Brewis, Joanna, and Stephen Linstead. *Sex, Work and Sex Work: Eroticizing Organization.* London and New York: Routledge, 2000.

Bridges, William. *Job Shift: How to Prosper in a Workplace without Jobs.* Reading, Pa.: Addison-Wesley, 1994.

Brown, Kurt, and Laure-Anne Bosselaar, eds. *Night Out: Poems about Hotels, Motels, Restaurants and Bars.* Minneapolis: Milkweed Editions, 1997.

Bruni, Frank. "My Week as a Waiter." *New York Times* online. http://www.nytimes.com/
2006/01/025/dining/25note.html?ei=5070&en=dfaf5bafcc47c3e4&ex=1141797600&pagewan
ted

Bryman, Alan. "The Disneyization of Society." In *McDonaldization: The Reader*, ed. George Ritzer,
52–60. Thousand Oaks, Calif.: Pine Forge, 2002.

Bubeck, Diemet Elisabet. *Care, Gender and Justice*. Oxford: Claredon, 1995.

Burawoy, Michael, ed. *Ethnography Unbound: Power and Resistance in the Modern Metropolis*.
Berkeley and Los Angeles: University of California, 1991.

———. "The Extended Case Method." *Sociological Theory* 16 no. 1 (1998): 4–33.

———. *Global Ethnography: Forces, Connections, and Imaginations in a Postmodern World*. Berkeley
and Los Angeles: University of California Press, 2000.

———. *Manufacturing Consent: Changes in the Labor Process under Monopoly Capitalism*. Chicago:
University of Chicago Press, 1979

Bureau of Labor Statistics. U.S. Department of Labor website. Accessed online at: http://www.bls
.gov/

Butler, Judith. *Gender Trouble: Feminism and the Subversion of Identity*. New York: Routledge, 1990.

Butler, Suellen, and James Skipper. "Working the Circuit: An Explanation of Employee Turnover in
the Restaurant Industry." *Sociological Spectrum* 3 (1983): 19–33.

Cancian, Francesca M., and Stacey J. Oliker. *Caring and Gender*. Thousand Oaks, Calif.: Pine Forge,
2000.

Carroll, Peter, and David Noble. *The Free and the Unfree*. New York: Penguin, 1988.

Cavan, Sherri. *Liquor License: An Ethnography of Bar Behavior*. Chicago: Aldine, 1966.

Chalmers, Lee V. *Marketing Masculinities: Gender and Management Politics in Marketing Work*.
Westport, Conn.: Greenwood, 2001.

Chase, Susan. *Ambiguous Empowerment: The Work Narratives of Women School Superintendents*.
Amherst: University of Massachusetts, 1995.

Chetkovich, Carol. *Real Heat: Gender and Race in the Urban Fire Service*. New Brunswick, N.J.:
Rutgers, 1997.

Cieraad, Irene, ed. *At Home: An Anthropology of Domestic Space*. Syracuse, N.Y.: Syracuse University
Press, 1999.

Citron, Zachary. "Waiting for Nodough: The Case against Tipping." *The New Republic* 200, no. 1
(1989): 9–11.

Ciulla, Joanne B. *The Working Life: The Promise and Betrayal of Modern Work*. New York: Random
House, 2000.

Clark, Candace. *Sympathy and Misery*. Chicago: University of Chicago Press, 1997.

Cleveland, Jeanette N., Margaret Stockdale, and Kevin R. Murphy. *Women and Men in
Organizations: Sex and Gender Issues at Work*. Mahwah, N.J.: Lawrence Erlbaum Associates,
2000.

Clifford, James. *Writing Culture: The Poetics and Politics of Ethnography*. Berkeley and Los Angeles:
University of California, 1986.

Cobble, Dorothy Sue. *Dishing It Out: Waitresses and Their Unions in the Twentieth Century*. Urbana:
University of Illinois, 1991.

———. "Organizing the Postindustrial Work Force: Lessons from the History of Waitress
Unionism." *Industrial and Labor Relations Review* 44, no. 3 (1991): 419–36.

Cohen, Lizabeth. *A Consumers' Republic: The Politics of Mass Consumption in Postwar America*. New
York: Knopf, 2003.

Cohn, Samuel. *Race, Gender, and Discrimination at Work.* Boulder, Colo.: Westview Press, 2000.

Coles, Nicholas, and Peter Oresick. *For a Living: The Poetry of Work.* Chicago: University of Illinois, 1995.

Collins, Jane Lou. *Threads: Gender, Labor, and Power in the Global Apparel Industry.* Chicago: University of Chicago Press, 2003.

Collins, Patricia Hill. *Black Feminist Thought: Knowledge, Consciousness and the Politics of Empowerment.* New York: Harper Collins, 1991.

———. *Fighting Words: Black Women and the Search for Justice.* Minneapolis: University of Minnesota, 1998.

Connell, R. W. *Masculinities.* Berkeley and Los Angeles: University of California Press, 1995.

Constable, Nicole. "Filipina Workers in Hong Kong: Household Rules and Relations." In *Global Woman: Nannies, Maids and Sex Workers in the New Economy,* ed. Barbara Ehrenreich and Arlie Russell Hochschild, 115–41. New York: Metropolitan Books, 2002.

Crang, Phillip. "It's Showtime: On the Workplace Geographies of Display in a Restaurant in Southeast England." *Environment and Planning* 12, no. 6L (1994): 675–704.

Creighton, Hannah. "Tied by Double Apron Strings: Female Work Culture and Organization in a Restaurant." *Insurgent Sociologist* 11 (1984): 59–64.

Crossley, Nick. *Intersubjectivity: The Fabric of Social Becoming.* London: Sage, 1996.

———. *Key Concepts in Critical Social Theory.* London: Sage, 2005.

David, Natacha. "Sexual Harassment at the Workplace; Stop It!" http://www.icft.org/english/equality/ecamsexharr.html

Davies, Margery. *Women's Place Is at the Typewriter: Office Work and Office Workers, 1870–1930.* Philadelphia: Temple University, 1982.

Dellinger, Kirsten. "Wearing Gender and Sexuality 'On Your Sleeve': Dress Norms and the Importance of Occupational and Organizational Culture at Work." *Gender Issues* (Winter 2002): 3–25.

Dellinger, Kirsten, and Christine L. Williams. "The Locker Room and the Dorm Room: Workplace Norms and the Boundaries of Sexual Harassment in Magazine Editing." *Social Problems* 49 no. 2 (May 2002): 242–57.

Delphy, Christine. "Sharing the Same Table: Consumption and the Family." In *The Sociology of the Family: New Directions for Britain,* ed. Chris Harris, 214–31. Keele, England: University of Keele, 1979.

Derber, Charles. *The Pursuit of Attention: Power and Individualism in Everyday Life.* Oxford: Oxford University Press, 1979.

Derber, Charles, and Ralph Nader. *Corporation Nation: How Corporations Are Taking Over Our Lives and What We Can Do About It.* New York: St. Martin's Press, 1998.

DeVault, Marjorie. *Feeding the Family: The Social Organization of Caring as Gendered Work.* Bloomington: Indiana University, 1991.

———. *Liberating Method: Feminism and Social Research.* Philadelphia: Temple University Press, 1999.

Dickinson, Torry D. *Fast Forward: Work, Gender, and Protest in a Changing World.* Lanham, Md.: Rowman and Littlefield Publishers, 2001.

DiLeonardo, Micaele. "The Female World of Cards and Holidays: Women, Families and the Work of Kinship." *Signs* 12, no. 3 (1987): 440–53.

Douglas, Mary. "Deciphering a Meal." *Daedalus* 101 (1972): 61–81.

————, ed. *Food in the Social Order: Studies of Food and Festivities in Three American Communities.* New York: Russell Sage, 1984.

Duneier, Mitchell. *Slim's Table: Race, Respectability, and Masculinity.* Chicago and London: University of Chicago Press, 1992.

Edwards, Richard C. *Contested Terrain.* New York: Harper Collins, 1979.

Edwards, Tim. *Contradictions of Consumption: Concepts, Practices and Politics in Consumer Society.* Buckingham and Philadelphia: Open University Press, 2000.

Ehrenreich, Barbara. *Nickel and Dimed: On (Not) Getting By in America.* New York: Metropolitan Books, 2001.

Ehrenreich, Barbara, and Arlie Russell Hochschild, eds. *Global Woman: Nannies, Maids and Sex Workers in the New Economy.* New York: Metropolitan Books, 2002.

Elam, Diane. "Speak for Yourself." In *Who Can Speak? Authority and Critical Identity*, ed. Judith Roof and Robyn Wiegman, 231–38. Urbana: University of Illinois Press, 1995.

England, Paula, Michelle Budig, and Nancy Folbre. "Wages of Virtue: The Relative Pay of Care Work." *Social Problems* 49 no. 4 (Nov. 2002): 455–73.

England, Paula, and Nancy Folbre. "The Cost of Caring." *Annals of the American Academy of Political and Social Science* 561 (Jan. 1999): 39–51.

Epstein, Cynthia, et al. *The Part Time Paradox: Time Norms, Professional Lives, Family and Gender.* New York: Routledge, 1999.

Erickson, Karla. "Bodies at Work: Performing Service in American Restaurants." *Space and Culture* 7, no. 1 (2004): 76–89.

————. "Service Smiles and Selves: Representations of Labor and the Sociology of Work." In *Sociology through Film*, ed. Jean-Anne Sutherland and Kathy Feltey. Thousand Oaks, Calif.: Sage, forthcoming.

————. "Tight Spaces and Salsa-stained Aprons: Bodies at Work in American Restaurants." In *The Restaurants Book: Ethnographies of Where We Eat*, ed. David Sutton and David Berriss, 17–24. Gordonsville, Va.: Berg, 2007.

————. "To Invest or Detach?: Coping Strategies and Workplace Culture in Service Work." *Symbolic Interaction* 4 no. 1 (2004): 76–89.

Erickson, Karla, and Jennifer Pierce. "Farewell to the Organization Man: The Feminization of Loyalty in High-End and Low-End Service Jobs." *Ethnography* 6 no. 3 (2005): 283–313.

Estlund, Cynthia. *Working Together: How Workplace Bonds Strengthen a Diverse Democracy.* Oxford and New York: Oxford University Press, 2003.

Estroff, Sue. "Whose Story is it Anyway? Authority, Voice and Responsibility in Narratives of Chronic Illness." In *Chronic Illness: From Experience to Policy*, ed. S. Kay Toombs, David Barnard, and Ronald A. Carson, 77–104. Bloomington: Indiana University, 1995.

Faludi, Susan. *Backlash: The Undeclared War against American Women.* New York: Bantam Doubleday, 1991.

————. *Stiffed: The Betrayal of the American Man.* New York: Perennial, 1999.

Farrell, James J. *One Nation under Goods: Malls and the Seductions of American Shopping.* Washington, D.C.: Smithsonian Institute, 2003.

Filby, M. P. "The Figures, the Personality and the Bums: Service Work and Sexuality." *Work Employment and Society* 6, no. 1 (Mar. 1992): 23–42.

Finch, Janet, and Dulcie Groves, eds. *A Labour of Love: Women, Work and Caring.* London: Routledge and Kegan Paul, 1983.

Fine, Gary Alan. *Kitchens: The Culture of Restaurant Work.* Berkeley and Los Angeles: University of California Press, 1996.

———. "Organizational Time: Temporal Demands and the Experience of Work in Restaurant Kitchens." *Social Forces* 69, no. 1 (1990): 95–114.

Finkelstein, Joanne. "Rich Food: McDonald's and Modern Life." In *Resisting McDonaldization*, ed. Barry Smart, 70–82. London: Sage Publications, 1999.

Fiske, John. "Shopping for Pleasure: Malls, Power and Resistance." In *The Consumer Society Reader*, ed. Juliet B. Schor and Douglas B. Holt, 306–28. New York: New Press, 2000.

Folgero, Ingeborg S., and Ingrid H. Fjeldstad. "From on Duty-Off Guard: Cultural Norms and Sexual Harassment in Service Organizations." *Organization Studies* 16 no. 2 (2005): 299–313.

Foucault, Michel. *The Archaeology of Knowledge and the Discourse on Language.* New York: Pantheon, 1972.

———. *Discipline and Punish: The Birth of the Prison.* London: Allen Lane, 1977.

———. *The History of Sexuality*, Vol. 1, An Introduction. New York: Vintage, 1980.

———. *Madness and Civilization: A History of Insanity in the Age of Reason.* London: Tavistock, 1967.

Frank, Thomas. *The Conquest of Cool: Business Culture, Counterculture and the Rise of Hip Consumerism.* Chicago: University of Chicago Press, 1997.

Fraser, Nancy, and Linda Gordon. "Social Criticism without Philosophy: An Encounter Between Feminism and Postmodernism." In *Feminism/Postmodernism*, ed. Linda J. Nicholson, 19–38. New York: Routledge, 1990.

Freeman, Carla. *High Tech and High Heels in the Global Economy: Women, Work and Pink-Collar Identities in the Caribbean.* Durham: Duke University, 2000.

Frenkel, Stephen J., et al. *On the Front Line: Organization of Work in the Information Economy.* Ithaca, N.Y.: Cornell University Press, 1999.

Fried, Mindy. *Taking Time: The Parental Leave Policy and Corporate Culture.* Philadelphia: Temple University Press, 1998.

Friedman, Susan Stanford. "Beyond White and Other: Relationality and Narratives of Race in Feminist Discourse." *Signs* 21, no. 1 (Autumn 1995): 1–43.

Fuller, Linda, and Vicki Smith. "Consumers' Reports: Management by Customers in a Changing Economy." *Work, Employment and Society* 5, no. 1 (1991): 1–16..

Gamarnikow, Eva, et al. *The Public and the Private.* London: Heinemann, 1983.

Gatta, Mary Lizabeth. *Juggling Food and Feelings: Emotional Balance in the Workplace.* Lanham, Md.: Lexington Books, 2002.

Geiger, Susan. "What's So Feminist about Women's Oral History?" *Journal of Women's History* 2, no. 1 (Spring 1990): 169–83.

Gibson-Graham, J. K. "'Stuffed If I Know!': Reflections on Post-Modern Feminist Social Research." *Gender, Place and Culture* 1, no. 2 (1991): 205–25.

Gini, Al. *My Job, My Self: Work and the Creation of the Modern Individual.* New York: Routledge, 2000.

Gini, Al, and T. J. Sullivan, eds. *It Comes with the Territory: An Inquiry Concerning Work and the Person.* New York: Random House, 1989.

Ginsberg, Debra. *Waiting: The True Confessions of a Waitress.* New York: Harper Collins, 2000.

Giuffre, Patti A., and Christine L. Williams. "Boundary Lines: Labeling Sexual Harassment in Restaurants." *Gender and Society* 8, no. 3 (Sept. 1994): 378–401.

Glazer, Nona Y. "Women's Work: Linking Separate Spheres." In *Women's Paid and Unpaid Labor*, ed. Nona Glazer-Malbin, 29–48. Philadelphia: Temple University Press, 1993.

Glenn, Evelyn Nakano. "From Servitude to Service Work: Historical Continuities in the Racial Division of Paid Reproductive Labor." In *Working in the Service Society*, ed. Cameron Lynne Macdonald and Carmen Sirianni, 115–56. Philadelphia: Temple University Press, 1996.

Goffman, Erving. *Encounters: Two Studies in the Sociology of Interaction*. Indianapolis: Bobbs-Merrill, 1961.

———. *Interaction Ritual*. New York: Doubleday and Company, 1967.

———. "The Nature of Deference and Demeanor." *American Anthropologist* 58 no. 3 (1956): 475–99.

———. *The Presentation of Self in Everyday Life*. New York: Doubleday Anchor, 1959.

———. *Relations in Public: Microstudies of the Public Order*. New York: Basic, 1971.

———. "Role Distance." In *People in Places: The Sociology of the Familiar*, ed. Arnold Birenbaum and Edward Sagarin, 121–38. New York: Praeger, 1973.

———. *Stigma: Notes on the Management of a Spoiled Identity*. New York: Simon and Schuster, 1963.

———. *Where the Action Is*. London: Allen Lane, 1969.

Goldberger, Paul. "The Sameness of Things." *New York Times*, section 6 (Apr. 6, 1997): 56.

Gregory, Raymond F. *Unwelcome and Unlawful: Sexual Harassment in the American Workplace*. Ithaca, N.Y.: Cornell University Press, 2004.

———. *Women and Workplace Discrimination: Overcoming Barriers to Gender Equality*. New Brunswick, N.J.: Rutgers University Press, 2003.

Gutek, Barbara. *The Dynamics of Service: Reflections on the Changing Nature of Customer/Provider Interactions*. San Francisco: Jossey-Bass, 1995.

———. *Sex and the Workplace*. San Francisco: Jossey-Bass, 1985.

Gutek, Barbara, and Theresa Welsh, eds. *The Brave New Service Strategy: Aligning Customer Relations, Market Strategies and Business Structure*. New York: Amacom, 2000.

Halford, Susan, Mike Savage, and Anne Witz. *Gender, Careers and Organizations: Current Development in Banking, Nursing and Local Government*. London: MacMillan, 1997.

Hall, Elaine J. "Smiling, Deferring, and Flirting: Doing Gender by Giving 'Good Service.'" *Work and Occupations* 20, no. 4 (1993): 452–71.

———. "Waitering/Waitressing: Engendering the Work of Table Servers." *Gender and Society* 7, no. 3 (1993): 329–46.

———. *Waiting on Tables: Gender Integration in a Service Occupation*. New Haven: University of Connecticut Press, 1990.

Hallett, Tim. "Emotional Feedback and Amplification in Social Interaction." *Sociological Quarterly* 44, no. 4 (2003): 705–26.

Halter, Marilyn. *Shopping for Identity: The Marketing of Ethnicity*. New York: Schocken, 2000.

Haney, Kathleen M. *Intersubjectivity Revisited: Phenomenology and the Other*. Athens: Ohio University Press, 1994.

Hanson, Susan, and Geraldine Pratt. *Gender, Work and Space*. London and New York: Routledge, 1995.

Haraway, Donna. "Situated Knowledges: The Science Question in Feminism and the Privilege of Partial Perspective." *Feminist Studies* 14, no. 3 (1988): 575–79.

Harding, Sandra. *Whose Science? Whose Knowledge?: Thinking from Women's Lives*. Ithaca, N.Y.: Cornell University Press, 1991.

Hartsock, Nancy. "The Feminist Standpoint: Developing the Ground for a Specifically Feminist Historical Materialism." In *Discovering Reality*, ed. Sandra Harding and Merrell Hintikka, 283–310. Dordrecht, Holland: Reidel Publishing Company, 1983.

Hays, Sharon. *The Cultural Contradictions of Motherhood*. New Haven: Yale University Press, 1996.

Henderson, Bruce Griffin. *Waiting: Waiters' True Tales of Crazed Customers, Murderous Chefs, and Tableside Disasters*. New York: Plume, 1995.

Henson, Kevin. *Just a Temp*. Philadelphia: Temple University Press, 1996.

Hershenberg, Stephen, John A. Alic, and Howard Wial. *New Rules for a New Economy Employment and Opportunity in Postindustrial America*. Ithaca, N.Y.: ILR Press, 1996.

Hewitt, Patricia. *About Time: The Revolution in Work and Family Life*. London: IPPR/Rivers Oram, 1993.

Hochschild, Arlie Russell. *The Commercialization of Intimate Life*. Berkeley and Los Angeles: University of California Press, 2003.

———. *The Managed Heart: Commercialization of Human Feeling*. Berkeley and Los Angeles: University of California Press, 1983.

———. *The Time Bind*. New York: Vintage, 1997.

Hochschild, Arlie Russell, and Anne Machung. *The Second Shift*. New York: Avon, 1989.

Hondagneu-Sotelo, Pierrette. *Domestica: Immigrant Workers Cleaning and Caring in the Shadows of Affluence*. Berkeley and Los Angeles: University of California, 2001.

Houghton Mifflin. "Reader's Companion to U.S. Women's History." Accessed online at: http://college.hmco.com/histoyr/readerscomp/women/html/wy_038500_waitresses.html

Howard, Theresa. "Keeping Servers Happy: A Real Competitive Advantage." *Nation's Restaurant News* 30, no. 23 (1996): 92–93.

Howe, Louise Kapp. *Pink Collar Workers: Inside the World of Women's Work*. New York: Putnam, 1977.

Hughes, Everett. *The Sociological Eye: The Selected Papers of Everett Hughes*. New Brunswick, N.J.: Transaction, 1951.

Hurley, Andrew. *Diners, Bowling Alleys and Trailer Parks: Chasing the American Dream in the Postwar Consumer Culture*. New York: Basic Books, 2001.

Husserl, Edmund. *Cartesian Mediations. Translated by Dorian Cairns*. The Hague: Martinus Nijhoff, 1970.

Iggers, Jeremy. "At Your Service." *Star and Tribune* (Mar. 29, 2001): T1–6.

Illouz, Eva. *Cold Intimacies: The Making of Emotional Capitalism*. Cambridge, England: Polity Press, 2007.

Jackman, Mary R. *The Velvet Glove: Paternalism and Conflict in Gender, Class and Race Relations*. Berkeley and Los Angeles: University of California Press, 1994.

Jackson, Eve. *Food and Transformation: Imagery and Symbolism of Eating*. Toronto: Inner City, 1996.

Jacobs, Jerry A. *The Time Divide: Work, Family, and Gender Inequality*. Cambridge, Mass.: Harvard University Press, 2004.

Janowitz, Morris. *The Community Press in an Urban Setting: The Social Elements of Urbanism*, 2nd ed. Chicago: University of Chicago Press, 1967.

Johnson, Allan. *The Gender Knot: Unraveling Our Patriarchal Legacy*. Philadelphia: Temple University Press, 1997.

Jones, Michael Owen, Michael Dane Moore, and Richard Christopher Snyder, eds. *Inside Organizations: Understanding the Human Dimension*. Newbury Park, Calif.: Sage, 1988.

Kanigel, Robert. *The One Best Way: Frederick Winslow Taylor and the Enigma of Efficiency*. New York: Viking, 1997.

Kanter, Rosabeth Moss. *Men and Women of the Corporation*. New York: Basic Books, 1979.

Kaplan, Jane Rachel, ed. *A Woman's Conflict: The Special Relationship between Women and Food*. Englewood Cliffs, N.J.: Prentice-Hall, 1980.

Kenny, Lorraine Delia. *Daughters of Suburbia: Growing Up White, Middle Class and Female*. New Brunswick, N.J.: Rutgers University Press, 2000.

Kerfoot, Deborah, and Marek Korczynski. "Gender and Service: New Directions for the Study of 'Front-Line' Service Work." *Gender, Work and Organization* 12, no. 5 (2005): 387–99.

Kessler-Harris, Alice. *Women Have Always Worked: A Historical Overview*. New York: Feminist Press, 1981.

Kirby, Diane. *Barmaids: A History of Women's Work in Pubs*. Cambridge, England: Cambridge University Press, 1997.

Kirp, David L. *Almost Home: America's Love-Hate Relationship with Community*. Princeton, N.J.: Princeton University Press, 2000.

Kondo, Dorinne. *Crafting the Self: Power, Gender and Discourses of Identity in Japanese Workplaces*. Chicago: University of Chicago Press, 1990.

Kovacik, Karen. "Between Language and Lyric: The Poetry of Pink-Collar Resistance." *NWSA Journal* 13, no. 1 (2001): 22.

Kress, Gunther, and Theo van Leeuwen. *Reading Images: The Grammar of Visual Design*. London: Routledge, 1996.

Kroc, Roy, and Robert Anderson. *Grinding it Out: The Making of McDonald's*. Chicago: Contemporary Books, 1977.

Kunda, Gideon. *Engineering Culture: Control and Commitment in a High-Tech Corporation*. Philadelphia: Temple University Press, 1992.

Kuttner, Robert. *Everything for Sale: The Virtues and Limits of Markets*. New York: Knopf, 1998.

Lamont, Michèle. *The Dignity of Working Men: Morality and the Boundaries of Race, Class and Immigration*. New York: Russell Sage Foundation, 2000.

Lamphere, Louise, et al. *Sunbelt Working Mothers: Reconciling Family and Factory*. Ithaca, N.Y.: Cornell University Press, 1993.

LaPointe, Eleanor. *Still Waiting: Gender and Job Power Among Waitresses*. New Brunswick, N.J.: Rutgers State University Press, 1991.

Larrabee, Eric, and Rolf Meyersohn. *Mass Leisure*. Glencoe, Ill.: Free Press, 1958.

Lears, Jackson. *Fables of Abundance: A Cultural History of Advertising in America*. New York: Harper Collins, 1994.

LeDuff, Charles R. "At a Slaughterhouse, Some Things Never Change." *New York Times* (June 16, 2000). The article can be accessed online: http://www.eco.utexas.edu/faculty/Cleaver/meatfactory.html

Lee, Jennifer. "From Civil Relations to Racial Conflict: Merchant-Customer Interactions in Urban America." *American Sociological Review* 67, no. 1 (2002): 77–98.

Leidner, Robin. "Emotional Labor in Service Work." *The Annals of the American Academy of Political and Social Science* 561, no. 1 (1999): 81–95.

———. *Fast Food, Fast Talk: Service Work and the Routinization of Everyday Life*. Berkeley and Los Angeles: University of California Press, 1993.

———. "Rethinking Questions of Control: Lessons from McDonald's." In *Working in the Service Society*, ed. Cameron Lynne Macdonald and Carmen Sirianni, 29–49. Philadelphia: Temple University Press, 1996.

———. "Serving Hamburgers and Selling Insurance: Gender, Work and Identity in Interactive Service Jobs." *Gender and Society* 5, no. 2 (1991): 154–77.

Leland, Karen, and Keith Bailey. *Customer Service for Dummies*. Foster City, Calif.: DG Books Worldwide, 1995.

LeMasters, E. E. *Blue-Collar Aristocrats: Life-Styles at a Working-Class Tavern*. Madison: University of Wisconsin Press, 1975.

Lerum, Kari. "Sexuality, Power, and Camaraderie in Service Work." *Gender and Society* 18 no. 6 (Dec. 2004): 756–76.

Liebow, Elliot. *Tally's Corner*. Lanham, Md.: Rowland and Littlefield, 1968.

Lincoln, James R., and Arne L. Kalleberg. *Culture, Control, and Commitment: A Study of Work Organization and Work Attitudes in the United States and Japan*. Cambridge, England, and New York: Cambridge University Press, 1990.

Linder, Staffan Burenstam. *The Harried Leisure Class*. New York: Columbia University Press, 1970.

Lipsitz, George. *Time Passages*. Minneapolis: University of Minnesota Press, 1991.

Longino, Helen. "Feminist Standpoint Theories and the Problems of Knowledge." *Signs* 19, no. 1 (1993): 201–12.

Lugosi, Peter. "Hospitality Spaces, Hospitable Moments: Consumer Encounters and Affective Experiences in Commercial Settings." *Journal of Foodservice* 18 (in press).

———. *The Production and Consumption of Hospitality Space*. Ph.D. diss., University of North London, 2003.

Lury, Celia. *Consumer Culture*. New Brunswick, N.J.: Rutgers University Press, 1996.

Luston, Meg, and June Corman. *Getting by in Hard Times: Gendered Labour at Home and on the Job*. Toronto: University of Toronto Press, 2001.

Lutz, Catherine. A., ed. *Language and the Politics of Emotion*. Cambridge, England: Cambridge University Press, 1990.

Lyman, Peter. "Be Reasonable: Anger and Technical Reason in Middle-Class Culture." Paper presented at the Society for the Study of Social Problems panel on Social Control and Everyday Life, San Francisco, Sept. 4, 1984.

Lynn, Michael. "Black-White Differences in Tipping of Various Service Providers." *Journal of Applied Social Psychology* 34, no. 11 (2004): 2261–71.

———. "Seven Ways to Increase Servers' Tips." *Corvell Hotel and Restaurant Administration Quarterly* (June 1996): 24–29.

Macdonald, Cameron Lynne, and Carmen Sirianni. "The Service Society and the Changing Experience of Work." In *Working in the Service Society*, ed. Cameron Lynne Macdonald and Carmen Sirianni, 1–29. Philadelphia: Temple University Press, 1996.

MacKinnon, Neil J. *Symbolic Interaction as Affect Control*. Albany: State University of New York Press, 1994.

Majors, Richard, and Janet Mancini Bilson. *Cool Pose: The Dilemmas of Black Manhood in America*. New York: Touchstone, 1992.

Manton, Catherine. *Fed Up: Women and Food in America*. Westport, Conn.: Bergin and Garvey, 1999.

Marar, Ziyad. *The Happiness Paradox*. London: Reaktion Books, 2003.

Mars, Gerald, and Michael Nicod. *The World of Waiters*. London: George Allen and Unwin, 1984.

Martin, Emily. "Flexible Survivors." *Cultural Values* 4, no. 4 (2000): 512–17.

Martin, Patricia Yancey. "'Said and Done' Versus 'Saying and Doing': Gendering Practices, Practicing Gender at Work." *Gender & Society* 17, no. 3 (2003): 342–66.

Marx, Karl. "Alienated Labor." In *Karl Marx: Selected Writings*, ed. David McLellan, 77–87. Oxford: Oxford University Press, 1977.

Mastracci, Sharon H. *Breaking Out of the Pink-Collar Ghetto: Policy Solutions for Non-College Women*. Armonk, N.Y.: M. E. Sharpe, 2004.

Maxwell, Richard. "Why Culture Works." In *Culture Works: The Political Economy of Culture*, ed. Richard Maxwell, 1–22. Minneapolis: University of Minnesota Press, 2001.

May, Elaine Tyler. *Homeward Bound: American Families in the Cold War Era*. New York: Basic, 1988.

McAllister, Jean. "Sisyphus at Work in the Warehouse: Temporary Employment in Greenville, South Carolina." In *Contingent Work: American Employment Relations in Transition*, ed. Kathleen Barker and Kathleen Christensen, 221–42. Ithaca, N.Y.: Cornell University Press, 1998.

McAllister, Matthew. *The Commercialization of American Culture*. Thousand Oaks, Calif.: Sage Publications, 1996.

McCormick, Albert E., and Graham C. Kinlock. "Interracial Contact in the Customer-Clerk Situation." *Journal of Social Psychology* 126 (1986): 551–51.

McNay, Lois. "Situated Intersubjectivity." In *Engendering the Social: Feminist Encounters with Sociological Theory*, ed. Barbara L. Marshall and Anne Witz, 171–86. New York: Open University Press, 2004.

Mehring, F. *Absolutism and Revolution in Germany, 1525–1848*. London: New Park Publications, 1975.

Meisenheimer, Joseph. "The Service Industry in the 'Good' versus 'Bad' Jobs Debate." *Monthly Labor Review* 121, no. 2 (1998): 24–47.

Mendez, Jennifer Bickham. "Of Mops and Maids: Contradictions and Continuities in Bureaucratized Domestic Work." *Social Problems* 45, no. 1 (Feb. 1998): 114–35.

Merriam Webster's Collegiate Dictionary, 10th ed. Retrieved from the World Wide Web: http://onelook.com.

Milkman, Ruth. *Farewell to the Factory: Auto Workers in the Late Twentieth Century*. Berkeley and Los Angeles: University of California Press, 1997.

———. *Gender at Work: The Dynamics of Job Segregation by Sex during World War II*. Urbana: University of Illinois Press, 1987.

Mills, Ami Chen. "Serves You Right." Retrieved November 21, 1999 from the World Wide Web: http://www.metroactive.com/papers/metro/03.14.96/waitprsn-9611.html: 1–21.

Mills, C. Wright. *The Sociological Imagination*. New York: Oxford University Press, 1959.

———. *White Collar*. New York: Oxford University Press, 1951.

Mirchandani, Kiran. "An Anti-Racist Feminist Critique of Scholarship on Emotion Work: The Case of Self-Employed Women." *Organization Studies* 24, no. 5 (2003): 721–42.

Mohanty, Chandra Talpade. "Women Workers and Capitalist Scripts: Ideologies of Domination, Common Interests, and the Politics of Solidarity." In *Feminist Genealogies, Colonial Legacies, Democratic Futures*, ed. M. Jacqui Alexander and Chandra Talpade Mohanty, 3–29. New York and London: Routledge, 1997.

Moody, Kim. *Workers in a Lean World*. London: Verso, 1997.

Morgan, David, Berit Brandth, and Elin Kvande, eds. *Gender, Bodies and Work*. Burlington, Vt.: Ashgate, 2005.

Morrison, Toni. *Playing in the Dark: Whiteness in the Literary Imagination*. Cambridge, Mass.: Harvard University Press, 1992.

Mount, Jeffrey. "Rethinking Turnover." *Restaurant Hospitality* 79, no. 4 (1995): 108–10.

Muirhead, Russell. *Just Work*. Cambridge, Mass.: Harvard University Press, 2004.

Mulcahy, Joanne B. "Waiting for What?" *Hurricane Alice* 9, no. 3 (1992): 1.

Mulvey, Laura. "Visual Pleasure and Narrative Cinema." *Screen* 16, no. 3 (Autumn 1975): 6–18.

Munk, Nina. "The Price of Freedom." *New York Times Magazine* (June 2000): 50–55.

Mutari, Ellen, and Deborah M. Figart. *Women and the Economy: A Reader*. Armonk, N.Y.: M. E. Sharpe, 2003.

Nelson, Margaret K., and Joan Smith. *Working Hard and Making Do: Surviving in Small Town America*. Berkeley and Los Angeles: University of California, 1999.

Newby, Howard. "Paternalism and Capitalism." In *Industrial Society Class, Cleavage and Control*, ed. Richard Scase, 59–73. London: Allen and Unwin.

Newman, Katherine. *Falling from Grace*. Berkeley and Los Angeles: University of California Press, 1988.

———. *No Shame in My Game: The Working Poor in the Inner City*. New York: Vintage, 1999.

Office Space. Videocassette, directed by Mike Judge. Los Angeles: Twentieth Century Fox, 1999.

Oldenburg, Ray. *The Great Good Place: Cafes, Coffee Shops, Community Centers, Beauty Parlors, General Stores, Bars, Hangouts and How They Get You through the Day*. New York: Marlowe and Company, 1989.

Omi, Michael, and Howard Winant. *Racial Formation in the United States*. New York: Routledge, 1986.

Owings, Allison. *Hey, Waitress! The USA from the Other Side of the Tray*. Berkeley and Los Angeles: University of California Press, 2002.

Oxford English Dictionary. New York: Oxford University Press, 1995.

Padavic, Irene, and Barbara Reskin. *Women and Men at Work*. Thousand Oaks, Calif.: Pine Forge, 2002.

Pardue, Derek. "Familiarity, Ambience, and Intentionality." *In The Restaurants Book: Ethnographies of Where We Eat*, ed. David Sutton and David Berriss. Gordonsville, Va.: Berg, 2007: 47–65.

Parker, Robert E. *Flesh Peddlers and Warm Bodies: The Temporary Help Industry and Its Workers*. New Brunswick, N.J.: Rutgers University Press, 1994.

Patai, Daphne. "U.S. Academics and Third World Women: Is Ethical Research Possible?" In *Women's Words: The Feminist Practice of Oral History*, ed. Sherna Berger Gluck and Daphne Patai, 137–53. New York: Routledge, 1991.

Paules, Greta Foff. *Dishing It Out: Power and Resistance among Waitresses in a New Jersey Restaurant*. Philadelphia: Temple University Press, 1991.

———. "Resisting the Symbolism of Service among Waitresses." In *Working in the Service Society*, ed. Cameron Lynne MacDonald and Carmen Sirianni, 264–90. Philadelphia: Temple University Press, 1996.

Perlik, Allison. "Fast Casual Profiling." *Restaurants and Institutions* 113, no. 8 (Apr. 1, 2003): 16.

Perrenas, Rachel Salazar. *Servants of Globalization: Women, Migration and Domestic Work*. Stanford, Calif.: Stanford University Press, 2001.

Philipson, Ilene J. *Married to the Job: Why We Live to Work and What We Can Do About It*. New York: Free Press, 2002.

Pieper, Josef. Translated by Alexander Dru. *Leisure: The Basis of Culture*. New York: Pantheon, 1952.

Pierce, Jennifer. *Gender Trials: Emotional Lives in Contemporary Law Firms*. Berkeley and Los Angeles: University of California Press, 1995.

———. "'Not Committed' or 'Not Qualified': A Raced and Gendered Organizational Logic in Contemporary Law Firms." In *An Introduction to Law and Social Theory*, ed. Reza Banakar and Max Travers, 155–71. London: Hart Publishing, 2002.

Poarch, Maria T. *Civic Life and Work: A Qualitative Study of Changing Patterns of Sociability and Civic Engagement in Everyday Life*. Ph.D. diss., Boston University, 1997.

Powers, Madelon. *Faces along the Bar: Lore and Order in the Workingman's Saloon, 1870–1920*. Chicago: University of Chicago Press, 1998.

Pringle, Rosemary. *Secretaries' Talk*. Sydney: Allen and Unwin, 1988.

Pringle, Rosemary, and Ann Game. *Gender at Work*. Sydney: George Allen and Unwin, 1983.

Prus, Robert. *Symbolic Interaction and Ethnographic Research: Intersubjectivity and the Study of Human Lived Experience*. Albany: State University of New York, 1996.

Putnam, Robert D. *Bowling Alone: The Collapse and Revival of American Community*. New York: Simon and Schuster, 2000.

Raz, Aviad E. Emotions at Work: *Normative Control, Organizations and Culture in Japan and America*. Cambridge, Mass.: Harvard University Asia Center, 2002.

Reichheld, Frederick, and Thomas Teal. *The Loyalty Effect*. Boston: Harvard Business School Press, 1996.

Reskin, Barbara, and Heidi I. Hartmann. "Cultural Beliefs About Gender and Work." In *Women's Work, Men's Work: Sex Segregation on the Job*, ed. Barbara Reskin and Heidi I. Hartmann, 38–43. Washington, D.C.: National Academy Press, 1986.

Riesman, David, Nathan Glazer, and Reuel Denney. *The Lonely Crowd*. Garden City, N.Y.: Doubleday, 1953.

Riessman, Catherine Kohler. "When Gender Is Not Enough: Women Interviewing Women." *Gender and Society* 1 (1987): 172–207.

Rifkin, Jeremy. *The Age of Access: The New Culture of Hypercapitalism, Where All of Life Is a Paid-for Experience*. New York: Putnam, 2000.

———. *The End of Work: The Decline of the Global Labor Force and the Dawn of the Post-Market Era*. New York: G. P. Putnam's Sons, 1995.

———. *The European Dream: How European's Vision of the Future Is Quietly Eclipsing the American Dream*. New York: Penguin, 2004.

Ritzer, George. *Enchanting a Disenchanted World*. Thousand Oaks, Calif.: Pine Forge, 1999.

———, ed. *McDonaldization: The Reader*. Thousand Oaks, Calif.: Pine Forge, 2002.

———. *The McDonaldization of Society: An Investigation into the Changing Characteristics of Social Life*. Newbury Park, Calif.: Pine Forge, 1993.

Roediger, David. *The Wages of Whiteness: Race and the Making of the American Working Class*. London: Verso, 1991.

Rogers, Jackie Krasas. *Temps: The Many Faces of the Changing Workplace*. Ithaca, N.Y.: ILR Press, 2000.

Rollins, Judith. *Between Women: Domestics and Their Employers*. Philadelphia: Temple University Press, 1985.

———. "Invisibility, Consciousness of the Other, and Re-sentiment among Black Domestic Workers." In *Working in the Service Society*, ed. Cameron Lynne Macdonald and Carmen Sirianni, 223–43. Philadelphia: Temple University, 1996.

Romero, Mary. *Maid in the U.S.A.* London: Routledge, 1992.

Rosaldo, Renato. "Imperialist Nostalgia." *Representations* 26 (Spring 1989): 107–22.

Roscoe, Will. "Writing Queer Cultures: An Impossible Possibility." In *Out in the Field: Reflections of Lesbian and Gay Anthropologists*, ed. Ellen Lewin and William Leap, 200–211. Chicago: University of Illinois Press, 1996.

Rose, Gillian. *Feminism and Geography: The Limits of Geographical Knowledge*. Minneapolis: University of Minnesota Press, 1993.

Ross, Andrew, ed. *Universal Abandon? The Politics of Postmodernism*. Minneapolis: University of Minnesota Press, 1988.

Rossi, Alice S., ed. *Caring and Doing for Others: Social Responsibility in the Domains of Family, Work and Community.* Chicago: University of Chicago Press, 2001.

Roth, Martha. "From a Waitress Journal." *Hurricane Alice* 1, no. 1 (1983): 7.

Roy, Donald F. "Banana Time: Job Satisfaction and Informal Interaction." *Human Organization* 18 (1959): 158–68.

———. "Work Satisfaction and Social Reward in Quota Achievement: An Analysis of Piecework Incentive." *American Sociological Review* 18, no. 5 (1953): 507–14.

Sack, Daniel. *Whitebread Protestants: Food and Religion in American Culture.* New York: St. Martin's Press, 2000.

Sacks, Karen Brodkin, and Dorothy Remy. *My Troubles Are Going to Have to Trouble Me: Everyday Trials and Triumphs of Women Workers.* New Brunswick, N.J.: Rutgers University Press, 1984.

Saguy, Abigail Cope. *What Is Sexual Harassment?: From Capitol Hill to the Sorbonne.* Berkeley and Los Angeles: University of California Press, 2003.

Sallaz, Jeffrey J. "The House Rules: Autonomy and Interests among Service Workers in the Contemporary Casino Industry." *Work and Occupations* 29, no. 4 (Nov. 2002): 394–427.

Salzinger, Leslie. *Genders in Production: Making Workers in Mexico's Global Factories.* Berkeley and Los Angeles: University of California Press, 2003.

Sartre, Jean-Paul. *Being and Nothingness: An Essay on Phenomenological Ontology.* Trans. Hazel E. Barnes. London: Philosophical Library, 1956.

Sawin, Philip, et al. *A Literature Guide to the Hospitality Industry.* Westport, Conn.: Greenwood Press, 1990.

Scapp, Ron, and Brian Seitz, eds. *Eating Culture.* Albany: State University of New York Press, 1998.

Schleumning, Neala. *Idle Hands and Empty Hearts: Work and Freedom in the United States.* New York: Bergin and Garvey, 1990.

Schlosser, Eric. *Fast Food Nation: The Dark Side of the All-American Meal.* Boston: Houghton Mifflin, 2001.

Schwarz, John E. *Illusions of Opportunity: The American Dream In Question.* New York: Norton, 1997.

Scott, Joan. "The Evidence of Experience." *Critical Inquiry* 17 (Summer 1991): 773–97.

Segrave, Kerry. *Tipping: An American Social History of Gratuities.* Jefferson, N.C.: McFarland and Company, 1998.

Seidman, Steven. *The Social Construction of Sexuality.* New York: Norton, 2003.

Sennett, Richard. *The Corrosion of Character: The Personal Consequences of Work in the New Capitalism.* New York: Norton, 1998.

Sennett, Richard, and Jonathan Cobb. *The Hidden Injuries of Class.* New York: Knopf, 1973.

Sewell, Graham, and Barry Wilkinson. "Someone to Watch Over Me: Surveillance, Discipline and Just-in-Time Labour Process." *Sociology* 26, no. 2 (1992): 271–89.

Shamir, Boas. "Between Gratitude and Gratuity: An Analysis of Tipping." *Annals of Tourism Research* 11, no. 1 (1984): 59–78.

Shapiro, Steve. "Building Proper Rapport Enhances Guest Relations." *Restaurants & Institutions* 99 (Aug. 7, 1989): 22–23.

Sherman, Rachel. *Class Acts: Service and Inequality in Luxury Hotels.* Berkeley and Los Angeles: University of California Press, 2007.

Shulman, Beth. *The Betrayal of Work: How Low-Wage Jobs Fail 30 Million Americans and their Families.* New York: New Press, 2003.

Simmel, Georg. *On Individuality and Social Forms.* Trans. Donald Levine. Chicago: University of Chicago Press, 1971.

Smart, Barry, ed. *Resisting McDonaldization.* London: Sage, 1999.

Smith, Dorothy E. *The Conceptual Practices of Power: A Feminist Sociology of Knowledge.* Boston: Northeastern University Press, 1990.

Smith, Vicki. *Crossing the Great Divide: Worker Risk and Opportunity in the New Economy.* Ithaca, N.Y.: Cornell University Press, 2001.

———. "Employee Involvement, Involved Employees: Participative Work Arrangements in a White-Collar Service Occupation." *Social Problems* 43 no. 2 (1996): 166–79.

———. "Institutionalizing Flexibility in a Service Firm: Multiple Contingencies and Hidden Hierarchies." *Work and Occupations* 21, no. 3 (1994): 284–307.

———. *Managing in the Corporate Interest: Control and Resistance in an American Bank.* Berkeley and Los Angeles: University of California Press, 1990.

Speer, Tibbett L. "The Give and Take of Tipping." *American Demographics* 19, no. 2 (1997): 50–55.

Spiegel, Lynn. *Make Room for TV: Television and the Family Ideal in Postwar America.* Chicago: University of Chicago Press, 1992.

Spradley, James P., and Brenda J. Mann. *The Cocktail Waitress: Woman's Work in a Man's World.* New York: John Wiley and Sons, 1975.

Steinberg, Ronnie J., and Deborah M. Figard. "Emotional Labor since the Managed Heart." *The Annals of the American Academy of Political and Social Science* (Jan. 1999): 8–26.

Sturdy, Andrew. "Customer Care in a Consumer Society: Smiling and Sometimes Meaning It?" *Organization: The Interdisciplinary Journal of Organization, Theory and Society* 5, no. 1 (1998): 2–53.

Supersize Me: A Film of Epic Portions. Videocassette, directed by Morgan Spurlock. New York: Hart Sharp Video, 2004.

Sutton, David E. *Remembrance of Repast: An Anthropology of Food and Memory.* New York: Berg, 2001.

———. "Tipping: An Anthropological Meditation." In *The Restaurants Book: Ethnographies of Where We Eat,* ed. David Sutton and David Berriss, 191–204. Gordonsville, Va.: Berg, 2007.

Sweeney, Ann. "Ladies in Waiting." *Magazine of the Detroit News* 1 (Jan. 1999): 5–11.

Szegedy-Maszak, Marianne. "Which of the following can't be found in fancy restaurants? (a) Salmon with dill, (b) Dom Perignon, (c) waitresses." *Washington Monthly* 20 (May 1988): 30–34.

Talwar, Jennifer Parker. *Fast Food, Fast Track: Immigrants, Big Business and the American Dream.* Boulder, Colo.: Westview, 2002.

Taylor, Frederick Winslow. *The Principles of Scientific Management.* New York: Harper and Brothers, 1911.

Terkel, Studs. *Working: People Talk about What They Do All Day and How They Feel About What They Do.* New York: Ballantine, 1973.

Theriault, Reg. *How to Tell When You're Tired.* New York: Norton, 1995.

Tolich, Martin B. "Alienating and Liberating Emotions at Work: Supermarket Clerks' Performance of Customer Service." *Journal of Contemporary Ethnography* 22, no. 3 (1993): 361–81.

Tönnies, Ferdinand. *Community and Society.* Trans. and ed. Charles P. Loomis. New York: Harper Torchbooks, 1957.

Trice, Harrison M., and Janice M. Beyer. *The Cultures of Work Organizations.* Upper Saddle River, N.J.: Prentice Hall, 1993.

"24 Hours at the Golden Apple." *This American Life*, Chicago Public Radio, WBEZ Chicago.

U.S. Bureau of the Census. Statistical Abstract of the United States, 1989.

U.S. Department of Agriculture, Economic Research Service. "National Food Review." Yearbook 10, no. 5 (1987): 24–33.

Van Maanen, John. "Afterword: Natives 'R' Us: Some Notes on the Ethnography of Organizations." In *Inside Organizations: Anthropologists at Work*, ed. David N. Gellner and Eric Hirsch, 233–61. Oxford and New York: Berg, 2001.

Van Maanen, John, and Gideon Kunda. "'Real Feelings': Emotional Expression and Organizational Culture." *Research in Organizational Behavior* 11 (1989): 43–103.

Vosko, Leah F. *Temporary Work: The Gendered Rise of a Precarious Employment Relationship*. Toronto and Buffalo: University of Toronto Press, 2000.

Wallulis, Jerald. *The New Insecurity: The End of the Standard Job and Family*. Albany: State University of New York Press, 1998.

Walters, Suzanna Danuta. "Wedding Bells and Baby Carriages: Heterosexuals Imagine Gay Families, Gay Families Imagine Themselves." In *Feminist Frontiers 6*, ed. Laurel Richardson, Verta Taylo West, Candace, and Don Zimmerman. "Doing Gender." *Gender and Society* 1 (1987): 125–51.

West, Jackie, and Terry Austrin. "From Work as Sex to Sex as Work: Networks, "Others" and Occupations in the Analysis of Work." *Gender, Work and Organization* 9, no. 5 (2002): 482–503.

Wharton, Amy S. "Service with a Smile: Understanding the Consequences of Emotional Labor." In *Working in the Service Society*, ed. Cameron Lynne Macdonald and Carmen Sirianni, 91–113. Philadelphia: Temple University Press, 1996.

———, ed. *Working in America: Continuity, Conflict and Change*. Boston: McGraw-Hill, 2002.

Wharton, Carol S. "Making People Feel Good: Workers' Constructions of Meaning in Interactive Service Jobs." *Qualitative Sociology* 19 no. 2 (1996): 217–33.

White, Deborah Gray. *Too Heavy a Load: Black Women in Defense of Themselves, 1894–1994*. New York: Norton, 1999.

Whyte, William Foote. *Human Relations in the Restaurant Industry*. New York: McGraw-Hill, Inc, 1948.

———. *The Organization Man*. Garden City, N.Y.: Doubleday, 1957.

Williams, Patricia. *The Alchemy of Race and Rights*. Cambridge: Harvard University Press, 1991.

Williams, Raymond. *The Long Revolution*. New York: Columbia University Press, 1966.

———. *Marxism and Literature*. Oxford: Oxford University Press, 1977.

Wilson, William Julius. *When Work Disappears: The World of the New Urban Poor*. New York: Knopf, 1996.

Wolf, Diane L. *Feminist Dilemmas in Fieldwork*. Boulder, Colo.: Westview, 1996.

Wolf, Naomi. *The Beauty Myth*. New York: William Morrow, 1991.

Wolff, Kurt H., trans. and ed. *The Sociology of Georg Simmel*. New York: Free Press, 1950.

Wolkowitz, C. "The Social Relations of Body Work." *Work Employment and Society* 16, no. 3 (2002): 497–510.

Woolridge, Adrian. "Come Back, Company Man!" *New York Times Magazine* (June 2000), 82–83.

Wuthrow, Robert. *Loose Connections: Joining Together in America's Fragmented Communities*. Cambridge: Harvard University Press, 1998.

XY Factor. "Sex During World War II." History Channel, Aug. 30, 2003.

Yano, Christine R. "Side-Dish Kitchen: Japanese American Delicatessens and the Culture of

Nostalgia." In *The Restaurants Book: Ethnographies of Where We Eat*, edited by David Sutton and David Berriss, 47–65. Gordonsville, Va.: Berg, 2007.

Zaniello, Tom. *Working Stiffs, Union Maids, Reds and Riffraff: An Organized Guide to Films about Labor*. Ithaca, N.Y.: ILR Press, 1996.

Zelizar, Viviana A. *The Purchase of Intimacy*. Princeton, N.J.: Princeton University Press, 2007.

Zubar, Amy. "Restaurant Workers Worst Drug Abusers." *Nation's Restaurant News* 31, no. 7 (1997): 1–2.

INDEX

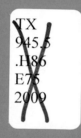